THE COUNTRY MUSIC STORY

THE COUNTRY MUSIC STORY

A Picture History
of Country and Western Music

photos by Burt Goldblatt
text by Robert Shelton

THE BOBBS-MERRILL COMPANY, INC.
A Subsidiary of Howard W. Sams & Co., Inc.
Publishers • Indianapolis • Kansas City • New York

First printing, 1966
Library of Congress catalog card number 65-25655
Copyright © 1966 by Robert Shelton and Burt Goldblatt
All rights reserved
Printed in the United States of America

Designed by Burt Goldblatt

This book is respectfully dedicated to two organizations that have worked for the greater understanding, acceptance and dignity of country music — The John Edwards Memorial Foundation at U.C.L.A. and The Country Music Association. They saw the light and helped spread it around the world.

CONTENTS

THE COUNTRY MUSIC STORY

1 Medicine show in the 1930's, Huntingdon, Tenn.

1 POOR MAN'S MUSIC BECOMES AN INDUSTRY

Vaudeville never died. It moved to Nashville, Tennessee.

The medicine show, whose glib salesmen hawked patent remedies for every ache and pain of body and spirit, never died. It just moved to Nashville.

The minstrel show, with its outrageous jokes strewing corn in every comic exchange, never died. It scrubbed the paint off its face and moved to Nashville.

Nor did the great American rural tradition of homemade music die in mountain shacks or at ranchland campsites. Just as the Industrial Revolution moved handicrafts from the hearth to the factory, so have the fiddle tunes and ballads moved to the music factory called Nashville.

Some of the noblest and some of the crudest elements in American show business have crystallized in the central Tennessee city. As the capital of an international country-music industry, Nashville has become the focal point of a forty-year-old entertainment phenomenon that is still growing with the vigor of a gangling adolescent.

There have, of course, been great changes from vaudeville and the medicine and minstrel shows of old. The world of country music has become sophisticated far beyond its backwoods origins. The Nashville music industry today is peopled by skilled musicians, astute businessmen, facile song writers, powerful promoters, adroit taste-makers and able technicians. But beneath the surface gloss of a business is a native art form that speaks for and to perhaps 35 million listeners around the world. Through the recording and radio microphones of country music passes a form of music, comedy, stage presentation, and personality that reveals as much about the American character as anything to be found on Broadway or in Hollywood.

If your entertainment tastes have been formed by the songs, films, shows and night clubs of Broadway or Hollywood, it may come as a surprise to you that America has *two* major popular musics. You will be familiar with, if, indeed, you can escape, the tunes and lyrics of Tin Pan Alley.

But from Nashville's Tin Pan Valley comes another breed of popular music. A chorus of names has been used to describe country and Western music: hillbilly, ballads, weepers, heart songs, Bluegrass, rockabilly, cowboy, event songs, breakdowns, folk songs, songs of the trail, ranch-house tunes, sacred, blues, gospel, mountain, old-time, Western swing, hoedowns . . . .

In the pages that follow, the lines of distinction will be made apparent, as will the frequent overlapping of types. Taken together, here is essentially another way of musical speech from the pop ballad, rhythmic blues, or novelty song of Tin Pan Alley. Here is a music that deals in simplicity, that roots itself in reality, that speaks of love, grief, and other basic emotions with frankness. Here is a music that is unashamed of being sentimental and nostalgic, a music that places sincerity higher on its ladder of values than refinement.

Country music is generally made on stringed instruments—guitar, banjo, mandolin, Autoharp, fiddle—rather than the saxophones, brasses, pianos, and percussion of city popular music. Country and Western singers consciously employ a distinctive twang which seems—or attempts to seem—as if it rose out of the gullies, flatlands, swamps, deserts, grazing grounds, or farmlands of rural America.

To the 35 million fans of country music, there is a totally different galaxy of stars than there is to the followers of the Broadway-Hollywood axis. The names of Buck Owens, Rose Maddox, Little Jimmie Dickens, Ray

Price, Marvin Rainwater, and Carl Butler are known to country-music fans better than those of Frank Sinatra, Perry Como, Ray Charles, Tony Bennett, or Rosemary Clooney. What is more startling, with the postwar surge of popularity of country music overseas, American music *means* country music to many listeners.

This book will try to summarize the forty-year history of country music: its folk origins, its growth through radio and phonograph recordings, the development of styles, the song writers, the personalities who produce America's other popular music. For the country-music listener, we will try, in words and pictures, to put together the beginning of a survey of country music. So many thousands of professionals and thousands of amateur country musicians crowd this canvas that selectivity had to be exerted continually. Each chapter heading is really only an outline for a book or series of books that would examine each phase of country music in great detail.

For the readers who have not encountered the color and the beauty of country music, this book will attempt to persuade you to take off the bandages of prejudice that have covered your ears and eyes. More complexity and more artistic beauty and truth have been

2 The "Little White House" at Warm Springs, Ga., 1933. President Roosevelt and his daughter, Anna, with group of musicians from Cove, Ga. They played "Soldiers' Joy" for the President.

4 Gene Autry, 1935

5 Bashful Joe Tryon, Bradley Kincaid, and Grandpa Jones

6 Panhandle Pete, Asheville, N. C.

7 Joe and Rose Lee Maphis

expressed in country music than you might imagine. If a few thousand readers who have dismissed this music as "hillbilly corn" can be impelled to listen with more sympathy, the work will have achieved its goal.

Two of the most convincing reasons for serious consideration of country music as part of the American heritage have been provided by the Administration of President Lyndon B. Johnson. The Johnsons, true to their Texas roots, are country-music fans and have frequently indicated their love of this music. More compelling, however, is President Johnson's War on Poverty. If we are being asked as taxpayers to help campaign against poverty, if we are asked to have sympathy for the victims of economic disparities, then we must certainly expand our knowledge of these people to include their culture.

Country and Western music has spread too far into the rural ethos of America to be pinpointed to any one area. But American folk music, and the hillbilly and commercial country music that grew out of it, found one of its richest sources in the hills of Appalachia, a ten-state area where poverty has been a particularly heavy burden. In these mountain regions, partially because of isolation, music sank its roots deeply. Even Tennessee, where the country music industry finally centered itself, is the nation's fourth-poorest state. Some of this "poor man's music" has been reflected, as we shall see, in country music lyrics, from the Carter Family's "Coal Miner Blues" to the recent Bill Anderson song "Poor Folks."

Partially because of the humble origins of many country music stars, the glamour of Nashville is part of the "American dream" of the rise from rags to riches. No one ever used money to measure the artistic worth of any creative product; yet so many country stars have moved from lives of privation into comfort and luxury, that it represents part of the lure and part of the legend of this whole field.

Eddy Arnold twenty-five years ago was a self-styled "Tennessee Plowboy" who would relax at the end of a furrow by swinging his guitar off his back to serenade his mule. Today, he walks into a Nashville recording studio in a neat hound's-tooth tweed jacket, Italian desert boots, and the generally relaxed air of a man with vast real-estate holdings. Webb Pierce was a Sears Roebuck

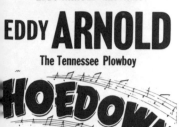

8   Eddy Arnold

clerk in Shreveport before he began singing professionally; now he drives a flamboyant car studded with silver dollars on the inside. Gene Autry rode to success on his voice and is now worth millions of dollars in West Coast hotel operations. Roger Miller, one of the newer overnight successes, was an elevator operator at the Andrew Jackson Hotel in Nashville before a few hit tunes catapulted him to financial security.

There are enough instances of this sort of dramatic success to form a trend. In some cases, it explains the motivation of many performers. In other cases, it explains how vast, how devoted is the country-music audience to have paved the way to wealth for scores of Nashville stars. Conversely, there are many dedicated country performers who have not been able to even make a living by their music, however gifted they are. Some of the old-timers who have seen others skyrocket to fame are quietly bitter about the way things are. Some must still work at farming or manual labor to afford the luxury of performing.

Every five years or so, the national press rediscovers the world of country music. A cycle of national magazine articles focuses on this or that outlandish antic or expensive costume or strange personal quirk of a country-music star. But a more probing approach to country music seems overdue. All too often the junketing Northern magazine or newspaper writer in Nashville will come away with a nearsighted, sensational, snobbish, and patronizing view of what he has seen. Content with superficialities, he may return with such hokey articles as "Sex Backstage at 'Grand Ole Opry' " or "Songs of Sex, Sin, and Salvation."

Understandably this furthers the tensions and suspicions between city slicker and country cousin. Rural people, in the age-old reflex of agrarians, tend to feel resentment toward the city snobs who do not pay attention or respect to their country ways, traditions, speech, and music. Can one ever forget the following lines from John Steinbeck's *Grapes of Wrath*? A white-shirted filling-station operator remarked about the Joad family, escaping the Dust Bowl for the hope of work in California:

" 'Well, you and me got sense. Them goddam Okies got no sense and no feeling. They ain't human. A human being wouldn't live like they do. A human being couldn't stand it to be so dirty and miserable. They ain't a hell of a lot better than gorillas.' "

Not only filling-station operators failed to understand the ways that hard times had impressed on the lives of the poor white; a scholar, W. J. Cash, in his classic study, *The Mind of the South*, asked:

"The ultimate test of every culture is its productivity. What ideas did it generate? Who were its philosophers and artists? And—perhaps the most searching test of all—what was its attitude toward these philosophers and artists? Did it recognize and nurture them when they were still struggling and unknown? Did it salute them before the world generally learned to salute them? One almost blushes to set down the score of the Old South here."

Unfortunately the learned Mr. Cash was evaluating only formal "culture," only the artistry of the academy, the philosophy of the intellectual. Had he examined the folk arts of the Old South, he might have come up with other answers. He might not have blushed to set down the score of the folk art, folk legend, and folk philosophy of the Old South. Nor would he have been so negative if he could have understood and evaluated the role of folk and popular music in the life of the average rural white Southerner.

This snobbery has not been all Northern, by any means. The aristocracy of Nashville, which prides itself on being the "Athens of the South," with so many leading universities and colleges within its city limits, took a dim view of the hillbilly musicians. There was a time when such troupers as Salt and Peanuts, who appeared at the old Princess Theater in Nashville, were made to feel unwelcome. More ironically, even the sponsor of "Grand Ole Opry," the National Life and Accident Insurance Company, was years behind in discovering what a fountain of rural culture it had in its own fine old radio program.

Is it any wonder then that there is a cockiness, a pride, and an aggressively "upward mobility" attitude on the part of the Nashville music community? They feel that theirs is an underdog art and entertainment medium that deserves recognition from the culture establishment.

9   Music made the long road easier for migrant workers.

10 The late Jim Reeves exchanging family photos with Bobby Bare, Anita Kerr, Chet Atkins

A researcher into American popular music with some standard reference works will see why the country-music industry battles for its place in the sun. David Ewen, a knowledgeable commentator, wrote a 229-page *History of Popular Music* (Barnes and Noble, New York, 1961) without a line about country and Western music. The vaunted *Encyclopaedia Britannica* and *Current Biography* can be searched with a magnifying glass for mention of country music and musicians.

To counteract this, country music has been receiving great attention in the music trade press and from a growing number of city folk-music devotees and students who have become expert on the growth of country music from traditional folk song. Also to counteract this is a fraternal feeling among most country and Western musicians and fans that reminds one city person of the dedicated, zealous attitude of people in the off-Broadway theater of a few years ago.

It would be naïve to think that the only factor motivating the country-music world is a belief in the music. Nashville has become the center for an international industry that yearly grosses nearly 100 million dollars. A personal appearance network run by more than a score of talent agencies grosses more than 10 million dollars a year in a total of nearly fifteen thousand engagements. There is a recording industry that is rivaling New York and Hollywood as centers. More than twenty recording studios, some working round the clock, produce nearly one out of every two recordings made in the United States.

11   Roy Drusky, Carl Butler, Minnie Pearl, and the late Hawkshaw Hawkins

Radio, along with recordings and personal appearances, is a keystone of country music. More than 2,200 radio stations in the United States and Canada program some country music every day. In November, 1963, the number of full-time country-music stations was 115. That number is now a total of 210. Television, too, has been gradually accepting country music. In 1963, the last year for which figures were available, 131 television stations were programing country music.

Two major television shows, conducted by Jimmy Dean in New York and by Carl Smith in Toronto, have established country music as entertainment fare for home viewers in the United States and Canada. The success of such shows as "Beverly Hillbillies," "Petti-coat Junction," "Bonanza" and "The Andy Griffith Show" must in part be attributed to the appeal of country and Western music directly, or the spirit of rural manners, wit, and mores indirectly.

That such a widespread industry should have grown out of the scrape of a fiddle at a square dance or the high, lonesome voice of a mountain balladeer speaks volumes about the hold that this music has had on rural America. (A common misconception is that this music, which started in the Southeast, is just a Southern phenomenon. One of the leading country talent agents, W.E. (Lucky) Moeller, reports that his artists make more personal appearances in the rural Midwest and the North than below the Mason-Dixon line.)

The country-music fan is distinguishable from the Tin Pan Alley fan in his loyalty. The admirer of Roy Acuff twenty years ago is likely to remain a Roy Acuff fan today. Whether it is the pop country song for entertainment or the sacred song of religious devotion, music plays an important part in the life of the rural or small-town American.

Political figures in the South have been aware of the deep hold music has on their constituents. You could hardly imagine a congressman from Brooklyn running for office with a rock 'n' roll band behind him! But many political figures in states with large rural populations have found that country music is invaluable to their campaigning. Jimmie Davis, a singer and song writer, rode two trips to the Governor's mansion of Louisiana singing such songs as "You Are My Sunshine." (His opposition has been quoted as saying: "You can't fight Davis—how in the devil can you fight a song?")

In Texas, the leader of a Western string band, the Light Crust Doughboys, W. Lee O'Daniel, was twice elected to the Governorship and the United States Senate with the help of such songs as "Please Pass the Biscuits, Pappy." Another Texas music-maker, Stuart Hamblen, who had written "Why Fool Around With Calico When You Have Silk at Home?", ran for President on the Prohibition ticket in 1952. The Leake County Revelers helped Huey Long win an election in Louisiana. In Kentucky, one Pleasant (Plez) Moberley of Manchester ran for county court clerk and later for the Congress astride an old mule, picking a guitar, and singing country ballads.

Of course, in Nashville today, a politician who is not attuned to country music would be committing suicide. Governor Frank Clement is one of country music's biggest boosters and has even gone to bat before a Congressional hearing to defend the songs of the hills. The late Tennessee Senator, Estes Kefauver, said at the Country Music Disk Jockey Convention in 1961:

". . . Country music has been the expression of the inner beings of our people. This is the only pure American music."

The Senator went on to discuss the alarm in Democratic circles when Roy Acuff ran for Governor in 1948: "The Democratic campaign strategists . . . couldn't decide whether the people were coming to hear Roy Acuff pick and sing or whether there was a revolutionary trend to the Republican nominees. Happily for our side, the people listened Republican but voted Democratic!"

The sound of country music has undergone great change in forty years, from the Golden Age of the 1920's to the Electronic Age of the 1960's. The rural electrification program has been so complete that it is difficult to find a country band without some sort of electric, amplified instrument.

The music has, by and large, moved from the simple to the more complex. In the beginning was the solo voice. Then a fiddle and a banjo were added. Around 1900, the guitar began to gain popularity.

12 Jimmy Davis

13 W. E. Lee O'Daniel

14 The Leake County Revelers, l to r, Dallas "Casey" Jones, guitar and lead vocal; Jim "Smoky" Wolverton, banjo; R. O. Mosley, banjo and founder of group, and Will Gilmer, fiddle

The drift toward a modern, sleek sound in country music has caused endless discussion among music circles. "Keeping country music country" has been vigorously debated recently, but the debate has been inconclusive. Traditionalists (including many city folk fans and musicians who have collected recordings and songs from the pre-1941 period and swear to its superiority over pop Nashville music) have argued that the great tradition has been betrayed. Others have defended the innovation of vocal backing, pedal steel guitars, electric banjos, and Fender basses as a way of keeping pace with the times.

Much of the change in country music can be explained in two words: Elvis Presley. The musical revolution wrought by the singer from East Tupelo, Mississippi, has haunted Nashville since the mid-1950's. Presley's mixture of country songs with a strong beat of Negro rhythm-and-blues formed a new style called rockabilly. He then carried this further into another new style called rock 'n' roll. The guitar-picking Pied Piper brought millions of city and rural teen-agers with him and began to have an effect on the thinking of arrangers, musicians, and recording officials in the country field. Drums were admitted to "Grand Ole Opry" and the battle between tradition and modernity grew in intensity.

Typical of the two points of view among even the taste-makers of Nashville is this straightforward remark by Chet Atkins, R.C.A. Victor's leading producer in Nashville: "I love unadulterated country music. But I'm in the business of selling records."

The stylistic picture of country music today is far from clear-cut. There are a dozen ways of singing and playing. Often one star will mix many of these styles in the course of several songs. This listener feels there is more evidence of a continuing grand tradition in country music than many purists will admit. It is possible to find traits of Chris Bouchillon's talking blues style of the 1920's in Jimmy Dean's "Big Bad John" and Roger Miller's "Dang Me" or "Chug-a-Lug." It is possible to find echoes of Rodgers-Williams-Cash singing in some of the work of Stonewall Jackson, Buck Owens, George Jones, and Bill Anderson. One can even discern some few remnants of the great women's voices of Molly O'Day, Cousin Emmy, and Rose Maddox in the singing of Kitty Wells and Loretta Lynn.

But it is just as easy to take a negative view about the changes in country music since the 1920's, to agree with the traditionalists that the modernization has been nothing but a series of unfortunate compromises to commercialism. It is easy to agree that "Grand Ole Opry" has lost the flavor it had in the 1930's under the strict traditional leadership of George Hay. The traditionalists feel that too much emphasis on hits, charts, ratings, and other popularity indicators has moved a pop country star like Marty Robbins so far to the front while the dedicated musicianship of old-timers like Sam and Kirk McGee has been all but ignored.

The debate will continue, as it always has in music circles, between traditionalists and modernists. The purpose of this book is not to feed the fires of that debate, but to sketch the great tradition and to find in what areas the modern innovators are stretching that tradition toward the future.

Country music has been making tremendous inroads among listeners in American

15 Chris Bouchillon, one of the first talking-blues men

cities in the last decade. Four main reasons can be advanced for this trend:

1. The organized effort of the country music industry to broaden its influence and audience. Such trade groups as the seven-year-old Country Music Association have taken the lead in approaching advertisers and others for spurring country-music programing on radio and television and in personal appearances.

2. The continuing declining spiral of quality in the content of Tin Pan Alley music. Increasingly, thoughtful commentators have indicated how popular music taste in America is dominated by a teen-age audience of single-record buyers and by a handful of powerful disk jockeys who manipulate tastes as if they were playing chess.

3. The major shift in population caused by World War II. To serve in defense industry, hundreds of thousands of rural and small-town residents headed toward the exploding urban centers of the Northeast, Midwest, and Far West.

The shift from an agrarian to an industrial economy drained away the youth of the countryside. The number of Southerners who have resettled in Chicago, Detroit, and Los Angeles is staggeringly large. But these emigrés took their cultural luggage with them. The longing for the good old days — and

16 Ernest Tubb

17 Jimmy Dean and the Everly Brothers recreating their early morning repertoire when Jimmy was starting out on radio

18 Roger Miller

the good old music – of their childhood has remained pervasive.

4. The growing disenchantment of city people with the impersonality, rootlessness, alienation, and loneliness of city life. This has stoked a hunger for a better set of values, for a link to the past that has continued to grow as metropolises grow into megalopolises, such as the one spreading down the East Coast from Boston to Washington. How many city youths are still hypnotized, in fiction, film, and television show, by such heroes of American life as the cowboy and the drifter? The hunger for personal freedom has grown even stronger in a pseudo-automated society. This has reflected itself in a tremendous postwar boom for do-it-yourself carpentry – and do-it-yourself music, of the folk and country variety.

Thousands of city and college youngsters in the last decade have taken on a strange identification with rural folkways, the self-reliant backwoodsman, the pioneer, the cowboy, the hobo, the wandering minstrel, the man who could rule his own life, not have it ruled for him by I.B.M. machines and computers.

For these reasons, country music has been making inroads on the city audience. It is a trend that can only grow, despite fads such as the British invasion of rock'n' rollers.

19   Little Jimmy Dickens

20   Salt and Peanuts

(Some observers find that the Beatles' music has a strong element of rockabilly. The circle of return to music with American roots continues.)

Perhaps the greatest irony of the postwar years has been not that the city person has longed for the vanishing country, but that the country person has longed for the benefits of city living. Who would deny that there are material improvements that can and should be sought? But what gets lost in the process are values. Gradually country isolation has broken down. Highways poked their concrete fingers into mountain pockets; television waves crossed the ridges and took Broadway and Hollywood faces, speech, and tastes into the back country. The Associated Press wires out of New York and Washington brought the same news at the same time to Bismarck, North Dakota, and Deep Fork, North Carolina.

Thus, the American countryside is gradually becoming urbanized, falling sway to the advertising of national magazines, the commercials of national television. Inevitably, the music of the country must reflect this break-

Wilma Lee and Stoney Cooper

Jimmie Rodgers and friend in front of Blue Yodeler's Paradise

ing down of rural-urban walls. The smoothness, the slickness, the polish of the city is gradually changing the beautiful, rough, natural sound of old-time country singers. A factory-made table is the new serving board, replacing the fine old Early American table.

Only a hopeless romantic would say "forward to the sweet tranquility of yesterday" on every level. But it is not hopeless romanticism that finds beauty in old songs, old truths, old poems, old fiddles. "Country people play their feeling and feel their playing," Tom Ashley, a rural music master, has said.

This, then, is the story of American country music, a crazy-quilt pattern of forty years of singing, playing, joking, tale-telling, dancing, and reminiscing. It should be played out not in words and pictures alone, but with a sound track. That sound track would have some of the most beautiful melodies and some of the roughest sounds in American music:

It would be the clang of an electric guitar; the subtle fretting of Merle Travis' unamplified guitar; the piercing, stirring "Gloryland March" of Wilma Lee and Stoney Cooper; the yodeling of Kenny Roberts; the devilish banjo tricks of Don Reno; the clunk of Stringbean's old banjo; Pappy McMichen's bow sliding across his 1723 Italian violin which he has to call a fiddle; Johnny Cash pointing his guitar at an audience as if he were going to hold them up; a screaming "Howdy" from beneath Cousin Minnie Pearl's straw hat; Jimmy Wakely singing to his horse; Zeke Clements explaining how to skin a cat to get a banjo skin; Archie Campbell telling a racy story one minute and singing a gospel song the next; Ralph Peer telling rustic auditioners in a hotel room to relax and sing out; Ernest Tubb speaking like a benign Lincoln in a ten-gallon hat; Hank Williams crying his lonesome words into a microphone; Jimmie Rodgers hearing a railroad whistle in the night. It is a rare and exciting sound.

23   L to r, unidentified, Fiddlin' John Carson, Land Norris with banjo, Earl Johnson and unidentified. Atlanta, Ga., 1919

2   THE GOLDEN AGE OF COUNTRY MUSIC

"When you call me hillbilly, just smile." — ERNEST TUBB.

"I've noticed in my 35 years of show business that there's 500 pairs of overalls sold to every one tuxedo suit. That's why I stick to swamp opera." — PAPPY MCMICHEN.

Home was where the music was. The Scottish-Irish-English settlers who populated the American colonies brought their music with them from the Old World. The fiddler's reels and hornpipes were to be as entertaining and serviceable on this side of the Atlantic as they had been on the other. The old ballads were to undergo change and forge a new ballad tradition here, but originally they came to this country with the settlers in their Old World forms.

Although the common storehouse of songs had come from the British Isles and Ireland to all the American colonies, it was in the South that they held their greatest sway. This happened partially because of a complex of conservative factors in the primarily agrarian economy of the South. Partly, too, it stemmed from the strong hold of frontier religious institutions, which included music. Although it is a popular romantic myth that isolated mountain areas held more tenaciously to old British ballads, there was ample evidence that all areas of the Southeast provided a particularly fertile nesting place and growing climate for the old songs. It was startling when the English folk-song collector Cecil J. Sharp came here to collect British ballads in World War I that he found survivals of British styles that were more intact than what he could collect in Britain.

Secular and sacred folk songs by no means remained totally static in the Southern countryside. There were many other influences at play: songs of the minstrel show, the sentimental composed song, the blues and other song forms of the Negro, and in some instances, the songs of other ethnic minorities, such as the Mexicans in the Southwest.

But it was the home-grown music that was to ultimately feed the pipe lines of the commercial country music. There were many functions at which rural folk would congregate for work, socializing, and the music that went along. There were logrollings, barnraisings, bean-stringings, apple-cuttings, or quilting parties. Tom Ashley calls some of his oldest songs "lassy-making tunes" from the old custom of communal molasses-making in the autumn.

Fiddling conventions and contests have been an institution in this country since the 1880's. Here was a great opportunity for fiddlers of a region to compete for honors while socializing and learning music. Although they have changed considerably, many fiddlers' contests and conventions are still going. The one at Union Grove, North Carolina, now in its forty-first year, has become a generalized country-music event, mixing traditional with modern styles, amplified instruments with the non amplified. The Galax, Virginia, annual country-music festival stresses the more traditional sound. But there are smaller fiddler's contests in many places in the Southeast, New England, and the Southwest.

Another medium in which the traditional music of the South spread was the medicine show. Three of the oldest musicians to have performed country music with medicine shows were Uncle Dave Macon, Fiddling John Carson, and Ashley. A description of this is given in the notes by Ralph Rinzler to the Folkways album "Old Time Music at Clarence Ashley's":

"He was about 16 (approximately 1911) when the 'doctor' of a medicine show, then camped in Mountain City, invited him to join up with the troupe and pick the banjo and sing some. . . .

"Tom traveled in the prairie-schooner type of covered wagon along with the platform, lanterns and rigging for the stage, while the doc rode in a smart little horse-drawn buggy. . . . The doctor always ran the show, headed the troupe, hired the performers and

arranged the runs in each town. Before World War I he had a license to sell his products, usually consisting of corn salve for foot ailments, liniments for all sorts of aches and pains, tonic for blood building and worm cure, special soap to cure dandruff, eczema and for a beautiful complexion, and little red boxes containing penny candies. . . . The doc rented a field on the edge of town, the platform was set up with prizes as a backdrop and large brilliant lamps on either side providing illumination. The show went on, consisting of separate pitches for different products, relieved by songs, blackface skits and tall tales told by the doc. . . ."

Ashley's career is otherwise a fascinating document of the early rural professional musician. He and his wife made some money by "busting," singing in the streets, at carnivals, outside miners' pay shacks. Afterward came the formation of string bands in groupings that were to set the style for the bulk of the music of the 1920's.

No one can say with authority when the first string band was formed. According to his

daughter, Dr. Humphrey Bate of Nashville, who was to be among the first country music-makers on WSM, had played with a string band in Tennessee from 1900 on. His group had performed at Cumberland River excursion boatings, at schools, and at cakewalks.

Typical of how the early professional country musicians started is the story of Fiddling Sid Harkreader, who worked for many years with the late Uncle Dave Macon. Sid got his first fiddle from a Sears Roebuck catalogue for $3.95. At the age of twelve, which was about 1910, he trapped rabbits and possums to save the money for his first fiddle. His great-great-grandfather had been a fiddler in Germany. He recalls how the postman in a horse and buggy delivered the coveted package from Sears Roebuck.

There was a Negro boy who worked on Sid's father's farm in Mount Juliet, Tennessee. "He tuned the fiddle for me at 1 P.M. By nightfall, I could play anything I had ever heard," Sid said. He went on to play at fiddling contests in Knoxville, Chattanooga, and Birmingham, winning at least twenty-five or thirty of the competitions.

Fiddling Sid Harkreader

The fiddle was to be an important instrument in the early history of country music. One of the first, if not the first, country musicians to record was Fiddling Bob Haines, who recorded "Arkansas Traveler" on Edison cylinders in the early 1900's. The first country musicians to record on disk were Eck Robertson and Henry Gilliland, who recorded fiddle tunes for Victor in June, 1922. The first real hillbilly record to enjoy popularity and to start the whole trend toward the recording of rural white musicians was Fiddling John Carson's "Old Hen Cackled" in June, 1923.

It was the development of two electronic mediums, ironically, that spread country music out of the South and lit the flame of the country-music industry. The development of disk recordings in 1921 and the birth of radio in 1920 were to move the music of the country fiddler and balladeer out to the world at large.

Radio, which was to do more to break down rural isolation than any other invention except the automobile, was to spread Southern music far from its environment. A few statistics will show how quickly radio became nearly a craze. Sales of radios in 1922 in the United States grossed 60 million dollars; by 1929 that figure had skyrocketed to almost 842 million dollars! By 1930, a census report showed, more than 12 million American families owned radio sets.

By 1922, there were more than five hundred radio stations of appreciable size operating in America, with about ninety of them in the South. The coming of radio to the South was to provide an immediate outlet for hundreds of professional or pseudo-professional music-makers. As happened with the first of the major Southern stations, WSB in Atlanta, country music was among the first material to be broadcast.

Among the favored groups playing on WSB

was one of the historic string bands, Gid Tanner and the Skillet-Lickers. The personnel of this band included Gid Tanner, Clayton (Pappy) McMichen, Riley Puckett, Fate Norris, Lowe Stokes, Bert Layne, and Ted Hawkins.

McMichen, now living in Louisville, remembers how the members of the Skillet-Lickers would congregate on some member's porch in Atlanta to pick and bow and sing. At the time, Pappy had been "firing an engine" on the Nashville, Chattanooga and St. Louis Railroad. "We didn't know there was any money in what we did with our music," he recalls.

The group's first name was Ye Old Hometown Band, a comic name taken from the "Toonerville Trolley" cartoon strip then popular. Later the band was called the Lick the Skillet Band. "Columbia Records finally heard about us, after we had been playing on WSB," McMichen said.

Although the growth of disk recording and radio occurred during almost the same years, radio put a lot of pressure on the recording industry, especially in 1923 and 1924. It is ironic to note that the period that John Edwards, the late Australian discographer and music historian, has called the "Golden Age of Country Music" was a period of the decline of the sales of recordings. The competition with radio and the national Depression both served to diminish the number of recordings sold. Despite this, the 1920's were a period of great activity in the recording of country artists and the recording of country songs by non-Southerners.

The first big hit in hillbilly music was released by Victor on November 16, 1923. Wendell Hall, the "Red-Headed Music-Maker" from Chicago, took an old country-dance tune, added some amusing new words, and recorded it as "It Ain't Gonna Rain No Mo'." The disk, Victor's top hit of 1923, caused a national sensation and is believed to have led directly to the search for authentic hillbilly talent.

There is no more fascinating story in the

25   L to r, Al and Joe Hopkins, Elvis Alderman, John Rector, Uncle Am Stuart, and Fiddlin' John Carson, 1925, Tennessee

Al Hopkins and his Buckle Busters. L to r, Elvis Alderman, Joe Hopkins, Charlie Bowman and Al Hopkins

history of country music than the work of such pioneer recording men as the late Ralph S. Peer, the late Frank Walker, and others such as Art Satherley and Eli Oberstein. Probably the most celebrated of these was Peer, who, while pursuing Negro, then white, rural talent, was to become one of the first major American folklore collectors. It was not until 1933 that the Library of Congress undertook recordings of field material. Thus, we have about ten years of recording when the commercial field men were capturing almost all the music of the rural folk.

Frank Walker had joined Columbia Records in 1921. Being from rural upstate New York, he was familiar with country music when he set out in 1922 to record a fiddler in a schoolhouse near Atlanta. The music he recorded caused some consternation at Columbia. They did not quite know what to do with it, but soon started a special 15,000 catalogue series. According to Mike Seeger, who interviewed Walker in 1962, he never used the term "hillbilly" for the gospel and religious songs, the jigs and reels, the heart and sentimental songs, and the event songs he recorded. Instead, they were carried in the catalogue as "Old Familiar Tunes," then

"Songs of the Hills and Plains," and finally just "Country."

Among Walker's major discoveries were members of the Skillet-Lickers. Many who knew of the Skillet-Lickers through recordings have slighted the reputation of Pappy McMichen, who did most of the lead fiddling. Tanner was really the front man and comic, more than a musician. As popular as the group's musical efforts, such as "Down Yonder," were, the comic skits, such as "Corn-Licker Still" or "A Bee Hunt On Hell-For-Sartin Creek," sold more disks.

One of the most important concepts in understanding the old-time country musician and entertainer is the quality of self-burlesque that dominates his work. Many a country string band of the 1920's and 1930's would choose purposely outlandish names to carry through this comic motif of the "Rube." Because they were lampooning themselves, it was all cast in a mold of genial spoofing of the outlandishly backward rural person.

Among the more accomplished of the early string bands were such aggregations as the Hoss-Hair Pullers, Arthur Tanner and His Cornshuckers, the Piedmont Log Rollers and the North Carolina Tar Heels.

Of the early figures in field recording, Ralph Peer probably looms over all others in the impact that he and his work were to have on the popularization of country music. Peer was the son of a storekeeper in Independence, Missouri, who sold sewing machines, phonographs, and records. When he was only eleven, he began to work two days a week in the store's record department and soon began to order records from Kansas City. At the time, Independence was a town of ten thousand and Harry S Truman was a county judge there.

At the end of World War I, Peer moved to New York and became an executive of the new record-manufacturing company, Okeh Records. In 1921, to use Peer's own recollection, "quite by accident I unearthed and developed the business of recording Negro artists to make records for sale to the colored population. Two years later, I had the good fortune to stumble across the fact that throughout our Southern states there existed a separate and distinct repertory of popular music, not connected in any way with the productions of New York and Chicago song writers.

"I supervised recordings of material taken from this folkloric gold mine using local artists. This led to the development and expansion of the traveling recording studio, and brought up the necessity for a name which would distinguish this special repertory from the New York brand of popular music. After trying several names unsuccessfully, the word hillbilly took the popular fancy and has since become universal. Actually, of course, 'hillbilly' is the local name given to a country people living in the Ozark mountains in northern Arkansas."

These comments by Peer, in *The Meridian* (Miss.) *Star* of May 26, 1953, were indicative of Peer's modesty. He had actually started a boom in so-called race recordings of Negro artists with his 1921 recording of Mamie Smith. His recording of Fiddling John Carson on June 14, 1923, was the real start of the country-music industry.

The early days of the recording of hill-country music have been documented in detail by Archie Green in a brilliant paper titled "Hillbilly Music: Source and Symbol." Green found four responses from the embattled recording industry to the competition of radio in the early 1920's: receivership, plugging of tested items, the change of the phonograph to an acceptable piece of home furniture, and

27 Frank Walker

28 Ralph Peer

29 Smith's Hoss Hair Pullers

The Possum Hunters. From left, Oscar Albright, bass; Staley Walton, guitar, seated; Jimmy Hart, guitar, standing; Oscar _____ one, fiddle, standing; Walter Leggett, banjo, seated, and Dr. Humphrey Bate, center, clapping. 1930

31   Uncle Dave Macon at the age of sweet-16

the "quest for new material and new market."

A key figure in that quest was Polk C. Brockman, an Atlanta record dealer who was the Okeh wholesale distributor in the headquarters of its largest regional market, Atlanta. On a trip to New York, in June, 1923, Brockman saw a newsreel of a Virginia fiddlers' competition at the Palace Theater and made a note to suggest that Okeh record Fiddling John Carson. The Atlanta session at which Brockman and Peer recorded Carson was the first major field recording by a major company in the South.

Carson was born on a farm in the Blue Ridge in Fannin County, Georgia. At the age of ten he began to play his grandfather's violin, a copy of a Stradivarius dated 1714. Carson had played fiddle while earning a living as a jockey, textile hand, and house painter. Green says: "He fiddled constantly at political rallies for friends Tom Watson and Eugene Talmadge, on trolley cars and at street corners, presenting topical ballads to casual audiences, at the many civic auditorium fiddlers' conventions, and, finally, on the then-infant radio."

Fiddlin' John Carson playing "The Little Old Log Cabin in the Lane"

32   Fiddlin' John Carson

Carson, who died in 1935, had appeared frequently with his daughter, Moonshine Kate. McMichen, who played with Carson on WSB in its first year, recalls that Fiddling John "could outfiddle Gid Tanner forty to one." Zeke Clements remembers Carson as "a crude country man. He drank the roughest whiskey, then fiddled all night."

Fiddling John's first record was "The Little Old Log Cabin in the Lane" and "The Old Hen Cackled and the Rooster's Going to Crow." Peer was unconvinced and remarked later that he found Carson's singing "pluperfect awful." But Brockman correctly assayed the fiddler's regional audience. Brockman offered to buy five hundred disks immediately after they were pressed. According to Green: "Peer acceded and issued the item as an uncatalogued special without a label number for local Atlanta consumption. He could not imagine a regional or national market for the disk."

Four weeks after the session, the disks arrived in Atlanta. Fiddling John hawked them over the footlights at a fiddlers' convention to which Elks reunion-goers were invited. Fiddling John sensed success and remarked to Brockman: "I'll have to quit making moonshine and start making records."

The first Carson disk was played on WSB. Brockman reordered more copies, which had then been listed in Okeh's popular catalogue. In October, 1923, Carson was sent to New York to record another dozen songs. His second release coupled "You Will Never Miss Your Mother Until She Is Gone" with "Papa's Billy Goat." Sensing the coming of another boom, Peer recalled that there was a test pressing from the spring of 1923 by Henry Whitter, a guitarist and harmonica player from Fries, Virginia, who had gone to New York four months before Carson had recorded in Atlanta. Peer took the Whitter tests off a shelf, got Brockman's advice on them, and "Lonesome Road Blues" and "The Wreck of the Old 97" were issued in early 1924.

Both recordings did well and Brockman stepped up his talent hunt. Okeh recorded in Atlanta such local talents as the Jenkins Family in gospel songs, and Land Norris, a banjoist. Bascom Lamar Lunsford (later known as the Minstrel of the Appalachians), who was to lead the long and lively country-music festivals at Asheville, North Carolina, recorded two traditional ballads. The string-band movement got its first shot in the arm. Carson formed the Virginia Reelers and Whitter recorded with a fiddler.

Peer had perhaps oversimplified the origin of the word "hillbilly." Green has traced the word's first appearance in print back to April 23, 1900, when *The New York Journal* reported that "a Hill-Billie is a free and untrammeled white citizen of Alabama who lives in the hills, has no means to speak of, dresses as he can, talks as he pleases, drinks whiskey when he gets it, and fires off his revolver as the fancy takes him." There is speculation that carries the word hillbilly back to sixteenth-century Scotland, but Green concludes "we know the word in print only from 1900 and only as an Americanism. . . . It is

33   Riley Puckett

34   The Skillet-Lickers. From left, Gid **Tanner**, Clayton McMichen, blind guitarist Riley Puckett, seated, and the band also included at times Fate Norris, Lowe Stokes, Bert Layne

35 Whitter's Virginia Breakdowners. L to r, Jim Sutpen, fiddle; Henry Whitter, guitar; John Rector, banjo

my thesis that the term 'hillbilly music' was born out of the marriage of a commercial industry — phonograph records and some units of show business — with traditional Appalachian folk song."

The actual use of the term hillbilly on records, Green finds, goes to two Okeh disks of early 1925. A group of musicians from Watauga County, North Carolina, and Grayson and Carroll Counties in Virginia made a second trip to New York to record. The group, Al and Joe Hopkins, Tony Alderman, and John Rector, had recorded in 1924 for Victor in New York, but the session was a failure.

The quartet returned to New York in January, 1925, to try their luck at the Okeh studio. Peer was in charge of the session, and six numbers were recorded. Here is how Green has reconstructed the famous session:

"At the end of the last number Peer asked for the group's name. Al (Hopkins) was unprepared. They had no name and he

36 Eck Robertson

7 Henry Whitter

38 The Blue Sky Boys, Bill and Earl Bolick

Successfully introduced and Recorded by Carson Robison and Bud Billings

39 The Callahan Brothers

40   Clayton McMichen's Georgia Wildcats. L to r, Carl Cottener, Buck Yates, Merle "Ridgerunner" Travis, and Blackie Case, WSM, 1937

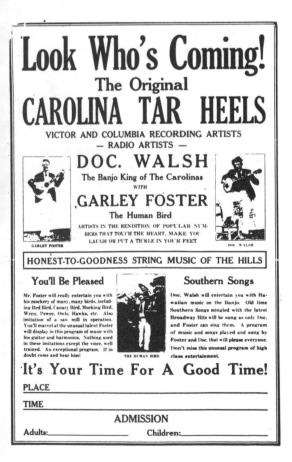

41   Alton and Rabon Delmore and Wayne Raney

The Carlisles, Bill and Cliff seated, young Tommy Carlisle
and Shannon Grayson, "Midday Merry-go-Round," Knoxville,
'50

J. E. Mainer's Mountaineers

searched for words. 'We're nothing but a bunch of hillbillies from North Carolina and Virginia. Call us anything.' Peer, responding at once to the humorous image, turned to his secretary and told her to list the Hill Billies on her ledger slips for the six selections."

Peer left Okeh to work for Victor in 1925. In January, 1928, he and Victor set up the Southern Music Publishing Company to handle copyrights for the company's music. The band that had helped give the name hillbilly to Southern white country music was to record later as the Hill Billies on Vocalion and as Al Hopkins and His Buckle Busters on Brunswick.

Although Peer was the leading field-recording official of the early period, Columbia Records, largely through the work of W.S. Fuhri and Walker, were to take an early lead in the recording of hillbilly music. Green puts it this way: "By January, 1925, the firm had enough folk material to begin a Columbia 15,000-D series 'Familiar Tunes—Old and New,' paralleling its own 14,000-D 'race' offerings. At this time Okeh was still releasing country material on pop labels. Hence, Columbia was the first company to see the possibilities in an exclusive white folk series."

Vocalion was anxious to get on the hillbilly music bandwagon and did so by recording Blind George Reneau, Uncle Am Stuart, and a major figure in country-music history, Uncle Dave Macon, who will be discussed at length in the "Grand Ole Opry" chapter.

Victor was the largest single recording company in the mid-twenties. Its entry into the country-music field was cautious, but destined to assume an almost dominating position. The Victor imprint on Southern country music was to be made largely through a singer of popular music and light opera, Vernon Dalhart. Born in Jefferson, Texas, on April 6, 1883, and reared on a ranch, he first recorded, for Emerson and Columbia, in 1916. Later Dalhart said his first real recording was the 1917 Edison Diamond disk "Can't You Hear Me Calling, Caroline?"

Dalhart's name at birth was Marion T. Slaughter, but in searching for a stage name he chose the names of two Texas towns, Vernon and Dalhart. He was later to record under nearly forty pseudonyms. By 1924, his fortunes were waning at Victor, and he asked the company's directors to let him try a hillbilly song. Their decision, finally, to let him do so helped to nationalize hillbilly music, helped pull Victor out of a financial plight,

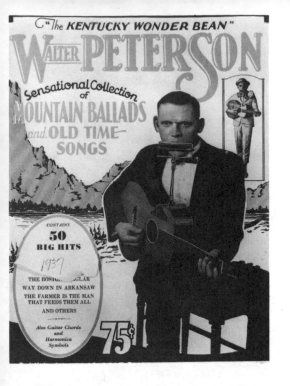

4 Clayton McMichen and friend Patsy, 1936

and made Dalhart one of the best-known recording figures of the 1920's.

It was reportedly at the suggestion of Thomas A. Edison's son, Charles, that he chose to record "The Wreck of the Old 97," the song that Henry Whitter recorded on Okeh. Whitter's performance had challenged several country musicians to improve upon it. The back of the Dalhart disk was "The Prisoner's Song." Dalhart used the lyrics from the Whitter Okeh recording of 1923, and also imitated his nasal style. "The Prisoner's Song," written by Dalhart's cousin Guy Massey, with additional words and melody by Nathaniel Shilkret, a Victor staff accompanist, was to become the best-selling Victor record before electrical recording.

From 1925 until 1931, Dalhart was one of the most affluent performers of country music. He recorded such songs as "The Death of Floyd Collins," "The Fatal Wedding," "Sydney Allen," and comedy tunes such as "The Little Black Mustache." For a time Dalhart was associated with the Hawaiian guitar of Frank Ferara, who came to the United States in 1900 and claimed to have introduced the Hawaiian guitar to this country. Later, Dalhart worked with Carson Robison, a giant in the field of writing country songs from the early 1920's until his death in 1957. (See song-writer chapter.)

If some of the most noted names of the 1920's were those of Fiddling John Carson, Vernon Dalhart, and Jimmie Rodgers, the story of the golden age of country music includes dozens of lesser figures who helped define and give shape to the new music. One such performer was Cliff Carlisle, who had become a well-known country star in the late 1920's. His story cuts across almost all lines of musical entertainment in the 1920's and 1930's.

"We drifted with the trend of the time," Carlisle recalled in an interview in 1964 in his Lexington, Kentucky, home.

Carlisle was born in a log cabin atop Mount Eden, near Taylorsville, Kentucky, in 1904. He remembers many cold winters when the snow would come through the cracks in the logs. "Me and my brother Bill come from the old school. We didn't have any silver spoons in our mouths."

He was born on a sharecropper's farm; half the tobacco crop went to the owner. He re-

Hezzie   Ken   Frank   Gabe

THE HOOSIER HOT SHOTS
On Your Radio - Coast-to-Coast - Every Week
for ALKA-SELTZER

45   Little Georgie Gobel

members walking •two or three miles to school. If the river rose, he would have to stay with a neighbor for two or three days. He recalls the hardship of carrying wood up the hill, riding eight or ten miles in a buggy to the nearest grocery store. "Mamma used to cut our hair. Our cabin must have been one of the coldest places in the world. There was nothing to knock the wind off."

The date of Cliff's first recording, for Gennett Records in Richmond, Indiana, is disputed, but he believes it was around 1924. He at one time worked with Wilbur Ball, another guitarist, as a duo called the Lullaby Larkers. He worked for several years on amateur shows at the six or eight theaters in Louisville that used this form of entertainment. "We had a Hawaiian act then," recalled Carlisle, reflecting the interest in Hawaiian music on early radio. But he also had the first blue-yodeling duet on records. He had learned the yodeling from Jimmie Rodgers records and from many subsequent meetings with the Singing Brakeman.

Carlisle played in every conceivable form of early rural entertainment: vaudeville on the B.F. Keith circuit, the Continental Chautauquas, etc.

Again, following the vogue of the times, Carlisle changed from Hawaiian music to hobo tunes, and has recorded some of the best in this genre, including "I'm Just a Lonely Hobo" and Rodgers' "Desert Blues."

"From Hawaiian to yodeling to hobo songs to strictly hillbilly music, was the way I went, until I retired in 1947," he said. Later, teaming with his brother Bill, the Carlisle Brothers were to make some of the best country vocal recordings of the 1930's.

Family or brother groups were popular in the early days of country music. Among these were Mainer's Mountaineers, headed by J. E. Mainer, a fiddler, and Wade Mainer, a banjoist. This string band worked in the traditional vein that was to lead to the Bluegrass style of the postwar period. At the time the Mainer band included another brother group, Wiley and Zeke and George Morris, two of whom made a successful appearance at the Newport Folk Festival of 1964. Of this group, which began to record on Bluebird in 1934, Billy Charles Malone has written: "The

46 Bradley Kincaid

Mainers remained primarily an instrumental organization. For the student of folk music they were an extremely important group because of their extensive traditional repertory and as an interesting survival of old-fashioned country fiddling."

Other family groups that had a part in building the country rural tradition were the Callahan Brothers, Bill and Joe, and the late Rabon and Alton Delmore of Elkmont, Alabama. The Delmore Brothers showed a strong influence of Negro style.

Bill and Earl Bolick, who call themselves the Blue Sky Boys, work with mandolin and guitar and have recorded some of the most beautiful vocal duet sounds to be heard in country music. In recent years, with the aid of the Northern folk audience, the Blue Sky Boys have been making a strong comeback.

The growth of radio in the 1920's did much to further the spread of country music. Although "Grand Ole Opry" on Nashville's WSM was to become the leading pacesetter for country music and ultimately lead to the development of Nashville as the center of the music industry, there were other important radio barn dances. With their attendant personal-appearance networks they were to play a pivotal role in the popularity of country music.

47 Charles Correll and Freeman Gosden, better known as Amos n' Andy

Bogtrotter's Band from Renfro Valley, Ky.

49   Renfro Valley Gang including Cousin Emmy, with ribbons in her hair, and Pee Wee King, third row from the bottom, first from the left

50 First stage show out of WLS "Merry-Go-Round," Linda Parker, third from left, with guitar

51 ·Barn dance view as they looked on stage in Renfro Valley, l to r, Jethro, Homer, Martha Lou Carson, Lillie May Ledford, Bertha Ambergay, Granny Harper, Doug Spivey, Aunt Idy, Marvin Taylor, Slim Miller, Shorty Hobbs; row two, l to r, first three, part of square dance group, Opal Ambergay, Judy Dell, John Lair, Guy Blakeman, Jerry (last name unknown), Roland Gaines, next four members of square dance group, Eller Long; third row, l to r, unidentified; Elsie and Janie, Gene Cobb, Jerry Byrd, Ernie Lee, Aychie Burns, 1940

The earlist country-music activity on radio had been, as we have seen, on Atlanta's WSB, shortly after the station opened in 1922. The nation's first commercial station, Pittsburgh's KDKA, started a barn dance in January, 1924. But the first radio station to feature a barn dance show of lasting significance was WLS in Chicago.

Some say that the two leading radio barn dances, from WLS in Chicago and WSM in Nashville, both began as accidents. One week after WLS opened on April 12, 1924, the first broadcast from "the old hayloft" in the Sherman Hotel went on the air. According to John Lair, who was later to be music director of WLS and then to head his own successful "Renfro Valley [Kentucky] Barn Dance," the WLS show began when "there was just nobody to put on the air." The station manager was in Evanston, and Tommy Dandurand, a janitor at the station, brought out a scratchy fiddle and somebody got a cowbell, and off it went.

Although the station was then owned by the Sears Roebuck Agricultural Foundation (Sears, the *W*orld's *L*argest *S*tore) and dedicated to "serve the people on the farms of America," some Sears officials were skeptical of the show. But the mail poured in, and the show was obviously a hit with the listeners.

52 John Lair

Among the early performers on the show, besides Dandurand's Fiddle Band, later named the WLS Barn Dance Orchestra, were Chubby Parker, banjoist and folk singer; Walter Peter, harmonica player and guitarist, called "The Kentucky Wonder Bean"; Tom Corwine, who imitated barnyard animals; Tom Owen, a square-dance caller; the singing team of Ford and Glenn; Grace Wilson; a Hawaiian guitar duo, Cecil and Esther Ward; and Ralph Waldo Emerson, an organist.

Prior to 1926, when the show was renamed "The National Barn Dance" and moved to the Eighth Street Theater in response to the demand for tickets, it had been called "The Aladdin Playparty" (sponsored by the Aladdin kerosene lamp company) and later "The Old Fiddlers' Hour."

George Dewey Hay, who was later to hold the decisive leadership of "Grand Ole Opry," was hired by WLS. The "Solemn Old Judge," as he titled his column in *The Memphis Commercial-Appeal*, had also been an announcer on WWMC. For fifteen or sixteen months he helped direct the course of the WLS "Barn Dance."

Program WLS Program

NATIONAL BARN DANCE

FIRST SHOW 7:00 p. m. Cent. Stan. Time

ALL TIME IS
CURTISS Candy Time
Buy Baby Ruth Candy

SECOND SHOW 9:45 p. m. Cent. Stan. Time

Masters of Ceremonies: HAL O'HALLORAN JACK HOLDEN

WLS welcomes you to the National Barn Dance a feature that millions of radio listeners in the United States and Canada have enjoyed since April, 1924. So many desired to witness the performances, that the Barn Dance "moved" to the Eighth Street Theatre in March, 1932. The entertainers who appear before you have become favorites of the air because they are just "home folks," striving to do their very best to lighten your cares by bringing you wholesome fun and entertainment. They hope that you will enjoy their show from the ringing of the first cowbell until "Good Night Ladies."

PRESENTATION OF ACTS   Entire Company

CUMBERLAND RIDGE RUNNERS   Old-Time Fiddling and Kentucky Mountain Songs
With Linda Parker, "Slim" Miller, Karl Davis, Harford Taylor, Clayton MacMichen, "Red" Foley and John Lair

Have you tried Curtiss Ic Candy Bars? ...

PRAIRIE RAMBLERS   Old Time Singing and Playing
    with Jack Taylor, "Chick" Hart, "Tex" Atchison and "Salty" Holmes

THE MAPLE CITY FOUR   In Songs, Chatter and Washboard Band Novelties
                    Al, Art, Fritz and Pat

GRACE WILSON   "Bringing Home the Bacon" Girl

GEORGE GOEBEL   "The Little Cowboy"

RALPH WALDO EMERSON — WLS Staff Organist   With His "Little Haywire Organ"

JOHN BROWN   WLS Staff Pianist   "At the Piano"

Baby Ruth Ic Candy Bars are delicious. Try them

43

53 The Prairie Ramblers, with Patsy Montana, l to r, "Happy" Jack Taylor, "Smiling" Charles (Chuck) Hurt, Shelby "Tex" Atchison, and Kenneth (Ken) Houchins, seated, Patsy Montana

54 Linda Parker, The Sunbonnet Girl

56 Homer and Jethro in the 1930's

55 Bob Atcher and Bonnie Blue Eyes

44

7   The big barn where the barn dance is broadcast

The first star of the WLS frolic was Bradley Kincaid, the leading country performer on the show from 1926 to 1931. Kincaid was billed as "The Kentucky Mountain Boy with His Houn' Dog Guitar." In later years he recalled that he and his wife had total possessions of $412 when called to WLS. "Four years later our worldly possessions consisted of twin daughters, a new Packard and more than $10,000 in the bank." Kincaid, who moved on to successful appearances on half a dozen other radio stations, was among the few of the early country professionals whose career survived the Depression.

By 1928, operation of WLS had been taken over by *The Prairie Farmer* newspaper. "The National Barn Dance" continued to be a prime attraction of the station, running to four and one-half hours each Saturday night. Between 1926 and 1960, when the show went off the air for about eight months, prior to switching to WGN, more than three million persons paid to see the Saturday night frolic. In March, 1961, the show ran ninety minutes on WGN radio and also became a half-hour WGN-TV show in September, 1963.

A long and distinguished list of country and other performers were helped to stardom by their appearance on "The National Barn Dance." Gene Autry was a leading attraction from 1930 to 1935. The Hoosier Hot Shots, a quartet, with their familiar greeting, "Are you ready, Hezzie?" were long-time favorites, as was the girl singer Patsy Montana.

58   The old mill still in operation at Renfro Valley

59   The interior of one of the reconstructed cabins

45

60 The Cumberland Ridge Runners, front row; second row, Harty Taylor, Karl Davis, and Linda Parker; third row, Slim Taylor, Hugh Cross and John Lair

61 L to r, Uncle Junie, Little Clifford and Aunt Idy

62 Ambergay Sisters

Lulu Belle and Scotty Wiseman were fixtures on the show with their colorful hit tune "Does the Spearmint Lose Its Flavor on the Bedpost Overnight?" Mack and Bob were two blind singers who conventionally closed the "Barn Dance" with a hymn. An early producer of the show, George C. Biggar, brought on Louise Massey and the Westerners, a group that included Curt Massey, now the music director of "The Beverly Hillbillies" and "Petticoat Junction," television shows.

Several comedians had their first wide exposure on the WLS "National Barn Dance." George Gobel began singing on the show when he was only ten years old. Being too small to play a guitar, he used a ukulele and just called it a guitar. Homer and Jethro, Correll and Gosden (Amos and Andy), Lum and Abner, and later Fibber McGee and Molly appeared on the WLS Saturday night show.

Within ten years of its founding, the WLS "Barn Dance" had become a one-hour network show as "The WLS-N.B.C. Alka-Seltzer Barn Dance."

The current roster of "The National Barn Dance" includes Arkie, the Arkansas Woodchopper, Bob Atcher, Red Blanchard, the Johnson Sisters, Dolph Hewitt, Bob and Bobbie Thomas, Cousin Tilford, Orion Samuelson, the Sage Riders, and others.

A description of "The National Barn Dance" sound is not easy to offer. After the noncountry performers had left WLS, the show began to have what has been described by Homer and Jethro, probably jocosely, as "uptown hillbilly." This was to distinguish it from the rougher "hungry hillbilly" style popular in such West Madison street cabarets of the early 1950's as La Conga, the 3022 Club, and The Casanova. In such clubs could be heard performers like Randy Barnett, who has been singing and fiddling for Chicago rural-music lovers for many years, many of them recently relocated residents of Kentucky, Tennessee, and North Carolina.

Shifts in country musical style have happened so often that there may well be more of the quality of country music of the 1930's on the WGN "Barn Dance" today than there is on the "Opry." One marked difference of

63 Whitey Ford, The Duke of Paducah

64 Emory Martin plucked banjo with teeth, toes and the stub of his arm

65 The Coon Creek Girls

66 Shorty and Little Eller

the WLS-WGN "Barn Dance," however, has been described by Green as a "synthesis embodying the tastes of those migrating from the Ozarks and Kentucky, those in the Appalachian tradition. Yet the Chicago station's listening audience is from the farm population of Northern Europe that settled in the area from Ohio westward to the Dakotas."

Consequently, one could hear on WLS such instruments as the accordion, which fused the music of the polka and schottische with that of a rural string band or fiddle-banjo combination. The sound of the WLS "Barn Dance" ranged from an Ozark reel to a Polish polka. It is another example of how quickly influences have affected all of popular music in America, and country music was to be no exception.

Of the many long-lasting radio barn dances that featured a Saturday night show and went on to influence an industry and a way of life, few have had a more colorful history than the "Renfro Valley [Kentucky] Barn Dance." In the light of the drift toward modernization in country music, Renfro Valley tells a particularly interesting story of faithfulness to tradition.

The Renfro Valley broadcasts and the building of a pioneer community centered around the radio show are largely the work of

one inspired man, John Lair. This "renaissance man" of country music was born in Livingston, Kentucky, in 1894. For twenty years he had a vision of one day owning all of Renfro Valley, south of Lexington, Kentucky, where he could build and maintain a pioneer rural community of the sort that might have grown on that spot after it was settled in the late eighteenth century.

There were to be many detours for Lair, detours that turned him into a teacher, an insurance executive, music director, band leader, and broadcasting official. Lair had organized a bright little string band called the Cumberland Ridge Runners, which was one of the first bands to incorporate a square-dance group. The band had appeared on the WLS "Barn Dance" from 1928 to 1937, during which time Lair also headed the station's large music library. While in Chicago, Lair continued to nourish "the idea of coming back to the valley, restocking the streams, taking off the weatherboard, and reconstructing a pioneer village that would feature a radio barn dance and ultimately become a tourist attraction."

Leaving WLS in 1937, he went to WLW in Cincinnati, where he simultaneously helped start that station's "Boone County Jamboree." In actuality the "Renfro Valley Barn

Granny Harper and Slim Miller and friends

68   Old Joe Clark

Dance" was started in Cincinnati two years before moving to the settlement. As the show in the city progressed, he helped ready the valley as a permanent home for what would become the only truly indigenous barn-dance show in the country.

Finally, on Saturday night, November 5, 1939, the group of musicians Lair had taken with him to Chicago and Cincinnati returned to their home environment, moved into the big wooden barn in Renfro Valley, and made the initial broadcast. There was no radio outlet then, but the show was carried over the telephone wires to the studios of WLWL and later WHAS. Among the notable musicians and comics associated with Lair and Renfro Valley have been Red Foley, Aunt Idy, Little Clifford and Uncle Junie, Carl and Hart, the Renfro Valley Boys, Linda Parker (the Sunbonnet Girl), and the famed rural comedian Whitey Ford, known familiarly as the Duke of Paducah.

One of Lair's earliest discoveries were the original Coon Creek Girls, which included Rosie and Lily May Ledford. They were to be the first all-girl country string band on radio. They made a bit of history in 1939 appearing in Washington at a performance before the King and Queen of England.

The "Renfro Valley Barn Dance" is only one of many folk-music and folklore activities of John Lair. On Sunday mornings, since 1942, have been held the "Renfro Valley Gatherings," religious music events. There have been for many years all-day sings on the first Sunday in August, and for many years a folk festival was run at the valley by Bascom Lamar Lunsford.

Lair also runs a museum and a lodge and woodworking and handicraft shops. Renfro Valley, although it has seen greater days on radio, is still a flourishing tourist center where one can see pioneer America brought back to life. Most remarkable, perhaps, is how Lair has managed to maintain the old-time folksy rural flavor on the Renfro Valley station, WRVK. The salty little 500-watter "serves 250,000 farm families" in its listening area, from sunup to sundown.

Aside from an hour and a half of pop music for the teen-agers and a "fine music show" at 6 P.M. for the family, the station's music diet is all country, with traditional and old-time music favored. A charming feature of the station is "The Renfro Valley Daily Newspaper of the Air," which is broadcast Monday through Friday.

"Well, friends and neighbors," gray-headed, gentle-voiced John Lair will almost confide into the microphone, "we couldn't afford a daily newspaper here, so we are just presenting our daily newspaper of the air." The clock in the WRVK studio, almost symbolically, is running thirty-two minutes late, perhaps an unconscious reminder of the station's link to the past. "Oh," Lair dismisses a city boy's question, "I never use that clock, I prefer my wrist watch."

With not only country music undergoing sophistication and modernization, but also the voice and content of rural-radio public-service features, WRVK remains uncompromisingly folksy and old-time. The station's chief disk jockey is Old Joe Clark, a banjo player, comic, singer, and word-fountain whom Lair considers "the greatest natural ad-libber I've ever heard." Old Joe Clark will greet a visitor by handing him a copy of a disk single he has cut. "This is my million seller. I bought a million copies and put them in my cellar for future use. If you get hungry on the road, try it with a little water. It's sort of like hardtack."

In between recordings by a Bluegrass band, "The Daily Newspaper of the Air" offers front-page news, then turns to the "woman's page." Lair's secretary gives some history of tulips, some homey advice about sewing curtains and darning socks. Then some "local news" about a car wreck, a funeral, a dinner party, a visit to somebody's aunt in Mount Vernon, Kentucky, down the road, announcement of a Baptist church revival, and so on. Then Old Joe Clark and the station's other disk jockey, Joe Fisher, do a satire of the "Huntley-Brinkley Report," which they call "Confusing the News." The O.K. Fertilizer Company offers a commercial and a weather report, and "the farm page" brings to the microphone the Fayette County Farm Agent, Lee Durham, "who has a few words to say about the clover mite." Then, as always, a recording of good old country music.

Radio has played, and continues to play, such a vital role in country music that a complete survey of all the leading country-music shows would fill a book much larger than this one. But passing mention should be made of a few of the major shows besides the WLS-WGN "Barn Dance" and WSM's "Grand Old Opry."

One of the leading shows featuring live country talent has been "The World's Original WWVA Jamboree," which began in Wheeling, West Virginia, on January 7, 1933. Among the stars of this show have been

69 L to r, Carl Davis, John Lair, Red Foley and Hardy Taylor

Grandpa Jones, Doc Williams, Cousin Emmy and Her Kinfolks, Red Belcher, Elton Britt, Lew Childre, and the Osborne Brothers.

"The Midwestern Hayride" began on WLW in Cincinnati before 1937, originally as "The Boone County Jamboree." Among the stars have been the Browns Ferry Four, Slim Bryant, the Delmore Brothers, Natchee the Indian Fiddler (who vied with Pappy McMichen for many national fiddling championships; he is believed to be of Italian, not Indian, descent), Joe Maphis, and Riley Puckett (the famed singer and guitarist of the Skillet-Lickers).

A postwar show that has had many listeners in the Southeast was "The Old Dominion Barn Dance" on WRVA, from Richmond, Virginia. Sunshine Sue was the leader of this program after 1946, and Carlton Haney became the kingpin in 1957, when the program was retitled "The New Dominion Barn Dance." Among the stars have been Crazy Elmer, Barbara Allen, Red Battle, the Knight Singers, Allen Shelton, Quincy Snodgrass, and Mac Wiseman.

"The Big D Jamboree" was the successor show on KRLD, Dallas, Texas, to "The Lone Star Barn Dance." Among the lone stars on the show have been the Callahans, Orville

70 Red Foley and Ozark Jubilee Crew

Couch, Merle Kilgore, Peach Seed, Bob Roy, and Billy Walker.

From Springfield, Missouri, another leading Midwestern show has been "The Ozark Jubilee," which started on KWTO radio, was renamed "Country Music Jubilee" in 1957 and 1958, on A.B.C. television, and is now known as "Jubilee, U.S.A." on KWTO-TV. Red Foley was long the star of this show. Others who have appeared include Cyp and Sap Brasfield, Arlie Duff, Flash and Whistler, the Foggy River Boys, Jimmy Gately, Wanda Jackson, Sonny James, Brenda Lee, Lenny and Goo, and Pete Stamper.

Two radio shows that have served as springboards for appearances on "Grand Ole Opry" have been the "Tennessee Barn Dance," on WNOX, Knoxville, which began in January, 1942, and "Louisiana Hayride," on KWKH, Shreveport, and KTHS, Little Rock, Arkansas. This show began on April 3, 1948, with Hank Williams as star.

The list is by no means complete, with new country-music shows beginning to have a powerful sway on audiences almost every day. One of the most interesting developments on radio in the 1930's and 1940's was the emergence of the Mexican border stations. A detailed study of this phenomenon is

to be found in the unpublished doctoral dissertation by Billy Charles Malone, "A History of Commercial Country Music in the United States, 1920–1964."

These powerful stations usually had call letters beginning with the letter X. They often operated on tremendous wattage that was two or three times the legal limit in the United States. Because of their strong signals these stations could be heard throughout the United States and often even in Canada. In 1932, it was estimated that XER reached as high as 500,000 watts.

Many of the Mexican border stations were owned by Americans. They provided a powerful advertising medium. Malone described them this way: "The type of products advertised ranged from old-time religion to medical cure-alls and were aimed at rural American listeners. The border station era was inaugurated in 1930 when Dr. J. R. Brinkley's XER (changed to XERA in 1935) began operations at Villa Cuna, Mexico."

Dr. Brinkley had touted a goat-gland operation for male potency on a station at Milford, Kansas, but his station license was revoked, so he moved to the Texas border to run the first X-station. He later acquired XEPN and XEAW. Besides his own nostrums, the good

71 Grandpa Jones

72 Ferlin Husky on his TV show

74 Del Reeves

73 Hugh and Shug's Radio Pals; front row, l to r, Ken Carlson, Shug Fisher; second row, Lenny Aylshire, Hugh Cross, Ted Grant and Buddy Ross

75 Red Belcher

Dr. Brinkley advertised other products, along with the fare that Malone describes as "a steady diet of religious evangelists, hillbilly singers (mostly by transcription) and on many occasions, right-wing politicians." In later years, one Norman Baker advertised his cancer "cure" on XENT before he was convicted of mail fraud. Carr Collins became a millionaire selling Crazy Water Crystals over XEAW and heavily relied on personal appearances by country musicians.

"The X-stations profited," Malone said, "from the popularity of hillbilly music in Southern and Midwestern rural areas. These powerful stations squeezed out their American rivals during normal operating hours, and pre-empted those hours after midnight most American stations neglected. Through this type of programing the border stations touched not only the farmer, who listened during the earliest hours, but also the truck driver, the night-shift worker, and the insomniac. If one could endure the seemingly never-ending advertising, he could occasionally hear a hillbilly song of the best quality. . . . On the border stations hillbilly music has continued to the present day to be of a more old-time and religious nature. . . ."

As Mexican border and American radio continued through the 1930's to popularize country music, so did the increasing number of personal appearances. WLS had pioneered in an artists' bureau that handled personal appearances for the well-known performers on its "Barn Dance" after a booking agent, Dick Bergen, made a successful arrangement for some musicians at a Peoria, Illinois, theater. WSM followed suit, and soon all the leading country-music shows fell in line. By the end of the 1930's personal appearances by country musicians and comedians had taken over where vaudeville, the minstrel show, and the medicine show left off.

It stood to reason that if, in the years 1932 to 1942, more than one million persons had paid some $660,000 to watch "The National Barn Dance" broadcasts in the heart of Chicago, there was a vast audience willing to pay to see and hear country musicians and comedians when they came to one's home area. Thus began the elaborate network of state and county fairs, schoolhouse and civic auditorium benefits and functions, tent shows, barn dances, and ballroom dates. The traveling country musician and comedian of the late 1920's and 1930's was only a preview of things to come when international tours and jet-age hillbilly circuits were to be commonplace.

From the first scraping sounds of the Skillet-Lickers on WSB and Fiddling John Carson's recordings of 1923, an industry and an entertainment medium were to emerge. From the early 1920's until the beginning of World War II, country music was to evolve from an unself-conscious folk music into a highly self-conscious entertainment form. Traditional music could still be heard, but new songs were entering the country-music storehouse, songs written for the new country-music audience provided by radio, disks, and personal appearances.

The music was to become more polished, more stylized and more professional. Because of the emergence of the jukebox and the honky-tonk, a need for a music that projected brought in electric instrumentation. Because of a shift of the stylistic center of country music from the Southeast to the Southwest during the 1930's, the old mountain music of the early string bands was to change into a new entity. But the major change in style and feeling of country music was to be caused by the role of one singer more than any other set of factors. Jimmie Rodgers introduced a sort of sweet crooning that was to be markedly different from the nasal mountain sound. While the fiddle remained an important instrument, the guitar and banjo were to move to the fore. For better or worse, country music was growing up.

3 "MY TIME AIN'T LONG": THE JIMMIE RODGERS STORY

If any one individual were to be chosen to stand as a symbol of the forty-year history of country music, it would undoubtedly be Jimmie Rodgers.

The man and his music represent everything that preceded and followed his brief, brilliant career. Here was a "little man" who sang *for* the rural Southerner as few have sung since. His death in 1933 at the age of thirty-five took away a musician who gave form, shape, and content to the music of the hillbilly and laid the foundation for commercial country music.

Paul Ackerman of *Billboard* magazine captured the importance of Rodgers when he wrote:

"Some regard him as America's 'truly native' balladeer. Others consider him the father of the country music field. And many more, thinking of Rodgers' big pop hits, which cut across all musical categories, place him in that select group whose compelling talent established the phonograph as an important medium of home entertainment. . . . Someone at that early date had to fuse and synthesize these musical elements (pop, folk, country, blues and jazz) to prepare the way for the Elvis Presleys and Johnny Cashes of today. It was Rodgers who did this."

Although Rodgers died in 1933, the sway of his music continues unabated. It is typical of the power of his image and his music that his LP's continue to sell as if he were still making one-night stands with the other country troupers. At least two Nashville stars of today, Hank Snow and Ernest Tubb, have been so heavily influenced by Rodgers, man and myth, that they help keep his tradition alive.

In six short years, 1927 to 1933, a tubercular railroad man was to become a star whose records were to sell more than another great tenor, Enrico Caruso, the opera star — some 20 million copies. In six short years, Rodgers was to write and record songs sung around the world today. Folklorists have collected versions of his songs in Scandinavia, Scotland, Australia, and North Carolina. Fan clubs are centered in England and Texas. Three labels in India have issued his recordings, and he is known elsewhere in Asia.

Rodgers was nothing if not versatile. He sang songs of nearly every category: railroad, jazz, country, Western, blues, folk, and pop. His nickname, the "Father of Country Music," moved from a promotional label to history when, in November, 1961, he was elected to the Country Music Association's Hall of Fame as "the man who started it all."

Rodgers was far from being the first country singer to record, but he is clearly the most influential. The number of singing stars who have acknowledged their debt to him, stylistically, is long. A few would be Ernest Tubb (who carries a Rodgers guitar given to him by Rodgers' widow), Hank Snow (who carries on the tradition of railroad songs), Cliff Carlisle, Obray Ramsey, Gene Autry, Tommy Duncan, Bob Wills, Eddy Arnold, Red Foley, Lefty Frizzell, Elton Britt, Hank Williams, Jimmie Davis, T. Texas Tyler, and many more.

The Jimmie Rodgers story, even told without romanticizing, is the raw material for legend. Perhaps more than any other country singer, Rodgers understood what the poor man of the South wanted to hear, because he was one of them. Roy Horton of Southern Music-Peer International says that in the early 1930's a customer in a general store almost anywhere in the South would approach the counter and say: "Let me have a pound of butter, a dozen eggs, and the latest Jimmie Rodgers record."

James Charles Rodgers was born in Meridian, Mississippi, on September 8, 1897. He was the son of Aaron W. Rodgers, a section

76 Gene Autry

foreman on the Gulf, Mobile and Ohio Railroad. His mother, Mrs. Eliza Bozeman Rodgers, died when he was four. He was to grow up in the boardinghouses, switch-shanties, and freight yards of the South. There, according to Nolan Porterfield of Southeast Missouri State College, on whose research much of this chapter is based, Rodgers was to learn "two essentials that were to mark the course of his life: (1) the human condition, at its best, is a tough proposition, and (2) music helps to lighten the load."

What was the strange appeal of this simple man and his simple, plaintive songs? His widow, the late Mrs. Carrie Rodgers, explains it this way in the 1935 biography of her husband:

"One of the reasons [for his success] was the many 'publics' Jimmie Rodgers could reach. Family groups delighted in his sentimental ballads. The poverty-stricken, gripped by sickness and troubles almost more than they could endure, knew that here was a fellow who understood; who had 'been there.' Far, lonely cabins on Western plains, on the high ranges, in distant forests; isolated dwellers in such places knew that this boy knew them, too.

"Railroad men and their families thrilled to his songs of the silver rails. Army men— hard-boiled, grim-faced he-men—scoff and wisecrack as they might, knew deep in their hearts a genuine liking for 'Soldier's Sweetheart.'

"Even the rowdies in poolrooms and barrooms—yes, he knew them, too.

"He talked the language of all of them. Sweethearts — mothers — fathers — hoboes —husbands and wives—even cops! For each, some gift of cheer, of sympathy, of broad or tender humor, Jimmie Rodgers reached them, every one, with his sobbing, lonesome yodels: held them with his whimsey, with his deliberate audacity. . . ."

Where had his music started, from what wellsprings did it start? As was to happen with Hank Williams later, it appears that the influence of Negro music had been very strong on Rodgers. Again, quoting *Jimmie Rodgers' Life Story:*

77 Elton Britt

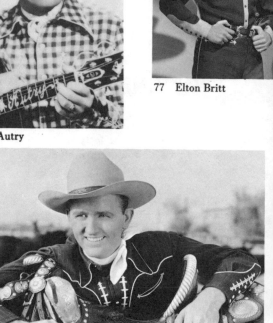

78 Jimmy Wakely

79 Bill Carlisle

80 T. Texas Tyler

81 Ernest Tubb

Eddy Arnold

83 Hank Williams

84 Lefty Frizzell

"The grinning, hard-working clacks who took Aaron Rodgers' orders made his small son laugh—often. Though small he was white. So, even when they bade him 'bring that water 'round,' they were deferential. During the noon dinner-rests, they taught him to plunk melody from banjo and guitar. They taught him darkey songs; moaning chants and crooning lullabies. . . . Perhaps that is where he learned that peculiar caressing slurring of such simple words as 'snow,' 'go,' so that, in later years when he crooned to the world: 'been away too long, up with the ice and snow-oo, somehow I crave to travel back where the warm, warm breezes blow-oo' listeners in faraway lonely shacks were enthralled."

It was from snatches of work songs and laments and blues songs that Rodgers later made his famous "blue yodels."

At fourteen, Rodgers' schooling ended as he went to work as an assistant foreman to his father. Later that year, 1911, he got a job as a brakeman on a freight-yard work train. A short time later, with the help of his older brother Walter, Jimmie became a regular on the New Orleans and Northeastern line between Meridian and New Orleans.

This began fourteen years of various railroad jobs. He was to work as callboy, flagman, baggagemaster, and brakeman. He would generally carry along a banjo or mandolin, singing to his crew buddies. In April, 1920, Rodgers married Carrie Williamson of Meridian, and the following January a daughter, Anita, was born. According to Porterfield:

"Growing up in foster homes and boardinghouses, riding freight cars across the Southland, unburdened and unattached, Jimmie had become accustomed to a rootless, restless, carefree existence. Marriage and the responsibility of a family seem to have had little effect on his wild, wandering spirit."

Although Rodgers had enjoyed the war boom in railroad jobs, spending $35 a week when he only earned $30, the easygoing days were soon to end. A losing streak, marked by poverty, bad health, and personal crises, began in December, 1923, with the death of his second child, June, six months old. At the time, Rodgers was job-hunting in New Orle-

85   James Charles Rodgers, age 19

86   The house Rodgers lived in during railroading days

ans and had to pawn his banjo to get back to Meridian for Christmas and the funeral of his daughter.

Briefly, things improved. He found a job on the railroads in Colorado and Utah, but although this offered economic security, it meant long separations from his family. Also, winters in the harsh cold of snow-covered freight yards and on lurching boxcars began to take their toll on a man whose physical condition was fragile at best. In the spring of 1924 he came home with a bad cold and an ominous, persistent cough. When flecks of blood began to appear, the onset of tuberculosis was evident.

In late 1924, Rodgers nearly died of a lung hemorrhage, and spent three days in a charity hospital. When he left, he knew that his railroad days were over. As John Greenway of the University of Colorado has written: "Like almost every incapacitated worker from ancient times in Greece to modern times in the South, Jimmie Rodgers finally became a singer."

In 1925, Rodgers joined a medicine show, plunking a banjo in blackface while touring Kentucky and Tennessee. But all he earned were his living expenses. Years before at twelve, Jimmie had won an amateur talent contest at a Meridian theater singing "Bill Bailey" and "Steamboat Bill." The years of strumming and singing in boxcars and railroad stations had improved his natural talents, but he had still to develop his distinctive guitar technique. After the medicine-show tour, he tried an adventure in show business of his own, investing in a Hawaiian road show and carnival. But the high winds destroyed the show's tent.

He returned to railroading in 1926. He worked as a brakeman on the Florida East Coast Railroad out of Miami, but the damp climate brought back the old TB. The Rodgers family got into a rickety old Dodge and headed for the high, dry air of Arizona. Rodgers worked briefly in Tucson on the Southern Pacific, but doctors warned him that railroading was too arduous. The Dodge was

7   Blue Yodeler's Paradise, the $50,000 home built by Rodgers in Kerrville, Tex.

sold, and the family was becoming desperate. After several months with his wife's family, Rodgers went alone to Asheville, North Carolina, where he got a job as a "special officer" on the city police force. It was soon obvious, though, that this was just charity on the part of a friend, Fred Jones, chief of detectives. Jimmie chose to quit rather than to featherbed. He supported his family that winter by working as janitor and furnaceman in an apartment house.

Music was still on his mind. "I'm trying to pick up a couple musicians to work with me," he told his wife. ". . . Boys who'll be willing to work whatever date I can get — schoolhouse, barn dance, roadhouse, beer joint — anything. . . . Folks everywhere are gettin' kind of tired of all this Black Bottom — Charleston — jazz music junk."

Out of this idea came the Jimmie Rodgers Entertainers. Rodgers played tenor banjo, Jack Price was on guitar, and the Grant Brothers, Claude on tenor banjo and Jack on mandolin banjo, rounded out what its leader called his "hillbilly ork." Everyone had his

ear on radio in those days, and the Entertainers felt hopeful when, in May, 1927, they got a three-times-a-week spot on WWNC in Asheville. They were paid a small sum by the city's Chamber of Commerce to tout the natural wonders of western North Carolina.

Despite heavy fan mail from "the folks out there in radio-land," by late June the band had lost its sponsor. The Jimmie Rodgers Entertainers barnstormed across the Southeast through the month of July, "playing the sticks, the tanks, the jerkwaters, the turkeys," enjoying moderate success in wayside school auditoriums. Soon, however, their one-night stands ran out, and the Entertainers and Rodgers' family were "busted." At this point, the "Singing Brakeman's" luck changed dramatically.

He made his first recording, for an initial royalty payment of $27.43, but within half a year his income from recording was to rise to $2,000 a month. In an era when banks were closing and bread lines were forming throughout the country, Jimmie Rodgers was to be the owner of a new Cadillac and Chrys-

88 In blackface during the early 1920's

89 Aaron Rodgers and son

ler, to wear tailor-made suits. He was to strum on a $1,500 guitar and build a $50,000 mansion—Blue Yodeler's Paradise—near Kerrville, Texas. In the words of Porterfield:

"Jimmie Rodgers was, in the parlance of press-agentry, an Overnight Success: from a penniless country boy bumming across the country in a second-hand Dodge, family in tow, playing for handouts and gas money, to wealth and national prominence—in less than a year. And hardly six years after he cut his first record, he was dead."

At a local general store in that unnamed hamlet, Mrs. Rodgers learned that a Victor talent scout was bringing a portable studio to Bristol, on the Tennessee-Virginia border, to audition country talent. Playing along the way for "beds, gas, oil and such food as we simply had to have," the Jimmie Rodgers Entertainers made their way to Bristol and a meeting with the Victor field engineer, Ralph S. Peer.

According to Clayton (Pappy) McMichen, the able fiddler with Gid Tanner and the Skillet-Lickers, it was McMichen who had introduced Rodgers to Peer, in Atlanta, in 1926 or 1927. Columbia, according to this account, had turned down Rodgers for recording, resting content in the knowledge that "we have Riley Puckett," the blind guitarist with the Skillet-Lickers.

McMichen recalls that Rodgers "was very high-strung, yet he was full of fun. He'd play any kind of trick on you he could. A born jokester, who didn't care about backstage Johnnies. If he saw someone he liked, he would give him fifty dollars, just like that."

In later years, at recording sessions with Rodgers in Camden, New Jersey, Pappy McMichen recalls taking care of the ailing Rodgers, even to the point of administering morphine shots. Rodgers told McMichen one day: "I'm not gonna lay in one of those hospital rooms and count the fly specks on the wall. I want to die with my shoes on."

However the initial meeting with Rodgers took place, Peer realized immediately that the "hillbilly ork" was mismatched, and he advised them to audition separately. On August 4, 1927, on the Tennessee side of State Street in Bristol, in an improvised office-studio of the Victor Talking Machine Company, Rodgers cut his first test records. That same week, the Carter Family also made their first recordings. For his test record, Rodgers chose "Sleep Baby Sleep" backed with "Soldier's Sweetheart."

"Sleep" was a traditional Southern mountain cradlesong and "Soldier's Sweetheart" was Rodgers' first composition, written during World War I for a railroad pal, Sam Williams, who had been killed in France. Here is how Porterfield describes the vacuum that Rodgers was to fill:

"Much of Rodgers' success and his subsequent influence upon so many commercial forms stems from the fact that he was the first big commercial success in the country and Western field. . . . It is important to note that he set many patterns and brought endless innovations to the form. He had few guidelines to follow. . . . There were no great names, no established styles, not even an exact delineation of the genre when Rodgers made his debut on the country-music scene.

"Although much of his material came from traditional sources, he imposed upon it his own innate concepts and left it indelibly stamped with the elements of his peculiar brand of back-country genius—the driving, unorthodox guitar runs, his freight-train whistles and lyrical yodels, his colorful, magnetic personality. . . ."

For the test record, Rodgers received twenty dollars. He and Carrie and their daughter Anita traveled to Washington, to await news from Victor. In the interim, Jimmie booked a few cheap dates in Washington suburbs and played between films in neighborhood theaters, and Carrie worked in the Happiness Tearoom.

In November, with still no word from Peer, Rodgers went to New York to see him. (Peer said later he wrote to him, but got no reply.) Peer arranged a second session for Rodgers at the Victor Studios in Camden, New Jersey. There, in the old Trinity Baptist Church, Rodgers cut "T for Texas" (the first of his famed blue yodels), "Away Out on the Mountain," "Ben Dew Berry's Final Run," and "Mother Was a Lady."

Ralph Peer told of the episode in an article in *The Meridian* (Miss.) *Star* on May 26, 1953:

"When I was alone with Jimmie in our

recording studio (a very old warehouse which had not been in use for many years) I was elated when I heard him perform without the unsuitable accompaniment. It seemed to me that he had his own personal and peculiar style, and I thought that his yodel alone might spell success. Very definitely he was worth a trial and he deserved my close personal attention.

"We ran into a snag almost immediately because, in order to earn a living in Asheville, he was singing mostly songs originated by the New York publishers—the current hits. Actually, he had only one song of his own—'Soldier's Sweetheart'—written several years before. When I told Jimmie what I needed to put him over as a recording artist, his perennial optimism bubbled over. If I would give him a week he could have a dozen songs ready, etc. Sticking to the established facts, I let him record his own song, and as a coupling his unique version of 'Rock All Our Babies to Sleep.' This I thought would be a

very good coupling as 'Soldier's Sweetheart' was a straight ballad and the other side gave him a chance to display his ability as a yodeler. In spite of the lack of repertoire, I considered Rodgers to be one of my best bets. Accordingly, I asked him to sign a managerial contract, explained to him the necessity to find new material, and talked to him about his future plans."

That winter in Washington still gave no evidence that fame and fortune were soon to hit Rodgers. He had several bouts with pleurisy and Carrie continued to work. But things were improving. Jimmie worked regularly in Washington theaters, had his own broadcast on WTFF. In February he returned to Camden for his third recording session. Billed as "Exclusive Victor Recording Star," the "Singing Brakeman," and "America's Blue Yodeler," he appeared with Gene Austin and went yachting up the Potomac on Austin's *Blue Heaven*.

By August, 1928, Rodgers headlined the

91 With one of his many cars

Jimmie, Mrs. Ralph Peer, Ralph Peer, Mrs. Rodgers, and daughter, Anita, at Blue Yodeler's Paradise, 1931

bill at the Earle Theater in Washington, and his recordings topped the best-sellers in Victor's list. In his six years Rodgers was to record 111 titles, from very commercial songs to the 13 blue yodels, authentic folk-styled recordings dealing with life's actualities. He was recorded with every sort of accompanists, from bad studio groups to blues background by Earl Hines and Louis Armstrong on "Blue Yodel No. 9."

Some of his songs and arrangements were pure commercial corn—"Desert Blues" and "Home Call," for instance. But through most of the blues, railroad songs, love ballads, cowboy songs, and the sentimental ditties rang the sound of a great artist.

Of all categories, the blues songs form the biggest number, with thirteen blue yodels and another twenty-five in a similar vein. In this most significant area of Rodgers songs, it is interesting to see to what degree he borrowed from Negro plantation spirituals, field hollers, and barroom ballads, and in turn, the influence he had on later blues and rhythm-and-blues singers, both white and Negro.

In a preliminary comparison, Porterfield says:

"It seems to me that much of the material

drawn upon by both Rodgers and various Negro artists simply derived from common sources, as so much lyrical gruel floating in the community soup. In some cases Rodgers apparently picked it up first; in others, he was borrowing from material already recorded."

Thus, a verse from his "Train Whistle Blues" of 1929 ends up in Peetie Wheatstraw's "C & A Blues" of 1931. Similarly a verse from "Blue Yodel No. 9" of 1930 pops up in "Number Runner's Blues" from Jimmy Gordon's Vip Vop Band of 1938. One of the most dramatic evidences of borrowing or influence of a Negro singer upon Rodgers is the couplet from a 1923 Paramount recording by Gertrude (Ma) Rainey of "Southern Blues":

If your house catch afire and there
   ain't no water 'round [twice]
Throw your trunk out of the window
   and let that shack burn down.

By 1928, the last line appears in Rodgers' "Brakeman's Blues" as:

Just put my trunk out the window and
   let the house burn on down.*

*© renewed 1956 by Peer International Corp. Used by permission.

93   Bill McWilliam, Lee Holden, Billy Burks, Jimmie and Clayton McMichen, Tupelo, Miss., 1930

94   Jimmy and Sunny Blevans on a picnic, 1930

95   Jimmie's Mickey

96   On tour, 1929

"America's Blue Yodeler"

JIMMIE RODGERS
EXCLUSIVE VICTOR RECORDING STAR
ENROUTE:

Meridian Miss,

July 27th 1932

Mr Clayton McMichen.
Radio Station W.H.K.
Cleveland Ohio.

Hello Clayton:

Well son heres the dope on Recording. I plan on leaving here about
Sunday morning July 31st ariveing in Washington D.C. the nation,s Capital
Wednesday evening the 3rd of August, and will expect you to meet me there then.
or not later than Thursday or Friday Aug the 4th or 5th. We will meet at my
Bro and Sister in Laws House Mr and Mrs Alex Nelson. The Adress is as follows
1148 Abbey Place North East. And Ole Fiddler and Violin playing fool I is Sho
looking for you to be there.

I am driving through in the ole Cadalic Mrs Rodgers and my little Daughter
Anita will be with me as far as Washington and we will go on to New York
togather. I am planing on having A good Banjo Player to go with us.
You may knaw him his name is Oddie McWindows. And boy can he play A banjo?
ll say he can. Mac he plays A 5 string Banjo ole style and also plays all the
popular stuff ████. I mean takes solos and playes leads. Well he beats any dam
hing I ever heard of Playing A banjo Baring no body..
r Peer says he wonts me to do at least 10 numbers so if you have any thing of
our own be sure to bring it along because Im pretty sure I can get several
f your Songs Recorded. Then after the Recording is all finished we all go
under the Hammer for the Audition with the N.B.C. which seams like A pretty
ood break as ther have been wonting me to work in Nwe York for the last 2 or 3
ears. Now about this guitar player you spoke to me about on the Phone A few days
go. I will do all I can to get Mr Peer to use him but I would Rather Not guarane
ny thing for him . But I will pay his expensesif he cares to come along with you
nd take chances on working. I mean eating and sleeping expensesas long as he is
with us.

Your Same Ole Pal Jimmie Rodgers

Porterfield shows that Rodgers' role in preserving and passing on certain lyrics and techniques of Negro singers is "perhaps shown even more extensively in a study of the phrases he shared with colored singers: 'good gal,' 'whole world,' 'ride the blinds,' 'let your drivers roll,' 'sweet lovin' daddy,' 'evening sun goes down,' etc."

The years from 1929 to 1932 were busy, profitable, and mainly happy ones for Jimmie Rodgers. In November, 1929, while in Camden to record, he made his only movie, a ten-minute short for Columbia, entitled *The Singing Brakeman*, in which he sang "Waiting for a Train" and "T for Texas" in front of a railroad café.

About 1930, the Rodgers family settled in Kerrville in the mansion he had built there to be near the TB sanitarium. There was to be a lot of traveling in those days also, when Jimmie played the Keith-Orpheum, Loew's, and Interstate circuits; going to Reynosa, Mexico, to help Will Horwitz, the Houston philanthropist, open the border radio station XED, or going to Oklahoma to be entertained by Pawnee Bill.

In January, 1931, Rodgers appeared with the humorist Will Rogers, who introduced him as "my distant son" at a benefit for Depression victims in San Antonio. In 1932, Rodgers went to Hollywood, where he held a recording session and met Stan Laurel and Oliver Hardy and their mentor, Hal Roach, the producer. In October, 1932, he made his farewell trip to Meridian, to celebrate the fiftieth wedding anniversary of Carrie's parents.

Rodgers' health was failing rapidly, not helped at all by hard work and hard living. In early 1933, he spent a month in the hospital and three months at home in bed. By early May, however, he had apparently recovered, and because his Victor contract was up for renewal, he traveled to New York to discuss new terms. He arranged to record twenty-four numbers starting May 17. Some accounts have it that Rodgers knew "my time ain't long" and that he didn't think he would return from New York alive. Always at the back of his mind was the thought of leaving Carrie and his daughter Anita with unreleased songs that would provide for them after his death.

97 Lani McIntire and his Hawaiians; Lani, third from left, second row

98 L to r, Billy Burks, Weldon Burks and Joe Kaipo with Rodge

99 Earl Hines, early 1930's

100 Louis Armstrong,

101 On tour with vaudeville group, Indiana, 1925

102 Jimmie Rodgers, Will Rogers

103 Theatre marquee on tour

By May 24, Rodgers had only recorded twelve songs. Among them were songs with such prophetic titles as "I'm Free From the Chain Gang Now" and "Yodeling My Way Back Home." The story persists that Rodgers was so weak for his final sessions at Victor's Twenty-fourth Street studio that he had to rest on a cot between trips to the microphone. But his voice remained relatively clear to the last.

On May 25, Rodgers began to hemorrhage as he was returning from dinner. Put to bed in his room in Manhattan's Manger (now Taft) Hotel, Rodgers lapsed into a coma. He died in the early hours of May 26, 1933.

The executor of his estate, Nate Williamson, described Jimmie's last railroad trip in the *Country Music Who's Who of 1960:*

"Jimmie was transported by train from New York to Meridian for interment, and even though this train reached Meridian in the nighttime, relatives and friends of Jimmie were at the station in great multitude. Many of them wept unashamed, as did I. Like a part of the night itself, a low, mellow train whistle, not the usual train whistle, but a long moaning that grew in volume as the train crept toward the terminal station continu-

104 With daughter, Anita, Kerrville, Tex., 1929

67

COLUMBIA-VICTOR GEMS
"THE SINGING BRAKEMAN"

THE CAST

Players   *Characters*

Jimmy Rogers   Jim

THE TECHNICAL STAFF

Directed by   Col. Jasper E. Brady

Cameramen   { Dal Clawson

                  { Frank Zukor

Stage Settings by   Eddie Kahn

Recorded by   Sooy Brothers

        Western Electric System

THE STORY IN BRIEF

THE SINGING BRAKEMAN is an instrumental and vocal presentation that is unique in conception and clever in execution. It features Jimmy Rogers, one of the cleverest guitar players on the professional stage. He has won international reputation for his songs with human appeal.

Against the picturesque background of a railroad station, Jim, the singing brakeman, strums his songs while waiting for a cup of coffee. He has been called for the 10.15 train and takes a hasty bite at the waiting-room lunch. The counter girl is fond of Jim's selections and requests him to render "Waiting for the Train," "Dear Old Dad," and "T for Texas." The last is a humorous ditty of many verses, each funnier than the previous. The music of the three songs is catchy and before Rogers has finished his first number, he has his audience with him.

As a short subject, "The Singing Brakeman" stands in a class by itself. It will round out any program in any theatre anywhere. Old and young alike of both sexes will enjoy the melodious voice of Jimmy Rogers, who has sung his way to the hearts of millions. The atmosphere of the railroad station, the kindly woman behind the refreshment counter and the characterization of Rogers are full of romance and recall the happy hours spent in the country during a vacation period or in childhood days. This is the reason why "The Singing Brakeman" has proved so popular wherever it has been shown.

105   Still photo from "The Singing Brakeman"

106   The converted church in Camden, N. J., no longer standing, where Jimmie did most of his recording and made his only sound movie, "The Singing Brakeman"

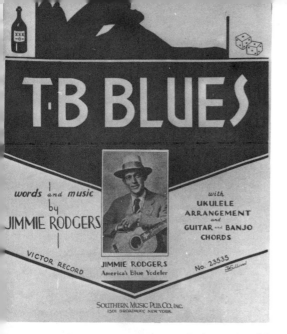

107 Hank Snow, Anita Rodgers, Ernest Tubb, Carrie Rodgers and Johnny Cash in front of the Jimmie Rodgers monument in Meridian, Miss., 1953

ously, never ceasing until the powerful engine breathed to a rest. The train crew knew Jimmie and how he loved the train whistle. It was their tribute to him."

The tributes have been sounding ever since. That year Bob Miller wrote a song, "The Death of Jimmie Rodgers," which enjoyed considerable popularity. The imitators, emulators, and disciples kept the blue yodels alive. Although it was the depth of the Depression (when records cost seventy-five cents and steaks forty cents) his records continued to sell. Estimates are difficult to arrive at, Brad McCuen of Victor explains, because of a fire after World War II in a Camden warehouse that held Victor sales data. Estimates of the number of single Rodgers disks sold have run from 5 to 75 million! A reliable compromise figure appears to be 20 million. The seven Victor LP reissues that McCuen has produced have sold more than half a million copies.

Among the more tireless proponents of the Rodgers legend has been Jim Evans, president of the Jimmie Rodgers Society in Lubbock, Texas. Evans has worked closely with all the researchers and record producers concerned with keeping the spirit of Jimmie Rodgers alive.

An annual country-music festival is held in Meridian in the third week in June, and the local hero is, of course, always recalled in song and story. Probably the most dramatic tribute to Rodgers was the Jimmie Rodgers Day held on May 26, 1953, to mark the twentieth anniversary of his death.

The event, which had the backing of Ernest Tubb and Hank Snow and Victor records, attracted political leaders and was simultaneously a tribute to the many railroad men of Meridian who had died in the pursuit of their occupation. Mrs. Casey Jones, widow of the legendary rail folk hero, was there, as were Governors Adlai Stevenson, Frank Clement and Jimmie Davis, and Senator James O. Eastland.

More than twenty thousand persons gathered to pay their respects to the "Singing Brakeman" as a stone monument carved in Italy was dedicated in Jimmie Rodgers Memorial Park. The Meridian and Bigbee line donated an old locomotive to be placed permanently in the park, and the Illinois Central donated a spur line to get the locomotive to its resting place. Railroad union officials, political leaders, and country stars spoke and sang the praises of Rodgers and the railmen for whom he spoke.

Mrs. Carrie Rodgers was to become an active figure in country music until her death in November, 1961. Johnny Cash now owns the screen rights to her biography of Rodgers, and there are discussions under way to turn this great story out of the American soil into a film.

A part of the Jimmie Rodgers story is retold around the world whenever one of his blue yodels is sung. A bit of him returns to life whenever a country musician carries on the grand tradition by singing in the high, lonesome, and stirring style of the tubercular railroad man who left such a deep mark on the face of American music.

4 THE INFLUENTIALS

The Carter Family - "Keep On The Sunny Side"

One of the strangest coincidences in American entertainment history occurred in August, 1927, in the town of Bristol, which straddles the Tennessee and Virginia border. Ralph Peer, the scout for Victor, met Jimmie Rodgers and the Carter Family, probably on the same day, August 1.

We have seen how the influence of Rodgers continued after his death in 1933. Although the Carter Family never hit the peaks of popularity that the "Singing Brakeman" did, this family group was to have a pervasively deep effect on all the currents of American country and folk music from 1927 until today.

Singing families have been a part of American life since colonial times. The Hutchinsons were one such notable group that flourished at the time of the Civil War. The Pickards, the Pritchetts, the Johnsons, the Ritchies are but a few better-known of nameless hundreds of groups that made home music for themselves, then spread out into the world of professional music-making.

Few singing families have had the impact on musical taste and style that the Carter Family, a trio of gentle-voiced Blue Ridge mountaineers, has had. The Carters established a style for close-harmony singing that was to become a pattern for dozens of professional groups to follow. The Carters' use of the Autoharp and guitar was a major departure for many selections that had earlier been sung without accompaniment. The Carters' guitar style, playing not only rhythm but also melodic accompaniment to voices, was another innovation. The roots of popular Bluegrass of the 1950's are traceable to this family from Clinch Mountain. The trio's hundreds of songs were to constitute one of the largest bodies of folk-country-hillbilly-popular songs we have.

Largely through recordings and recent appearances by Mother Maybelle Carter, the last of the original trio still performing, the city folk revivalists are very familiar with the original Carters. The group's fine songs are known in the city folk movement, too, either as performed by Joan Baez, Pete Seeger, the New Lost City Ramblers, Jean Ritchie, Doc Watson, and others, or as rewritten and adapted by Woody Guthrie, Bob Dylan, and others.

The Carter Family comes from a region rich in rolling country, and richer still in the colorful names that exude mental pictures of Southern rural life: Poor Valley between Pine Ridge and Clinch Mountain in Maces Springs, Scott County, Virginia. In this pocket of the Blue Ridge, Alvin Pleasant (known generally as A.P. or Doc) Carter was born on December 15, 1891. There had been Carters in this area since 1784, when they built Carter's Fort, a station on the old Wilderness Road from North Carolina to Kentucky.

According to Archie Green in his fine study, *The Carter Family's "Coal Miner's Blues"*: "Family tradition has it that when A.P. met Sara (Dougherty) she was singing the mournful railroad disaster ballad, 'Engine One-Forty-Three.'" A.P. and Sara were married on June 18, 1915, and settled in Maces Springs. The group called the Carter Family was formed in 1926 when Maybelle Addington, Sara's cousin, was married to A.P. Carter's brother, Ezra J. Carter. Maybelle moved to Poor Valley, bringing her guitar, banjo, and Autoharp.

The group's fame spread like wildflowers on a hillside. They sang at church affairs and local gatherings. In late July, 1927, the trio went to Bristol to audition for Peer. Sara Carter described the session in a letter to the

110   Jimmie Rodgers and the original Carter Family—Maybelle, A. P. and Sara, 1931

111   Recording session, Louisville, Ky.

LOOK!

Victor Artist

A. P. CARTER

and the

Carter Family

Will give a

MUSICAL PROGRAM

AT *Roseland Theater*

ON *Thursday August 1.*

The Program is Morally Good

Admission 15 and 25 Cents

A. P. CARTER, Mace Spring, Va.

late Australian discographer, John Edwards:

"So there was an ad come out in the Bristol, Va.-Tenn., paper for all talent to come to Bristol to try out on records. So we three decided to go. We made three records. 'Single Girl, Married Girl' tipped it off. The Carter Family and Jimmie Rodgers made a hit out of the talent that went."

A.P. was the group's leader. He sang bass and occasionally lead. Sara took most of the solos or lead in the part singing, playing Autoharp or guitar. Maybelle sang the tenor parts and was the guitar soloist. Her style of flat-picking melody on the bass strings, rather than treble strings, was distinctive. Coupled with the so-called church lick, a rhythmic device employing an upstroke, her playing is called Carter Family style.

In the next seventeen years, the Carter Family recorded more than 250 songs on 273 masters on a dozen labels that sold millions of copies. Soon they were traveling far from their Clinch Mountain home. Mother Maybelle recalls playing in theaters and schools in the late 1920's by lamplight, as they began their first tours through the Southeast. Sara and A.P. were divorced in 1932, but the trio stayed together until Sara was married to Coy Bayes in Texas in 1939 and settled in Angels Camp, California. For the following four years, the group worked six months out of the year.

112   Maybelle, A. P., and Sara

113 A. P., Maybelle, Jeanette, and the Phipps Family, Salt Gum, Ky.

Between 1938 and 1941, the Carters worked at the Mexican border station XERF across from Del Rio, Texas. During the early war years, the children of Sara and A.P.: Gladys, Jeanette, and Joe, and Maybelle's three daughters: Helen, June, and Anita, performed with the original trio. The group disbanded while they were at WBT in Charlotte.

A.P. died in retirement on November 7, 1960, and was buried in the Mount Vernon Methodist Church cemetery in Maces Springs. Johnny Cash described a visit to the cemetery:

"Having never heard a description of his monument nor a mention of it, I walked around and read 'A.P. Carter.' No date, no flowering verse, but just under that name was imbedded a gold record, which stated A.P. Carter's appropriate words simply and boldly: 'Keep On The Sunny Side.'"

Mother Maybelle continued to work with her three daughters, the Carter Sisters, on WRNL and WRVA in Richmond, and moved to "Grand Ole Opry" in 1950. Ralph Rinzler has aptly described why Mother Maybelle has had such popularity with city folk audiences at various collegiate festivals and at the Newport Folk Festival:

"Maybelle's singing and guitar playing have neither altered nor faltered since the days of the original Carter Family. The same deft

114   Texas, 1938-39, while they were on radio

15   Maybelle's three girls, Jeanette, and radio announcer, Bill Rinehart, 1938, Texas

116   Bob Dylan

117   Pete Seeger

118   Joan Baez

119   Doc Watson

120   Part of the Carter Family in 1965

Maybelle Carter

hand picks out tunes on the same Gibson guitar (purchased in 1929) with the assurance and rhythmic drive that characterized the instrumental work of the best of the old recordings. Her voice has lost none of its warmth and subtlety, and she has even expanded her approach somewhat by reviving the five-string banjo technique developed during childhood but never used with the original trio."

While the Carter Sisters lean toward modern country music, many traditionalists find it difficult to believe that Mother Maybelle should be appearing on "Grand Ole Opry" with drums behind her. With or without drums, here is a great woman singer and guitarist in the grand American mountain folk tradition.

If the original Carter Family cannot be heard today, there are fortunately several excellent reissues of the disks they made between 1927 and 1943. There are such touching songs as "Keep On The Sunny Side," "My Clinch Mountain Home," "Bury Me Under the Weeping Willow," "Cowboy Jack," "Foggy Mountain Top," "Poor Orphan Child," "Worried Man Blues," "Can the Circle Be Unbroken," "You Are My Flower," "Coal Miner's Blues," or "Wildwood Flower." Many Carter Family tunes have been recorded by Flatt and Scruggs, Johnny Cash, and a Kentucky group that has a remarkable similarity to the style and repertory of the Carters, the Phipps Family.

The songs of the original Carter Family comprise one of the finest bodies of traditional country music we have in America.

About the closest thing to a father-figure in country music is a thin, wispy man with a warm smile, a deeply lined face, and a yo-yo which he plays with on stage. If something good happens for country music in Nashville, more than a handful of musicians might remark, "Roy would like that" or "That would really please Roy."

The Roy invoked is Roy Acuff, who bears his title of "The King of Country Music" with a humility rare to most royalty. Since 1938, Acuff has held a peculiar position of eminence in this field, conditioned by his perennial popularity with audiences as much as by the kindly concern he shows toward most everyone in the field, as if they were his children.

Acuff is a millionaire several times over. He has been performer, song writer, band leader, publisher, and even political figure. Some of the songs he made famous during the late 1930's and World War II were to become as strongly symbolic of country music as had the blue yodels of Jimmie Rodgers before him. Was there a United States Army barracks anywhere around the world that didn't at one point ring to the sounds of Acuff's "Great Speckled Bird," "Wabash Cannon Ball," or the mournful, moralizing dirge by Dorsey Dixon, "Wreck on the Highway"?

In 1961, Acuff became the first living musician elected to the Country Music Hall of Fame. The citation read:

"Roy Acuff: The Smoky Mountain Boy . . . Fiddled and sang his way into the hearts of millions the world over, oftentimes bringing country music to areas where it had never been before. 'The King of Country Music' has carried his troupe of performers overseas to entertain his country's armed forces at Christmastime for more than twenty

years. Many successful artists credit their success to a helping hand and encouraging word from Roy Acuff."

The son of a judge who was also a Baptist preacher, Acuff was born in the Smoky Mountains of eastern Tennessee near Maynardsville. His first hope was to become a professional baseball player, but a serious sunstroke ended that dream. As he was recuperating, he learned to play the fiddle and began to appear on WNOX in Knoxville in 1933. He then worked with a small group called the Crazy Tennesseeans. He recalls backwoods schoolhouse one-nighters with twenty-five dollars total gate receipts.

One story has it that it took Acuff five years of trying to get onto the "Grand Ole Opry" roster. Finally, in February, 1938, he was invited. His first great hit was with the sacred song "The Great Speckled Bird," which has been his trade-mark since. The title is a symbol of the Bible, and is mentioned in the twelfth chapter of Jeremiah. Another great Acuff number, done with his customary fervor and sincerity, was a sacred number, "Radio Station S-A-V-E-D," in which the Saviour becomes, by a twist of modernity, the owner of a station that presents "news direct from Heaven."

This was to begin the first stage of Acuff's popularity. After Uncle Dave Macon, he was the second major star born on the "Opry." Acuff was one of the most sought-after performers in the first "Opry" tent shows and subsequent appearances in schoolhouses, at fairs, in parks, and in auditoriums.

Acuff appeared with Pap and His Jug Band, and with the Smoky Mountain Boys, Howdy Forrester, Jimmy Riddle, Shot Jackson, Robert Lunn, Bashful Brother Oswald and Sister Rachel, and later, June Stearn.

Acuff has recorded on six labels and sold

122   L to r, Lonnie "Pap" Wilson, Jess Easturday, Rachel Watson, Roy Acuff and Pete "Oswald" Kirby

123   L to r, Walter Bailes, Roy Acuff, Johnny Bailes and Oswald

124   L to r, Jimmy Riddle, Pete "Oswald" Kirby, Lonnie "Pap" Wilson, Joe Zinkans, Howdy Forrester and Roy Acuff in the 1950's

considerably more than 25 million disks. He is generally considered a "discovery" of the talent scout Art Satherley. By 1943, Acuff was undisputedly the biggest figure in country music, earning $200,000 a year, owning half interest in the powerful Acuff-Rose Music Publishing Company.

That year also saw Acuff's first brush with politics. As reported in *The Saturday Evening Post* of February 12, 1944, by Maurice Zolotow:

"Gov. Prentice Cooper was invited to grace the stage [of Ryman Auditorium] as guest of honor. Governor Cooper declined, stating that he would not be party to a 'circus,' and

that Acuff was bringing disgrace to Tennessee by making Nashville the hillbilly capital of the United States.

"Governor Cooper is supported by political boss Ed (Red Snapper) Crump, who is said to run Shelby County and Memphis with an iron-clad grip. And thereby hangs a tale. It being an off-day for news in Nashville, Beazely Thompson, a reporter for *The Nashville Tennesseean*, decided to stir up a little excitement. He reported Governor Cooper's acid comment to Acuff, and said it would be a fitting revenge if Acuff were to run for Governor. Acuff absently nodded, and that was all the encouragement Thompson needed. He immediately got up a petition, and now Acuff has been entered in the 1944 Democratic primaries. Boss Crump has been reported as much worried for the first time in his career. . . ."

The concern of the professional politicians was premature, however. Acuff bowed out of this campaign, but his friends from the stanch East Tennessee Republican area were insistent again in 1946. Finally, in 1948, while Acuff was making a film in Hollywood, his name was entered in the Republican primary. Without a campaign, Acuff defeated the other primary rival eight to one and entered the campaign in earnest. With his Smoky Mountain Boys he began to play and politick around the state. He noticed that the crowds

thinned out when the music ended and the politics started, but a Republican in Tennessee is foredoomed to trouble. Acuff conceded defeat to his old friend Gordon Browning, but later consoled himself by saying: "As Governor, I would have been just another politician. As a singer, I can be Roy Acuff."

"The King" has made repeated efforts to abdicate the country-music throne, but with little success. "Let's face it," he has stated publicly, "I just can't quit. I love that roar of the crowd. I have no idea how much longer I'll go on. My career should have been terminated long ago. We aren't an act that has something new or different every season. We have been doing some of our comedy and songs since we started. I suspect the public

125 Crowd at Dunbar Cave, Clarksville, Tenn., with members of Acuff's group performing

126 On tour in the Middle East

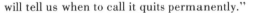

127 Roy Acuff today

will tell us when to call it quits permanently."

There seems little likelihood of that happening to the man *Collier's* magazine called the "Caruso of Mountain Music." Long behind him are the hundreds of thousands of miles on four continents where he has brought warmth and nostalgia to so many country fans.

Besides pursuing a rigorous performing schedule, Acuff has had a variety of outside interests. For a time he ran a tourist attraction, Dunbar Cave at Clarksville, Tennessee. His museum at Gatlinburg is being moved to Nashville, with its famous collection of old fiddles, hand-painted neckties, two thousand miniature bottles, coins, music boxes, and memorabilia of country music for the last thirty years.

Musically and temperamentally, Acuff wears his crown as "King of Country Music" with a gentle dignity. The sincerity he brings in his high tenor voice to the old songs is a thing of wonder. Backstage at the "Opry," he told a visitor who had admired his singing of "Little Birdie": "Thank you, son. I nearly got a tear in my eye. My mamma's favorite song, and she's been ailing. I'm glad you liked it."

Acuff is a millionaire who has never forgot his days of poverty, his homespun childhood days. This has been one of the sources of his perennial appeal to millions of listeners.

How ironic that the country singer best known in the cities for the last twenty-five years is virtually unknown by most country fans! But Woody Guthrie has probably told more city people about country everyman than any other performer. Guthrie wrote one thousand songs and ballads—and hundreds of stories, articles, and letters, plus three novels—that realistically described the everyday life of the country dweller. Some of his songs are classics that will live as long as music lives. "This Land Is Your Land," "Grand Coulee Dam," "Pastures of Plenty" are celebrations of the glories of America that make them almost anthems of patriotism.

Woodrow Wilson Guthrie was born in Okemah, Oklahoma, in 1912. His most active period as song writer, singer, author was between 1935 and 1950. By the late 1940's a vicious nerve disease had begun to still his voice and his pen. Now he lies ailing of incurable Huntington's chorea in a hospital in Brooklyn, New York.

A lot of verbal honors have been bestowed on Guthrie. He has been called "our best contemporary ballad composer," "the best folk ballad-maker whose identity has ever been known," "a rusty-voiced Homer," "an influence on America as strong as Walt Whitman."

Here is how Woody Guthrie defined the sort of songs he believed in writing:

"I hate a song that makes you think that you're not any good. I hate a song that makes you think that you are just born to lose. Bound to lose. No good to nobody. No good for nothing. Because you are either too old or too young or too fat or too thin or too ugly or too this or too that. Songs that run you down or songs that poke fun at you on account of your bad luck or your hard traveling. I am out to fight those kinds of songs to my very last breath of air and my last drop of blood.

"I am out to sing songs that will prove to you that this is your world and that if it has hit you pretty hard and knocked you for a dozen loops, no matter how hard it's run you down and rolled over you, no matter what color, what size you are, how you are built, I am out to sing the songs that make you take pride in yourself and in your work. And the songs I sing are made up for the most part by all sorts of folks just about like you."

In recent years, with the overlap of country music and the city folk-music boom, a few country artists have recorded some of the great Guthrie songs and ballads. Flatt and Scruggs have taped several and the Jordanaires have an album titled "This Land," after one of Guthrie's songs.

The country-music world knew of Guthrie heretofore through the popularity of his witty "Philadelphia Lawyer," and through his collaboration on such songs as "Oklahoma Hills" with his cousin Jack Guthrie. Jack, who had been a popular country singer in the Southwest, died in 1948 at the age of thirty-four.

Woody Guthrie followed the paths of the typical Oklahoma rural singer, driven out of the Dust Bowl of the mid-1930's with the suffering displaced farmers. After running a music show on WKVD, Los Angeles, in the late 1930's, Guthrie went East and fell in with the then leading members of the folk-song world, people like Pete Seeger, Burl Ives, Alan Lomax (who taped him for the Library of Congress in 1940), Leadbelly, Josh White, and others. For a time in the early 1940's, Guthrie sang with the Almanac Singers, one of the first city folk-song groups, and also traveled widely with his contemporary, the late Cisco Houston, and his disciple, Jack Elliott.

128 Bonneville Dam, Oregon

129 Tractored out, abandoned farm in the 1930's

130   Lee Hays, Burl Ives, Cisco Houston and Woody Guthrie

131   Jack Guthrie

THE SECRETARY OF THE INTERIOR

WASHINGTON

April 6, 1966

Dear Mr. Guthrie:

It gives me great pleasure to present you the Department of the Interior's Conservation Service Award. In conjunction with this award we are also naming a Bonneville Power Administration sub-station in your honor. It will be known hereafter as the Woody Guthrie Substation in recognition of the fine work you have done to make our people aware of their heritage and the land.

You sang that "this land belongs to you and me," and you sang from the heart of America that feels this about its land. You have articulated, in your songs, the sense of identification that each citizen of our country feels toward this land and the wonders which it holds. You brought to your songs a heart as big as all outdoors and we are fortunate to have music which expresses the love and affection each of us feels, though we are unable to express it so eloquently, toward this land... "from California to the New York Island—from the Redwood Forest to the Gulf Stream waters."

Yours was not a passing comment on the beauties of nature, but a living, breathing, singing force in our struggle to use our land and save it too. The greatness of this land is that people such as you, with creative talent, worked on it and that you told about that work—told about the power of the Bonneville Dam and the men who harnessed it, about the length of the Lincoln Highway and the men who laid it out. You have summarized the struggles and the deeply held convictions of all those who love our land and fight to protect it.

Sincerely yours,

Secretary of the Interior

United States Department of the Interior

CONSERVATION SERVICE AWARD

In recognition of honorable contributed services performed in connection with this Department's conservation activities

Woodrow W. Guthrie

is hereby awarded this certificate

Given under my hand and seal this sixth day of April 1966

Secretary of the Interior

Although Guthrie has stayed firmly in the folk world, he was a country singer who became a self-made intellectual. Almost all of the songs he wrote were new words and arrangements to traditional folk songs. He was strongly influenced by the singing of the Carter Family. Among Carter Family songs he reworked or adapted were "Wildwood Flower," which he converted into a topical song of World War II, "The Reuben James"; "The Wabash Cannonball" became, at Guthrie's hand, "The Big Grand Coulee Dam," one of many songs he wrote for the United States Government to help put across the Bonneville Power Project to the residents of the Pacific Northwest. Similarly, he converted the tune the Carters sang to the sacred "When the World's On Fire" and their secular "Little Darling Pal of Mine" into his famed "This Land."

The fact that Guthrie borrowed so much of traditional melody did not make him the lesser composer. He was following an age-old "folk process" of building a new song on the skeleton of an old song.

Probably the most famous Guthrie contribution was "Dust Bowl Ballads," which he recorded originally for Victor. Here, in song, was a small-voiced but large-scaled epic of the tragedy that afflicted so many in the Southwest. It was the tragedy that John Steinbeck was to recapture in *The Grapes of Wrath* and that John Ford re-created on film in a feature of that name.

The irony of Guthrie's having a large following in the cities and on the campuses, but still being largely unknown to most country-music fans, is strange indeed. A large crop of topical singers in the cities are considered "Woody's children." As more country artists and fans discover the wealth in the songs and writings of Woody Guthrie, they may yet find in him one of their greatest champions, one of their most dedicated and articulate interpreters.

Hank Williams — "I'm So Lonesome I Could Cry"

Much has been made of the tragedy that seems to stalk country music makers, from the death of Jimmie Rodgers from TB in 1933 to the death of Jim Reeves in an airplane crash in 1964. Musicians and poets have always been cursed by the tension of adjusting to their environments, and often their destruction is no accident, but self-destruction caused by themselves.

Hank Williams, an extraordinary poet and musician, died at twenty-nine of too much living, too much sorrow, too much love, too much alcohol and drugs. The cadaverous, lean six-foot man who was to hold a powerful sway over perhaps 15 million country fans around the world was born in a log cabin and died with five Cadillacs. He couldn't read or write music, yet composed 125 songs that include many classics of popular music.

Williams was the first country song writer to have become solidly entrenched with the pop singers of Tin Pan Alley, almost single-handedly bringing about the union of pop and country music which followed his death on New Year's Day, 1953. The thirteen years since his death have not diminished his stature. M-G-M continues to repackage his old recordings in more than twenty LP albums, leading many to believe that Williams is still alive. *Your Cheatin' Heart*, a film that had its premiere in Montgomery, Alabama, in November, 1964, helped keep the Williams story alive. The emergence of his son, Hank (Bocephus) Williams Jr., as a young Nashville star perpetuates the Williams legend.

The word "legend" is used with hesitation because the realities of Williams' short life are fanciful and dramatic enough without the embellishment of fiction. The real story may never be fully told while some of the other principals are alive. Williams had no greater enemy than himself, but he did antagonize many persons in his bursts of drinking and egomania. The role of his wife, Audrey, is one of inspiration or driving ambition, depending on whom you listen to.

But the enigmatic aspects of Williams' behavior pale in the light that he spread in his songs like some great folk bard of the Southland. That light cannot be eclipsed by the shadowy parts of his biography.

Hiram (Hank) Williams was born in a two-room log cabin outside Georgiana, Alabama, on September 17, 1923, to the poor family of a shell-shocked veteran of World War I. At the age of seven his mother gave him a $3.50 guitar, and soon thereafter "the hillbilly Shakespeare" was taking his first and only music lessons. His teacher was Tee-tot, a Negro street singer who instructed Hank while the boy was shining shoes and selling peanuts on the curbstones of Alabama towns.

Williams was to write songs in a variety of veins: "weepers," touching on the tragedy of love ("Cold, Cold Heart"); happy songs ("Hey, Good Lookin'"); philosophic pieces often in monologues under the name Luke, the Drifter; novelty tunes ("Kawliga"); and sacred songs ("I Saw the Light"). But he was essentially a white blues singer, probably the greatest ever known. Some of his songs, such as "Alone and Forsaken" and "I'm So Lonesome I Could Cry," although not strictly in the blues form, are among the most blistering statements of bitterness and sorrow ever put to melody.

It was one of his blues songs, "W.P.A. Blues," that won him fifteen dollars in an amateur contest in Montgomery's Empire Theater, when he was twelve. He immediately decided to form a band, the Drifting Cowboys, to bring to life his adolescent dream of being a cowboy. At the age of seventeen, he

132   Frank Walker and Hank Williams

133   Hank and Audrey Williams

134   Hank, Audrey and the Drifting Cowboys

ran off to Texas to become part of a rodeo. Fortified with whiskey, he tried riding a restless bronc, but the horse threw him and gave him a back injury that was to trouble him until his death.

He was playing a medicine show, selling and singing, in Banks, Alabama, when he met Audrey Shepherd, who was to become his bride. After a stormy courtship, in which he alternated between his need for the bottle and his need for her, she joined Williams' band. A year later, at a gas station near Andalusia, Alabama, Hank and Audrey were married.

Williams had a large following around Montgomery, and he deeply impressed Ernest Tubb when they played on a bill there together. Tubb recommended Hank to the late Jim Denny, then general manager of "Grand Ole Opry," but Denny was afraid of Hank's reputation as a hellcat. With the refusal of the "Opry" to sign him, he went to sing on the Shreveport "Louisiana Hayride" show. He continued to write songs, and later had a decisive meeting with Fred Rose, partner of Roy Acuff in the Acuff-Rose publishing house.

Rose was a thorough professional in the music business. He had established himself in the pop-music and Dixieland fields, and had written "Red Hot Mama" for Sophie Tucker and "Be Honest With Me" for Gene Autry. The initial meeting was between Audrey Williams and Fred and his son, Wesley Rose, as the Roses had just finished a game of ping-pong. Audrey said: "My husband has written some songs and I'd like you to hear them."

They went to the WSM studios for an audition, where, Wesley Rose has recalled: "We saw a tall, scrawny, sharp-featured kid, wearing pants too small for him and looking awfully frightened."

Hank sang several songs: "Move It On Over," "I Saw the Light," "Honky Tonkin'" and "When God Gathers His Jewels." Fred Rose, who was looking for material for Molly O'Day, was impressed. One account has it that he gave Hank a test to prove that he had really written his songs. He gave him an imaginary situation and sent Hank into a room for thirty minutes. He emerged with a version of "Mansion on the Hill." On April 12, 1948, Williams signed his first exclusive contract with Acuff-Rose. Rose facilitated another turning point for Hank — getting him to record for Frank Walker of M-G-M records, who bought some earlier Williams recordings on

135   Hank Williams

136   Lucrecia Ann and Randall Hank

the Sterling label. The help of Rose and Walker in guiding the turbulent talents of Williams cannot be overestimated.

"Move It On Over" was the first Hank Williams hit, and led Denny to book him on the "Opry." On June 11, 1949, Hank sang "Lovesick Blues" at the "Opry." Here is how it was retold in an excellent profile of Williams by Ed Linn in the January, 1957, issue of *Saga* magazine:

". . . he stopped the show colder than it has ever been stopped, before or since, in its 31 years. After Hank had gone through six encores, Red Foley had to make a little speech to quiet the place down and get the show back on schedule. . . ."

For the next two years, probably the happiest period in Williams' life, he kept his drinking in check and stayed out of hospitals and sanitariums. The money began to pour in, but Hank's old bitterness was there, and the birth of his son did not seem to halt it. At least one friend of Hank's has attributed part of his downfall to a success he felt he had not really earned. According to Minnie Pearl:

"Hank Williams was a strange man. Trying to cope with him was like riding a tiger; you couldn't ride it, and you couldn't get off. He was not prepared for the sudden fame or money. Money was a big pressure on him. Yet Hank was just as authentic as rain. A rough sack of bones who could tackle a buzz saw."

The Williams legend is filled now with stories of his shooting up hotel rooms, his tossing money around, his helping younger singers, his verbal fencing with hecklers in the audience, his recurring bitterness, and the strife with Audrey. For most of his three years on the "Opry," Hank was a luminary and well-behaved. But after his final break with Audrey in January, 1952, he fell apart. In a painful session for both men, Denny had to fire Hank from the "Opry" in September.

The time that followed his leaving Nashville was all falling action, as they say in the theater. Weeks after leaving Nashville, Hank married Billie Jones, a singer, on the stage of the New Orleans Auditorium as part of the show.

Officially, Williams died of a heart attack. To quote Ed Linn: "There have always been strong rumors, though, that he died of an overdose of drugs. The rumors are based on the fact that he was known to have been using sedatives to counteract the pain in his back (he had been operated on for two slipped discs). After he died, his wife got a bill from a 'Dr. Toby Marshall' for $736.39. Marshall, who turned out to be a paroled forger rather than a doctor, admitted that he had violated Federal narcotics regulations by giving Hank a prescription for 24 grains of chloral hydrate, a sedative usually prescribed for alcoholics. It is also a strong heart depressant."

Williams died in the back seat of his Cadillac as it was being driven to an appearance in Canton, Ohio, on January 1, 1953. Charles Carr, the chauffeur, was concerned about Hank's condition and stopped to look at him at Oak Hill, West Virginia. He touched Hank's hand and found it cold. Hank Williams was dead at 29.

At the Canton theater where he was scheduled to appear, a spotlight was thrown on the empty stage and a record of Hank singing his "I Saw the Light" was played. The audience rose and, crying, sang with the record. The funeral in Montgomery was called by Eli Waldron in a May 19, 1955, article in *The Reporter*, "the greatest emotional orgy in the city's history since the inauguration of Jefferson Davis."

Hank Williams' body lay on view at Montgomery's Municipal Auditorium. A throng of twenty-five thousand tried to attend the funeral, but only three thousand were able to gain entrance. "Luke, the Drifter" lay in state in a silver casket as Ernest Tubb sang "Beyond the Sunset," Roy Acuff sang "I Saw the Light," and Red Foley sang "Peace in the Valley." That year, 1953, Hank Williams records were to sell more than they had while their tortured, frustrated, lonely, bitter creator had lived. That year, his song "I'll Never Get Out of This World Alive" outsold all his other disks.

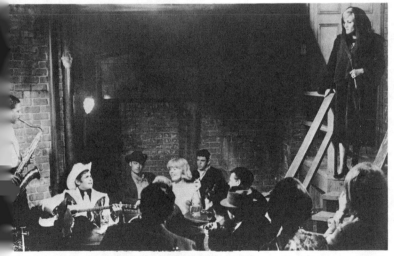

Movie Still from "Your Cheatin' Heart" starring George Hamilton

139   Hank Williams Jr., a star in his own right

138   Still from "Your Cheatin' Heart"

Few of the younger stars hold such a strong place in the grand country-music tradition as Johnny Cash. This lean, tall, mournfully intense singer and song writer has carried the folk ballad into the modern era.

In some instances the career of Johnny Cash, thirty-three years old in 1965, is similar to that of Elvis Presley's. Both rose through the world of folk, country, and blues to discovery by the Sun Recording Company of Memphis and then on to a major label. In other aspects, the personality of Cash reminds one of Rodgers and Williams. They, too, were gifted, driven men with almost embattled lives of hardship, either from the outer world or from the private torments that they inflicted upon themselves. Cash has been vexed by accidents, poverty, hard luck, sickness, and perhaps a singer's greatest curse — throat trouble.

Cash is an important influence on several levels. He and his music form a bridge between commercial country music and the folk tradition. He has an equally large following in city and country. He is a versatile performer who can move through blues, railroad songs, ballads, hymns, narrative "story" songs, love and Western songs with equal ease. He also stands at one end of the "rockabilly" trend in modern country music, with drums and an electric bass providing a strong, appealing rocking beat.

But above and beyond his "modern" sound, Cash sings with a deep soulfulness that is consistently convincing of his sincere identification with his lyrics. He is proud of his origins as a cotton farmer from Arkansas. He is proud of his descent from a Cherokee Indian.

He is finding a new identification with city folk audiences through his friendship with the young leader of the city folk-song writing

fraternity, Bob Dylan. (At the conclusion of the Newport [R.I.] Folk Festival of 1964, Cash, who had delivered a striking set of masterly story-telling songs, gave his guitar to Dylan. It was an age-old country singer's tribute to a fellow musician.)

Cash was born on February 26, 1932, to a family that lived in the dire poverty of the Depression in a shack near Kingsland, Arkansas, on the St. Louis and Southwestern Railroad. He nearly died of malnutrition before his mother stole some goat's milk to nurse him to health. His father, Roy Cash, was a hobo with a purpose: to scrounge up enough work to support his family of seven devout Baptists who sang hymns and folk songs almost by instinct. The father cut pulp wood for twelve hours a day for forty cents a day, picked cotton for thirty cents a hundred, railroaded. A passing train might mean "daddy was coming home."

President Roosevelt's New Deal meant a shift for the Cashes to twenty acres and a mule in the snake-infested delta farmland in Dyess, Arkansas, fifty miles from Memphis. A flood in 1937 sent the family to the hills. More cotton-picking and alternating bad-crop and good-crop years.

By the time Johnny entered junior high school, he had begun to write poems, stories, and songs, sometimes neglecting his studies for this "daydreaming." His first public singing was at seventeen, when he walked on trembling legs into a local talent contest and strode off, more confidently, with a five-dollar first prize. His mother secretly took in washing to earn fifty cents for voice lessons for Johnny, but his teacher wisely knew that he had natural talent that needed little shaping.

By 1944, the cotton land at Dyess Colony was becoming less fertile, and the Cashes took over an abandoned neighboring twenty acres and tried rotating crops to squeeze out a living. As late as 1946, the Cashes had no electricity in their home. Kerosene lamps provided light, and wood stoves were for cooking and heating.

At fourteen, Johnny took on a job of waterboy, because the stagnant stream of the Tyronza was full of snakes, turtles, and alligator-gar. He would sneak away from this job to listen to a Memphis radio show on a car radio. By the time he was graduated from high school, his heart was set on music. He traveled to Memphis to see his radio favorites, but ended up sitting bashfully at the back of the audience. He decided he wasn't ready to try selling his talents, and enlisted, instead, in the Air Force for four years. During basic training, at San Antonio, Texas, he overcame his great shyness about singing for others and entertained his barracks mates.

While at San Antonio he met Vivian Liberto, the girl whom, after a three-year separation while he served in Europe, he was to marry. It became such a post-office romance that they called it "our write-um, fold-um, lick-um, stick-um letter love." On July 4, 1954, Cash celebrated his independence from the Air Force and returned to his family and sweetheart in Memphis.

140   "The House I lived in from the time I was 3 to 18" (Dyess, A

141   "The road I walked down all my life"

142   "Dyess Colony Administration Building from the days of the New Deal. Mrs. Eleanor Roosevelt came to Dyess to dedicate the building in 1935"

143   "Where I went to the movies on Saturday night to see favorite pictures of Tex Ritter, Gene Autry, and all of them"

144   Johnny's home today, Casitas Springs, Calif.

While serving in Germany, Cash sang a lot with Air Force buddies and bought his first guitar, a cheap German instrument. Cash, who has been described as exceedingly self-critical, studied the styles of Rodgers, Williams, Hank Snow, and Ernest Tubb to develop his own manner. Johnny and Vivian were married August 7, 1954, in San Antonio. Still champing for a career in music, but not knowing how to approach it, he worked at a job he was ill-suited for, as a door-to-door appliance salesman.

A turning point occurred when his older brother, Roy, introduced Johnny to Luther Perkins, a guitarist, and Marshall Grant, a bass player. Johnny's songs seemed to blend in with their style. Impressed by the work of the new singer on Sun Records called Elvis Presley, Johnny arranged to have an audition with Sun's Sam Phillips. A month later, Phillips heard a half-dozen of Cash's songs without showing interest. "What else do you have?" Phillips asked him, and Cash sang six more, ending with "Hey, Porter." Phillips recorded that one on the spot, in one take. He asked Johnny for a love song better than any he had heard. That night, Cash wrote a "weeper" called "Cry, Cry, Cry."

145   On stage at Newport Folk Festival

146   Johnny Cash and Johnny Horton on a fishing trip

When Phillips called Cash in to sign the recording contract, Johnny had only fifteen cents in his pocket. His first record was released in June, 1955, and his first royalty check was for $6.40. After the record was beginning to catch on, Bob Neal, a Memphis disk jockey who was Presley's manager, asked him to be on a show with Presley. That night Neal asked Cash to tour Mississippi, Louisiana, and Texas. A second record by Johnny Cash and the Tennessee Two, "Folsom Prison Blues" and "So Doggone Lonesome," became a national hit. The trio moved on the "Louisiana Hayride" show.

By 1956, Cash's national stardom seemed assured. His song "I Walk the Line" was a hit for forty-four weeks, and trade papers named him the most promising new country artist. Soon he was on the roster of "Grand Ole Opry." By 1957, the trade papers were calling Cash the top country singer. The "promise" had been fulfilled.

Television and concert work followed, and Cash joined Columbia's label in the fall of 1958. He and his family moved to a trailer park and ranch at Casita Springs near Ventura, California, and he began acting. He had roles on four TV Western series and starred as a sadistic killer in the film, *Five Minutes to Live*. Other films include *The Night Rider* and *Hootenanny Hoot*. Tours of Europe and Australia, Japan and Korea followed.

Cash, who writes his songs anywhere, including in the back of his car, has had such hits as "Don't Take Your Guns to Town," "I Got Stripes," "What Do I Care," and "Next in Line." Among his most artistically successful albums are "Ride This Train," a spoken and sung epic of American rural life, and "Bitter Tears," a musical plea for better treatment for the American Indian, with songs by the star and by Peter LaFarge, a part-Indian folk singer.

Although a comfortable millionaire whose LP's have not sold less than 100,000 since 1958, Cash retains his feeling for the poor soil out of which his artistry grew. Onstage, generally dressed in black, he moves with a nervous, compelling grace, often pointing his guitar like a rifle at the audience. To this day, his favorite song of the thousands he knows and the hundreds he has written remains a song about his childhood in Arkansas. "Pickin' Time":

I got cotton in the bottom land
It's up, and growing, and I got a good stand.
My good wife and them kids of mine
Gonna get new shoes come pickin' time. (*)

*(C) Johnny Cash Music. Used with permission.

5 "GRAND OLE OPRY"—THE HILLBILLY CARNEGIE HALL

"Keep it down to earth, boys" —GEORGE D. HAY, THE SOLEMN OLD JUDGE

Few radio shows in the history of broadcasting have had such wide-ranging effect as "Grand Ole Opry." The show, which began on November 28, 1925, has become the longest continuous radio program ever presented in the United States. The "Opry" has probably done more to stimulate the growth of the music industry in Nashville than any other factor.

It is estimated that more than 10 million persons hear the Saturday night "Opry" broadcast over Nashville's WSM, or one of several subsidiary syndicated "Opry" broadcasts. Listeners in nearly every state and Canada keep swearing their allegiance to the grand old dinosaur of American radio.

Besides the impact the "Opry" has had on American musical tastes, the show has become a major tourist attraction. On July 4, 1964, a record for attendance at the show was established when 5,863 fans turned out. Many had lined up to get into the Grand Ole Opry House at 2 P.M., waiting for the show to start its four-and-a-half-hour run at 7:30 P.M.

A night at the "Opry" is a concoction of color, confusion, country culture, and corn. To observe the show is to see a spectacle rooted in the American grain. Only part of that spectacle is provided by the audience. More than 7,500,000 persons have viewed the show since its inception forty years ago.

The audience is made up of young lovers, old farmers, whole family groups who have traveled by bus for two days. Babies are dandled on knees, camera flashbulbs pop as favored stars amble to the microphone. Popcorn is crunched and soda pop swilled as if it were a picnic or a circus rather than a radio show.

On the stage, huge backdrops tout the products of such sponsors as the makers of evaporated milk, flour and corn meal, starch, salt, and rat eradicators. The procession of stars begins. A corral of cowboy types—Ernest Tubb, Hank Locklin, Bill Anderson, Billy Walker, Hank Snow, to name a few—outsplendor each other with mother-of-pearl guitars, fancy hand-tooled boots, wide-brimmed Stetsons, and jackets studded with colored sequins or rhinestones. It is a dazzling hubbub.

"New York advertising people just don't believe it when they see it," said Ott Devine, general manager of the "Opry," in an interview in Nashville in 1961. "They just don't understand the informality. When we start producing it, we kill it."

There seems no danger of the show's being killed, or even dying a natural death. The Saturday night show has stretched to four and one-half hours. The "Friday Night Opry" has outgrown its studio setting at WSM after fifteen years and has moved to the Grand Ole Opry House, which became in 1964 the official name of the Ryman Auditorium when the station bought the famous old tabernacle. In addition, taped radio broadcasts of each week's "Opry" are syndicated five days a week for fifty-five minutes each to more than four hundred stations in the United States and Canada. The movement of the "Opry" to television seemed imminent, and negotiations in this direction were announced at the thirty-ninth birthday party in November, 1964.

Already, several television shows by present or former "Opry" stars were bringing some of the flavor of the show to viewers. These include the Jimmy Dean show out of New York, the Carl Smith show out of Toronto, the Flatt and Scruggs and the Porter Wagoner shows out of Nashville. Another "Opry" star, Bill Anderson, was at work taping his TV show in the spring of 1965.

It is doubtful that any radio show has had such an impact on the city from which it emanates, or played such a powerful role in the

REV. SAM P. JONES.

NEW YORK.

147　Dr. Walter Damrosch

development of an industry. In large part, because of the vortex provided by the "Opry," Nashville was to become the center of the country-music business.

The origin of "Grand Ole Opry" can be traced to a Memphis newspaperman who loved country people and country music. George D. Hay was assigned by *The Memphis Commercial-Appeal* to cover the funeral of an Ozark-born marine who had died a hero in World War I. After the funeral, Hay filed his story and stayed the day in the town of Mammoth Spring. As he wrote in 1945:

"I sauntered around the town, at the edge of which, hard by the Missouri line, there lived a truck farmer in an old railroad car. He had seven or eight children and his wife seemed to be very tired with the tremendous job of caring for them. We chatted for a few minutes and the man went to his place of abode and brought forth a fiddle and a bow. He invited me to attend a 'hoedown' the neighbors were going to put on that night until 'the crack o' dawn' in a log cabin about a mile up a muddy road. He and two other

old-time musicians furnished the earthy rhythm. No one in the world has ever had more fun than those Ozark mountaineers did that night. It stuck with me until the idea became 'Grand Ole Opry' seven or eight years later. It is as fundamental as sunshine and rain, snow and wind and the light of the moon peeping through the trees. Some folks like it and some dislike it very much, but it'll be there long after you and I have passed out of this picture for the next one. . . ."

After this experience, Hay went on to be an announcer on WMC, Memphis, where his identifying signature was an old railroad whistle. He took his flair for announcing, his love of country music, and his whistle to WLS, Chicago, in the early days of that station's "Barn Dance." By the opening night of WSM, October 5, 1925, he had been hired by the Nashville station.

The official story and the popular legend of the birth of the "Opry" centers on an old Texas fiddler, Uncle Jimmy Thompson, who got things rolling on November 28, 1925. However, it appears certain that several of the old-timers who are still to be heard on the "Opry" preceded Uncle Jimmy playing country music on WSM.

At the death of Dr. Humphrey Bate in 1936, Judge Hay wrote in the house organ of the station's sponsor, the National Life and Accident Insurance Company: "He was among the very first on the program, which started in the fall of 1925. As a matter of fact, he played on the station before the barn dance started. . . ."

Dr. Bate was a respected physician and surgeon from Castilian Springs, Tennessee, who had served as an Army medic during the Spanish-American War. Folk music and playing the harmonica were his hobbies. Dr. Bate had learned most of his songs, according to his daughter, Mrs. Alcyon Bate Beasley, from an old Negro slave when he was a boy. He had formed a country string band around 1900. With a band called the Possum Hunters, Dr. Bate made his first appearance on WSM on October 25, 1925, before the opening of the "Opry."

Here history reaches an impasse. The popular story is that Uncle Jimmy Thompson and his niece, Mrs. Eva Thompson Jones, were the *only* performers on the night the WSM "Barn Dance" started, Saturday, November 28. Mrs. Beasley maintains that three members of the opening night broadcast also played, are still appearing on the "Opry," and deserve recognition. The three are Staley Walton, Burt Hutcherson of the Gully Jumpers, and herself, then a thirteen-year-old piano player with the Possum Hunters.

For some apparent symbolic reason, it was Uncle Jimmy Thompson who won the honors of that first night. His niece had introduced him to Judge Hay the previous night, and the judge had said that he would let the fiddling champion, then eighty years old, play old tunes, while his niece would play piano. The bearded fiddler was seated in front of an old carbon microphone, and the judge asked if there were any requests. At the end of the third number, another announcer jumped to the middle of the studio floor with a handful

of telegrams asking for listener requests. By 9 P.M., an hour after the fiddling had started, Hay asked Uncle Jimmy if he hadn't done enough fiddling. "Why, shucks, a man don't get warmed up in an hour. I just won an eight-day fiddling contest down in Dallas, Texas, and here's my blue ribbon to prove it," the fiddler replied.

The "Barn Dance" show was obviously off and running as a popular success. Uncle Jimmy soon was on the front page of *The Nashville Tennessean.* Fiddlers were all the national rage then, helped somewhat by the publicity over the encouragement given to square-dancing and fiddling by Henry Ford, the auto-maker. One of the first champions of Mr. Ford's competitions was one Mellie Dunham, an old Maine fiddler. WSM suggested a duel between Dunham and Uncle Jimmy, but there was not to be a Ford fiddler in Uncle Jimmy's future. "He's afeared of me," Uncle Jimmy remarked when Dunham refused the challenge. It added up to more publicity for the young "Barn Dance" show.

Among the other early performers on the WSM "Barn Dance" were a Mrs. Cline, who played the zither, and three old-time string bands besides the Possum Hunters. There were the Gully Jumpers, the Fruit Jar Drinkers, and the Crook Brothers. Another early string band was the Dixieliners, made up of Arthur Smith, fiddler, and Sam and Kirk McGee, guitarist and banjoist. The Dixieliners, by the way, recently played concerts in New York, Boston, and Philadelphia under the sponsorship of the Newport Folk Foundation.

The McGee Brothers and the Possum Hunters were among the first members of the "Opry" to record, in the mid-1920's, for Vocalion and Brunswick in Atlanta and New York. As Sam McGee reminisced later, with typical hillbilly self-burlesque: "They recorded us because we were outstanding in the field. And that's where they found us —out standing in the field." (In the early 1940's, Sam McGee tried to play an electric guitar on the "Opry," probably the first member of the troupe to do so. The Solemn Old Judge pulled out the restraining line that he was often to use whenever he felt the musicians were forgetting the country tradition of the show: "Keep it down to earth." The advent of the modern sound of country music was to be delayed for a while, at least.)

The actual naming of the show as "Grand Ole Opry" appears, from the close study of

149   Mellie Dunham and Henry Ford

150   Uncle Jimmy Thomson and niece, Eva Thompson Jones

151 Detail from facade of Ryman Auditorium

Nashville newspaper files by Don G. Cummings, to have occurred on December 10, 1927. Here is how it happened:

For two years the WSM "Barn Dance" was progressing on its merry way. The Nashville station, although geographically in the center of the Southeast, had varied its program fare and had joined the National Broadcasting Company network. From the network, on Saturday nights, WSM carried "The Music Appreciation Hour" directed by the great conductor and popularizer, Dr. Walter Damrosch, from New York. Here is how Hay described the episode in "The Story of the Grand Ole Opry," a pamphlet published in 1945:

"Dr. Damrosch always signed off his concert a minute or so before we hit the air with our mountain minstrels and vocal trapeze performers. We must confess that the change in pace and quality was immense. But that is part of America, fine lace and homespun cloth.

"The monitor in our Studio B was turned on, so that we would have a rough idea of the time which was fast approaching. At about five minutes before eight, your reporter called for silence in the studio. Out of the loudspeaker came the very correct, but accented voice of Dr. Damrosch and his words were something like this:

"'While most artists realize that there is no place in the classics for realism, nevertheless I am going to break one of my rules and present a composition by a young composer from 'Ioway,' who sent us his latest number, which depicts the onrush of a locomotive. . . '

"After which announcement the good doctor directed the symphony orchestra through the number which carried many 'shooshes' depicting an engine trying to come to a full stop. Then he closed his program with his usual sign-off.

"Our control operator gave us the signal which indicated that we were on the air. . . . We paid our respects to Dr. Damrosch and said on the air something like this: 'Friends, the program which just came to a close was devoted to the classics. Dr. Damrosch told us that it was generally agreed that there is no place in the classics for realism. . . . However, from here on out for the next three hours we will present nothing but realism. . . . It will be down to earth for the earthy.

"'In respectful contrast to Dr. Damrosch's

Judge Hay

153 DeFord Bailey

presentation of the number which depicts the onrush of the locomotives, we will call on one of our performers, Deford Bailey, with his harmonica, to give us the country version of his "Pan American Blues."' Whereupon, DeFord Bailey, a wizard with the harmonica, played the number. At the close of it, your reporter said: 'For the past hour we have been listening to music taken largely from Grand Opera, but from now on we will present "The Grand Ole Opry."' The name has stuck. . . . It seems to fit our shindig, hoedown, barn dance or 'rookus.'"

DeFord Bailey was the first and only Negro to be a regular on the "Opry." He started as a crippled boy and remained with the "Opry" some fifteen years. Judge Hay said Bailey knew about a dozen numbers but refused to learn more and was consequently dropped from the roster. Bailey is now in his seventies, running a shoeshine stand in Nashville adorned with a sign forbidding the use of profanity. Ralph Rinzler of the Newport Folk Foundation describes Bailey as still a powerful musician in 1965.

The first star of "Grand Ole Opry" was a vibrant, energetic oldster named Uncle Dave Macon, one of the most fascinating figures in country-music history. Uncle Dave epitomized many elements of country music: the freewheeling, high-kicking oldster with energy, capriciousness, and a warm heart. The banjoist would frail high-ringing, happy strums from his instrument. The alternately puckish and pious man knew the Bible "from kivver to kivver." The imitators or continuers of Uncle Dave Macon's style are many, from Grandpa Jones to Old Joe Clark. There was, for a time, even a citybilly descendant of Uncle Dave in Peter Stampfell.

If Jimmie Rodgers is to be considered the "father of country music," then Uncle Dave Macon probably deserves the title of "grandfather of country music." He has also been called the "Dixie Dew-Drop," the "king of the banjo-pickers," the "king of the hillbillies" and the "squire of Readyville."

The most typical remembrances of Uncle Dave by those who knew him well—Zeke Clements, Minnie Pearl, Sam McGee, Fiddling Sid Harkreader—show a slightly grizzled old-timer wearing a Senator's black plug hat, a red tie and his high gates-ajar wing collar. He had a mouth full of gold teeth, dating back to the fad for such dental jewelry in the mid-1920's.

155 Herald Goodman

Dorris and Uncle Dave Macon on stage at the "Opry"

Another view of Uncle Dave

David Macon was born in Cannon County, Tennessee, in the township of Smart Station, on October 7, 1870. He was of a large family of prosperous farmers who moved, when he was still young, to open a hotel on Broad Street in Nashville. It was here that Uncle Dave was bitten by the virus of show business, a virus that mixed with his traditional folk heritage. The Macon hotel was a stopping-over place for many in the entertainment world. While he attended the Hume-Fogg High School in Nashville, he was also studying at the feet of the entertainers at the family hotel, getting an education in music, comedy, and the ways of show folk.

Uncle Dave mastered the banjo and would carry three of them with him, each tuned to a different key. He developed a large repertory of secular and sacred songs. According to Hay, it was not until Macon was forty-eight years old (which would be in 1918) that he left his farm and decided to become a professional musician. Here is how Uncle Dave explained his decision to be a professional performer:

"All my life I had played and sung for fun. My neighbors always asked me to play at picnics and special occasions. Finally one very self-important farmer approached me and asked me to play at a party he was plan-

156 Crowd at the "Grand Ole Opry" for tickets

MINNIE PEARL'S
Grinder's Switch Gazette
OPRY
INDUSTRY · AGRICULTURE · TRANSPORTATION · COMMERCE
ONE YEAR $2.00   "The Sun Never Sets On The Grinder's Gazette"   25¢ PER COPY
Volume 1   Grinder's Switch, Tennessee, March, 1945   Number 7

Minnie Pearl Buys Auto

157   Minnie Pearl's own paper, 1945

ning. I was very busy and a bit tired, so I thought I would stop him. I told him I would play at his party for fifteen dollars. He said, 'Okay, it's a deal!' It was a large affair and in the crowd was a talent scout for Loew's Theaters."

The Loew's man offered him a booking at a leading theater in Birmingham at several hundred dollars a week. He was held over for several weeks, and then offered bookings throughout the country. "I was in the show business and I have been in it ever since," Macon said.

The career of Uncle Dave then becomes enmeshed with a frequent musical companion, Fiddling Sid Harkreader, who was interviewed in Nashville in March, 1964. According to Fiddling Sid, a Loew's theater man had heard him and Uncle Dave playing at Melton's barbershop on Second Avenue North in Nashville, in "19 and 21," and this led to further theater booking. "Uncle Dave had an act in which he had a little wagon drawn by two mules and he would ride on with me to get things started. We were with five other acts on the Loew's circuit, but we stopped the show every time. We were booked into the old Bijou in Birmingham and they packed them in so much the manager of the theater got arrested."

According to Fiddling Sid, Dave could turn almost anything into a joke. When the two went to New York to record in 1925, Uncle Dave went to a barbershop near the Times Square Hotel, where they were staying. Although Macon had only a fringe of hair, he asked the barber for a trim and a shoeshine. The barber, evidently sighting an easy mark from the country, charged Dave $7.50. Macon said, "That is cheaper than I expected." In his expense records, he made a notation for the episode: "$7.50: robbed in a barbershop."

Between 1921 and 1925 Sid and Uncle Dave toured the Loew's circuit and also played in many schoolhouses and small auditoriums. In early 1925, the first Nashville station, WDAD, began operations, and he played with his fiddler there on a variety show with Hawaiian guitarists such as Bob Martin and Tom Field. Sid started on the "Opry" in November, 1925, he recalls, which would also have put him on the first "Barn Dance" broadcast, and Uncle Dave joined him the next month.

Cousin Minnie Pearl recalled the "Opry" tent shows with Uncle Dave during World War II. "Uncle Dave used to carry a black satchel with him on these tours. In it was a pillow, a nightcap, his bottle of Jack Daniels (Tennessee Sour-Mash Bourbon) and a checkered bib. He was quite a ladies' man, who proved to me that some men never cease to believe themselves irresistible, no matter how old they are. We would often sit in the back of the tent while others were performing, and Uncle Dave would talk of religion. He complained about preachers departing from the Bible. He could quote at great length from Scripture and use it to solve all the problems of the world.

"Uncle Dave loved Jack Daniels," Minnie Pearl continued. "He would usually take a toddy at night. Many people thought he'd be drinking all the time, but he didn't need it for

162 On stage at "Opry." First row, l to r, Bobby Castleman, Jack Shook, Napp Bastian, Kirk Polton, Tommy Lefew, How Ragsdale, George Wilkenson, Claude Lampley, Gale Binkley, Amos Binkley, Tom Andrews, Mr. George; second row, Dee Simm Walter Ligitt, Dr. Humphrey Bate, Sally, Sarah, Uncle Dave Macon, Ed Poplin, Jack Woods, Robert Lunn, Paul Womack;

163 Robert Lunn

164 The Gully Jumpers, Paul, Burt and Charlie

, David Stone, DeFord Bailey, Buster Bates, Roy Hardison, Staley Walton, Oscar Stone, Honey Wild, Lasses White, Dorris
...on, Burt Hutcherson, Rabon Delmore, Alton Delmore, Sam McGee, Kirk McGee, Mr. Albright; 4th row, Charles Arrington,
...is Crook, Herman Crook, Ed Poplin Jr., Sid Harkreader, Arthur Smith, Judge Hay, Dixie Tabernacle in East Nashville, 1929

Sam and Kirk McGee and Fiddlin' Arthur Smith
...ing the 1930's

166   Sam and Kirk McGee today

113

that wonderful burst of energy. He was a born showman."

Judge Hay recalled a few changes that had to be made in the early 1930's when Uncle Dave was emerging as the first star of the "Opry." "When Uncle Dave came on we moved him back so that he would have plenty of room to kick as he played. He has always been an actor who thought the microphone was just a nuisance. It took a long time to 'hitch' him to it," Hay wrote.

The judge recalled the events around the first film of the "Opry," started by Republic Studios in 1939. The studio sent a man to case the "Opry" and evaluate the possibilities for a film. Uncle Dave was asked to entertain the Hollywood man at his farm in the Cannon County Hills. After a sumptuous meal for the producer, they sat for a spell and talked. The producer remarked to the judge later: "I have never met a more natural man in my life. He prays at the right time and he cusses at the right time and his jokes are as cute as the dickens."

The film was released in 1940, produced by Armand Schaefer and directed by Frank McDonald. Uncle Dave was one of the stars, with Roy Acuff and Judge Hay.

Macon frequently appeared with one of his seven sons, Dorris, who is still performing at the "Opry." Uncle Dave never retired. He continued his sprightly songs and instrumentals on the "Opry" until just a few weeks before his death in March, 1952, at the age of 81.

We can digress here for a moment to speak about rural comedy in general. This has always been a popular form of entertainment. One of the first rural-style entertainers to record on cylinders was Arthur Collins, who recorded such comic rural monologues as "The Preacher and the Bear" around the time of World War I. Cal Stewart, another rural humorist, had also recorded on cylinders his famous "Uncle Josh" stories, which utilized some country fiddling.

As we have seen, many of the early string bands used humorous names for their bands

158   Archie Campbell **relaxing backstage at the "Friday Night Opry"**

and featured a lot of comedy material. For a while, the Skillet-Lickers comedy records sold better than their music recordings. The "Opry" was always to be rich in the rural-comedy vein, drawing from the varied comedy traditions of the minstrel show, the medicine show, vaudeville, and the TAB circuits.

One early comedian and musician on the "Opry" was Zeke Clements, whose talents have spanned almost every aspect of the country-entertainment world. Clements was a Georgia-born guitarist who had known the early musicians on WSB when he was a boy. He started his radio career at the WLS "Barn Dance" in 1928 and joined the "Opry" about 1930. He had crossed paths with the successful vaudeville "rube" act of the Weaver Brothers and Elviry, and for a time had worked with a pioneer Western band, Otto Gray and the Oklahoma Cowboys.

Zeke had been a comedian in burlesque shows and found it easy to transform his material to a country format. Later he brought his own Western band onto the "Opry," Zeke Clements and the Bronco Busters. He also introduced the talented comedian Rod Brasfield to Judge Hay. Rodney Leon Brasfield was born in 1910 on a farm near Smithville, Mississippi. At sixteen he joined a traveling tent show with his brother Lawrence. Later the brothers worked together in an act with the Bisbee Comedians. After serving in the Air Force, Rod joined the "Opry" in 1944, and was one of the stalwarts until his death of a heart attack in 1958.

The story of country comedy would touch on such film and stage stars as Chic Sale and Will Rogers on up to Andy Griffith. The invention of the Clampetts on "The Beverly Hillbillies" is a continuation of this lively tradition of rural humor. Inevitably it turns on a native intelligence behind unsophisticated backwoods speech and manner. For a time, there was a girl named Dorothy Shay, who styled herself "The Park Avenue Hillbilly." To this list would be added such self-burlesquing types as Lum and Abner, Judy Canova, Bob Burns, and Jim Nabors.

Often country musicians invented subsidiary personalities. Bill Carlisle's comic alter ego was called "Hot-Shot Elmer." Later Ferlin Husky was to call his comic side-kick "Simon Crum."

One of the favored country comics and musicians with the city folk revival group is Grandpa (Louis Marshall) Jones, who works

159   Zeke Clements

160   The late Rod Brasfield, and Ferlin Husky filming a TV show

161   Cousin Wilbur

115

167 Lonnie "Pap" Wilson

168 Odie and Pap, Curley Rhodes and Lonnie Wilson

169 Homer and Jethro and Jimmy Dean on his TV show

170 Cousin Jody

171 Stringbean (Dave Akeman)

172 Lasses White and Honey Wild

73 Lasses and Honey in blackface

very much in the vein of Uncle Dave Macon. He had performed in the middle 1930's with Bradley Kincaid in New England. He wore his false mustache and whiskers then, and although only in his twenties, people used to ask how old he was. Grandpa brought his high-kicking boots and his banjo to the "Opry" in 1947, but since has left to do personal appearances and television from Nashville's WLAC.

Still another old-time banjoist on the "Opry" was Stringbean, who wears an outrageously funny costume that brings the junction of his shirt and belt well below his middle. Stringbean, who is Dave Akeman in private life, is a fine old-time banjoist with a delightful comic flair.

Another of the WSM comics and musicians who has remained popular for years is James C. Summey, who calls himself Cousin Jody. Under his squashed, beat-up hat, Jody looks like a man who left his dentures sitting in a glass beside his bed. He plays an old steel guitar he calls a "biscuit board." He joined the "Opry" in 1938 with the Roy Acuff band and has also worked with the Pee Wee King band. Someone has remarked that Jody was destined to be a country comic because he was born in a town called Possum Hollow, Tennessee.

Another "Opry" star of the mid-1930's was Robert Lunn, called "the original talking blues man." He took a style that had been recorded in the 1920's by Chris Bouchillon of speaking against a guitar vamping that became the format called "talking blues." Among his comedy numbers was "Tooth Pickin' Time in False Teeth Valley." For a time, Lunn worked closely with the Roy Acuff band, besides his own group, called the Talking Blues Boys. Biographical information on Lunn is scarce, because he would speak to this writer about his career in country music only if he would be paid a sum of five hundred dollars! Evidently Mr. Lunn has a case of the blues talking without compensation.

A good deal of country humor is predicated on a prime rural crop, corn. Crazy Elmer, a clownlike figure who has long been with the WWVA "Jamboree," will tell you about how he went on a garlic diet and lost five pounds and twenty-two friends in only one week. Then, too, humor pops up in strange places. An early announcer on WSM said in introducing the President of the United States:

174   Beecher Kirby (Oswald) and Miss Rachel Veach

175   The Girl from Grinder's Switch, Minnie Pearl,

"Here is Herbert Hoover." The announcer then asked, under his breath, "And who the hell wants to hear Hoover?" The microphone was still live; the indiscretion cost that announcer his job.

One of the finest country comedians to have come out of "Grand Ole Opry" is Benjamin Francis (Whitey) Ford, who is popularly known as the Duke of Paducah. His closing line, "I'm going back to the wagon, boys, these shoes are killing me!" became a well-known signature. Ford was born in DeSoto, Missouri, in 1901. He began on station KTHS, Hot Springs, Arkansas, in 1924. He served in the Navy, then toured the country with a band called Benny Ford and His Arkansas Travellers. He next worked the Keith vaudeville circuit with Otto Gray's Oklahoma Cowboys and for a time was Gene Autry's master of ceremonies. It is indicative of how much the medicine-show experience has contributed to country music and comedy that the Duke of Paducah has credited his work on this circuit as the most valuable.

Although the Duke of Paducah was far from being unsophisticated, he kept his humor riveted to the level that would catch on most readily with rural audiences. A few quotations from his "Joke Boke," published in 1947, will give a bit of the flavor of his wit:

"I'd rather live in the country than in the city. That's why I own a farm. Not long ago, a fellow asked me how to find my farm, and I told him. I said: 'You turn north and head out of town five miles, then you turn east and go eight miles, then you turn west and go four miles.' He said: 'Yeah, but how will I know it's your farm when I come to it?' And I said: 'You can't miss it. There'll be a horse looking out the kitchen window.' . . . . I got a wonderful mule out there on my farm. That mule is really intelligent. Anytime anybody yells: 'Hey, there—you jackass!' both of us turn around. . . . But I'm an expert farmer. I've got what it takes to make things grow. In fact, the fertilizer company just sent me another big load of it recently. . . ."

76 Minnie Pearl and Buddy Ebsen of "The Beverly Hillbillies"

177 Lonzo and Oscar, 1965

A comedienne who has become something of the grand old lady of "Grand Ole Opry" is Cousin Minnie Pearl. Pearl, as she is familiarly known at the "Opry," spreads natural joy about her like a frontier preacher dispensing benedictions. She has been on the "Opry" since 1940 and is considered one of its chief stars.

Ironically, Cousin Minnie Pearl is an "invented" role for Mrs. Sarah Ophelia Colley Cannon, who attended a swank social school, Ward-Belmont College in Nashville. Here is how she described the origin of her comedy character role, in an interview in March, 1964: "I was 'city broke,' having graduated from a finishing school. For six years after leaving Ward-Belmont I worked in rural areas producing amateur musical comedies out of Atlanta. It gave me a chance to really make a study of country girls. I became Minnie Pearl in 1936 at Brenlea Mountain in Baileyton, Alabama, at a show. I was staying in a mountain cabin and met a fine old mountain woman there who told so many tales and funny stories. After spending ten days with her, I began to quote her, and people would laugh. She was like Granny on 'Beverly Hillbillies,' a sprightly, brittle, hardy woman with a bun of hair on the top of her head."

This mountain woman was to provide the matrix for Minnie Pearl's appearance on the "Opry." Pearl remembers asking the Alabama woman if she had children, and she replied: "I've had sixteen young 'uns. Never failed to make a crop." Her father, who had been in the lumber business until the Depression hit the family hard, had advised Pearl simply: "If you keep it kind, you would make a million dollars."

Pearl has kept it kind, and she has kept her strong hold on the audience for twenty-five years. She will walk on stage in a cotton dress with a straw hat with a price tag hanging from its brim. "Howdy," she will trumpet, and the audience will greet her warmly. "I'm just so proud to be here!" Then, she'll break into her homespun routine of family humor. Describing the character of Minnie Pearl, Mrs. Cannon almost speaks of her as another person: "Minnie Pearl is not an unattractive country woman, but is a warm, lighthearted, zany kind of girl who needs some way to get men's attention. She is still hopeful of getting a man."

Many other comics have appeared on the "Opry" in its forty years. Among them are Cousin Wilbur (Bill Westbrook), known for his dunce cap with a spring in it; Lonzo and Oscar and Archie Campbell.

In Hay's story of "Grand Ole Opry," he recounts how the noted blackface minstrel comedian Lasses White joined the station in 1932. Social change has gradually eliminated this form of entertainment, but for a time Lasses White and his partner Lee Davis (Honey) Wild remained strong on the show. White was born on a Texas farm, attracted to the theater, and worked in stock and played for a time with the Swor Brothers. He became an understudy of the well-known minstrel Honey Boy Evans and completed shows for Evans after that star's death. White went on to a successful career in films.

Not the least of the factors for the popularity of the Roy Acuff band, which joined the "Opry" in 1938, was a long and distinguished series of comedians who worked with the Smoky Mountain Boys. Among these were Lonnie Wilson, who as "Pap" led a jug band for twenty years. Wilson had modeled this "rube" character after his uncle, whom he described as "truly a character; his cheerful humor made him the spark of his community."

Other comic-musicians who appeared with Acuff were Beecher R. Kirby, known as Bashful Brother Oswald, Rachel Veach, and Joe Zinkans.

Probably the best-known country comics today are two men who have only done two guest spots on "Grand Ole Opry," Homer and Jethro. Here are a few of their own words of self-description:

"Homer (Henry D. Haynes) and Jethro (Kenneth C. Burns), the Everly Brothers of the Stone Age, have been a team since 1932. Their home town is Knoxville. We don't publicize this fact; when we left there we agreed to keep it quiet if they would. After serving in World War II, they appeared on several low-budget radio shows. . . . We got a record contract with King Records. . . . Our records were an instant hit in shooting galleries. . . ." Actually, since they have been recording for R.C.A. Victor, and appearing on national radio and television, Homer and Jethro have been enjoying great popularity. They report that "our children are boys and girls. We drive Cadillacs when we can't get a taxi."

The story of country comedy is a long and fascinating one which should some day be fully documented. But the role of humor as a vital element in the history of country music cannot be underplayed. Minnie Pearl gets an ecstatic look on her face describing how warming it was to see the first of her audiences laughing at her jokes. "They come to see me because we share a mutual affection. We like to enjoy human frailties."

Picking up the thread again of the early music-makers on the "Opry," we must be

178 Asher and Little Jimmie Sizemore

179 The Arizona Wranglers, in the 1930's. Rear, l to r, Sleepy, Slicker, Hungry, Dynamite, Robbins, Irontail, Sherrif

180   Pee Wee King's Golden West Cowboys, l to r, Fiddling Redd Stewart, Eddy Arnold, San Antonio Rose, Cowboy Joe (Joe Zinkans) and Pee Wee King

cursory in describing many of the early performers. There were so many. It is believed that the first group on the "Opry" to bring in Western cowboy dress was Ken Hackley's. Slim Smith and the Arizona Wranglers and the Zeke Clements Bronco Busters, also in Western dress, followed, all about 1930 or 1931. An early family group was the Pickard Family and Theron Hale and his two daughters, Elizabeth and Mamie Ruth.

The judge described an interesting problem he faced in directing the musical course of the "Opry." "One of the bands which played with us for several years with good results was known simply as Ed Poplin and his Band. . . . They played well, specializing in folk music, although once in a while, before we could or did stop it, Uncle Ed would slip in an old popular song, such as 'When You Wore a Tulip and I Wore a Red, Red Rose.' There is not much difference between that number and for instance, 'Darlin' Nellie Gray,' except that we have always regarded the latter as strictly folk music. The line of demarcation between the old popular tunes and folk tunes is indeed slight. We have just as much trouble, if not more, now sorting them out. We have tried to keep the 'Opry' Southern in flavor, although any folk tune is okay."

Other early "Opry" performers were two blind men, Uncle Joe Mangrum and Fred Schriver, the former a fine old-time fiddler, and the latter a pianist and accordionist. Very popular with audiences were Asher and Little Jimmy Sizemore, the little one starting on the show when only six. The judge had high praise for Asher Sizemore as a shrewd showman who had first worked in the coal mines of eastern Kentucky.

One of the more flamboyant showmen of the "Opry" was Pee Wee King, who brought his Golden West Cowboys onto the show in the late 1930's. Pee Wee was, with Redd Stewart, the composer of the country evergreen "The Tennessee Waltz." King was the son-in-law of a famous early country-music promoter and manager, J. L. Frank.

181 Eddy Arnold at 6, in first suit his mother made for him

182 Eddy Arnold, Center; behind him, Howard McNatt, on St. Louis broadcast, 1938; others unknown

183 At age of 17 with Howard McNatt,

184 Eddy Arnold and Gov. Frank Clement, 1964

The first few years of the "Opry" were dominated by instrumental music rather than vocal music. It was not, indeed, until the rise of Roy Acuff that the show had a singing star. But in 1931 the first important vocal group joined the show. Three minister's sons, Herald Goodman, Dean Upson, and Curt Poulton, formed a group called the Vagabonds, which did some religious material and such "heart" songs as their very popular "When It's Lamp Lighting Time in the Valley."

Among the earliest women to score a success on the show were Mrs. Edna Wilson and Mrs. Margaret Waters, who appeared as Sarie and Sally. They did rural dialect stories on WSM starting in 1933, dressed in huge sunbonnets and aprons. Along with Uncle Dave they were the most popular performers at the early tent shows or picnics put on by the "Opry." The first such picnic, 1932, in

185 Ernest Tubb's first home, Crisp, Tex.

West Tennessee, attracted eight thousand persons at ten cents a head.

Back in the days when an old-time fiddler was still important to any radio barn dance, Curley Fox was one of the most reputable musicians in the country field. He had won competitions against some of the best fiddlers in the nation, started on Atlanta radio in 1933, and came to the "Opry" from WLWL, Cincinnati, in the late 1930's. He first worked with Texas Ruby Owen, who was called "Radio's Original Yodeling Cowgirl," and they later married. Texas Ruby died in a tragic fire in 1963. Curley Fox continues one of the esteemed old-time fiddlers in Nashville. Another early band was Jack Shook and his Missouri Mountaineers, two well-known members of which were Napp Bastian and Dee Simmons.

Even in the 1930's the "Opry" was developing its role as "the hillbilly Carnegie Hall," the place where the most popular and most accomplished country performers ultimately gravitated. Among these were Lew Childre from Alabama, Clyde Moody from North Carolina, and the Poe Sisters, Nell and Ruth, from Mississippi. The Bailes Brothers, John and Walter, joined the show from West Virginia, and Dan Bailey and his country band came from East Tennessee.

Between the periods when Roy Acuff and Hank Williams were, with Uncle Dave Macon, the major stars on the "Opry," three musicians who represented other forms of country music were to rise to stardom. The three, known wherever country music is known, have grown to become leaders of the Nashville music community—Ernest Tubb, Hank Snow, and Eddy Arnold.

On several levels, Ernest Tubb is a major figure in country-music history. He was one of the leading carriers of the Jimmie Rodgers tradition into the modern era. He was one of the first bandleaders to help develop the "honky-tonk" style, a fusion of Western swing and country vocal style. Tubb was among the first to use the electric guitar as a regular instrument in his band, the Texas Troubadours.

Tubb is a tall, lean, gaunt Texan who resembles the epitome of the cowboy singer as well as a sort of latter-day Abe Lincoln. He is one of the most highly respected figures in the Nashville and "Opry" scenes, sharing with Roy Acuff the paternal role in helping many young performers to get started.

Tubb was born near the town of Crisp, Texas, in 1914. A recording of Jimmie Rodgers' "T for Texas" made a lifelong impression on him from the time he was thirteen. Although he was living in San Antonio in the early 1930's while Rodgers was flourishing there, Tubb never met his idol. After his first radio job, on KONO in San Antonio, he met Mrs. Rodgers. She took him under her wing, presented him with one of her late husband's guitars, and helped him plan his first theater tour. At this point he was still riding on the Rodgers vogue, having mastered the yodeling style of the "Singing Brakeman."

Tubb recorded "I'll Get Along Somehow" for Dave Kapp of Decca in San Antonio. In 1941 his song "Walking the Floor Over You" became a national hit and in 1942 he joined the "Opry." There will be more discussion of the "honky-tonk" style in the chapter on Western swing. But as it pertains to Tubb, the change in his style marked something of a landmark in country music. This is how Billy Charles Malone described the transformation:

"The development of Ernest Tubb's career is suggestive of what was happening to country music as a whole. In his earliest appearances he accompanied himself, a la Jimmie Rodgers, on the guitar. Later, another musician joined him as lead guitarist, while Tubb

186 Ernest Tubb, elected to the C.M.A. Hall of Fame in 1965

provided the rhythm. Therefore, as his success increased, so did the size of his band. In the early 1940's, as the jukebox became a firm fixture in roadside taverns, some of the honky-tonk operators complained to Decca that it was difficult to hear the Ernest Tubb records after business picked up at night.

"Prior to this time, the Tubb instrumentation had consisted of two unamplified guitars. At his next recording session, he was accompanied by an electric guitar played by Fay (Smitty) Smith, the staff guitarist at KGKO in Fort Worth. Tubb then instructed his regular guitarist, Jimmie Short, to attach an electric pick-up to his conventional Martin guitar. Ernest Tubb, therefore, was one of the first country performers to feature an electric guitar, and the process through which he came to do so is representative of what was causing other entertainers to do likewise. Whereas the jukebox caused tavern operators to desire a louder type of music for the

187 Ernest Tubb, 1937

188 Justin Tubb

machine, hillbilly performers were deciding among themselves that the honky-tonk conditions necessitated an amplification of their instruments."

The introduction of the electric guitar to "Grand Ole Opry," however, preceded Tubb. In 1940, Pee Wee King's band, the Golden West Cowboys, had an electric guitar played by Clell Summey. King still expresses pride in the innovations in country music that his band made on the "Opry" from 1937 to 1947. Harold (Sticks) McDonald introduced drums with the Cowboys in 1947, and probably the first trumpet on the show was played by a King sideman, Buddy Herold, in 1945 as taps for the death of President Franklin D. Roosevelt. The guitar that Sam McGee had tried to play on the "Opry" was an amplified Spanish guitar, but King's man played an electric steel guitar.

The advent of drums on the "Opry" was equally controversial, meeting the opposition of Judge Hay as well as many of the tradition-directed musicians and fans. King said in the spring of 1964 that there had been so much of a stir about the drums in his band that he was told not to announce their use. After two or three "Opry" appearances with the drums, King had to exclude them. In 1945 or 1946, Bob Wills, the Western swing bandleader, brought drums on, but, according to one story, hid them behind a stage curtain at the "Opry." It is the recollection of several

189 Curley Fox and the late Texas Ruby

Nashville veterans that the drums finally were admitted on the "Opry" to accompany Ferlin Husky in his song "Wings of a Dove."

Tubb was otherwise to make history in Nashville as one of the first country artists to record there. Paul Cohen, a record scout for Decca, holds the honor of being the first man to record in Nashville, a pioneer event that was to lead to the city's ultimately rivaling New York and Hollywood as a recording center.

The first country star to actually record in Nashville appears to have been Red Foley. This was in Studio B at Station WSM. The date, despite repeated efforts, cannot be established beyond March or April, 1945.

Foley, by the way, had been a star on the "Opry" for about eight years prior to his wife's death in 1952. He migrated in 1954 to Springfield, Missouri, to run "The Ozark Jubilee" on KWTO. The show eventually was televised on the A.B.C. network to more than one hundred stations.

The date for Tubb's first Nashville recordings is clearly authenticated, however. Also at WSM, Tubb cut the single "It Just Don't Matter Now" and "When Love Turns to Hate" on September 11, 1945. This session was run by Paul Cohen for Decca, and Tubb was thus the second artist to have been commercially recorded in Nashville, aside from transcriptions.

I had a long interview with Tubb in the back of his music store on Broadway, around the corner from the Grand Ole Opry House. Tubb had opened the record and book store in 1946, and it does a thriving business. "The 'Opry' is like the Palace Theater to country musicians. After the 'Opry,' there is no place to go. You either go down professionally or you stay here," Tubb said.

He described how strongly the "Opry" had affected his own popularity. In his first six months on the show, Tubb's record sales doubled. Both he and Red Foley were riding high during World War II, each having standing orders for 200,000 copies of their records.

Tubb was one of the "Opry" stars who brought country music to Carnegie Hall for two performances in 1947. "We could have played all week there," he said. (Another "Opry" troupe visited Carnegie Hall in November, 1961, and sold out the hall.)

Tubb has actively fought for the dignity of the music and musicians. He long opposed the term "hillbilly" as degrading, and called

190   Hank Snow today

191   Hank, the Singing Ranger

126

this to Hay's attention. Tubb asked Decca not to list his recordings as "hillbilly" on the release sheet, but to call it "country music" instead.

After the start of recording in Nashville at WSM, two of the station's engineers, Aaron Shelton and Carl Jenkins, opened the Castle Studio in the old Tulane Hotel on Eighth Street. After Decca pioneered in recording in Nashville, other record companies followed suit.

The career of another performer on the "Opry" has had many similarities with the Ernest Tubb story. Hank Snow began as a musical disciple of Jimmie Rodgers and today also owns a music shop in Nashville, his store specializing in instruments. Snow has been a member of the "Opry" roster for fifteen years, has been recording for R.C.A. Victor for twenty-nine. Snow was born in Liverpool, Nova Scotia, Canada, in 1915. At the age of twelve he started three years' service on the Atlantic as a cabin boy on fishing schooners. In 1937 with an appearance on a Halifax radio station he got the nickname the "singing ranger," although he had never been a ranger. In 1947 he left his prosperous traveling show in Canada and traveled to Hollywood.

"Hollywood, as the saying goes, obviously wasn't ready for me—or vice versa," Snow was quoted by Red O'Donnell in a profile in *The Many Worlds of Music*, the B.M.I. journal. Snow headed for Dallas, where a disk jockey had been playing some of his Canadian recordings. He picked up bookings in Texas, including one with a show headed by Tubb. It was largely through the efforts of Tubb that Snow got his first "Opry" audition. He made his first "Opry" appearance on January 7, 1950.

"I don't mind telling you that I bombed. The people just sat there while I sang. And sat. No applause, no nothing, almost. Just sat."

Discouraged, Snow was thinking of returning to Texas when one of his own songs, "I'm Movin' On," caught fire, and then "Opry" audiences began to take notice of all he was singing. "I'm Movin' On" was in a genre in which Snow is particularly adept—the train song.

Both Tubb and Snow have moved from styles heavily derivative of Jimmie Rodgers to a more modern, suave pop country format. But the links to the great tradition are still to be found in their singing.

Another major singing star, Eddy Arnold,

192 **Hank Snow and his band**

has changed almost completely from a singer with country roots to a pop singer. In the late 1940's Arnold was one of the biggest figures in country music, reaching, if not eclipsing, the dominant position held by Roy Acuff. When Arnold came off his farm at Madisonville, Tennessee, he called himself the "Tennessee plowboy." At first he worked with the Pee Wee King Golden West Cowboys band, singing in a style reminiscent of Gene Autry. Actually, it is closer to say that Arnold, and later Marty Robbins, was influenced in his smooth, easy vocal style by a blind performer named Pete Cassell, a favorite on "Crossroad Follies" on Atlanta's WSB in the 1930's. Arnold made his first recordings, for R.C.A. Victor, in 1944. Here is how Malone described the subsequent changes in Arnold's career.

"As the years passed and as his success mounted, Arnold's singing style changed. By 1947, when he recorded the very popular 'Bouquet of Roses,' Arnold had taken on a more sustained and more forceful approach. Arnold's career is representative of that of many country singers, who, after a period of initial success, become dissatisfied with their original rural style and strive to achieve a more polished and smoother approach. On so doing, they become, perhaps, more accomplished, self-conscious vocalists; but with an attending loss of rustic simplicity and sincerity. By the mid-1950's Eddy Arnold could no longer be pictured as strictly a hillbilly singer. Instead, he had greatly modified his vocal delivery, and was making a determined effort to attract attention as a 'popular' singer."

Stylistic changes aside, Arnold is a leading figure in Nashville life today. February, 1964, was designated by Tennessee's Governor Frank G. Clement as "Eddy Arnold Month" to mark the twentieth anniversary of his recording for Victor. Arnold is not only close to political leaders in Tennessee, but is a friend of the Lyndon Johnsons, and has himself often been mentioned as a likely political contender.

The changes in style of these three "Opry" stars match in essence many of the developments that were to affect the "Opry" in its forty-year history. The show kept moving to provide more space for the growing roster of performers and the growing number of spectators. (By 1965 the show had 50 stars and 150 sidemen or guests.) The broadcast at an early time had moved to Studio B, which

193   War Memorial Auditorium, Nashville

194   Backstage room where older musicians congregate

195   The Crook Brothers backstage

196 "Friday Night Opry" broadcast as it was held in the WSM Building

had large plate-glass windows so that several hundred could watch. The "Opry" audiences soon outgrew that environment and the station built an auditorium studio which seated about five hundred persons, with a portable stage and acoustically treated walls and ceilings. One night, however, the crowds so filled up the entrance to the home of the National Life and Accident Insurance Company that two of the officials couldn't get into their offices. The audience was politely asked to leave the building, and for a while the "Opry" was broadcast without listeners present. This soon robbed the show of much vitality, and another site was sought.

The Hillsboro Theater, a neighborhood movie house, was rented and two separate audiences 'would fill the small theater each Saturday night. Agents of the insurance company distributed free tickets to prospective or actual clients. (The password of an agent paying a home call had become, simply: "I'm from the 'Grand Ole Opry,' " which opened many a rural door to him.) The show moved in 1939 into the War Memorial Auditorium, which seated twenty-two hundred. Even though by then twenty-five cents admission was charged, the War Memorial proved too small. Finally, the "Opry" moved in 1941 to its present site, the Ryman Auditorium, the largest hall in central Tennessee.

Ryman Auditorium had been built in 1892, the same year as Carnegie Hall, by a Capt. Tom Ryman, who owned a line of Cumberland River excursion boats. Ryman had been converted by a famous revivalist, the late Sam Jones of Cartersville, Georgia, in a

197 Billy Walker

198 The Browns, rehearsing backstage at "Friday Night Opry"

preachment on the subject of mothers. Ryman was so moved, he undertook to raise the money for a tabernacle "so Sam Jones wouldn't have to preach in a tent."

The ungainly old building has beautiful acoustics and curved wood church pews that hold thirty-five hundred persons. Despite the fact that Actors Equity recently found the dressing-room facilities beneath its standards, the hall continues to serve country music well. The Ryman has also been the site for many all-night religious sings, such as those run by Wally Fowler. In early 1964, WSM purchased the auditorium, renamed it the Grand Ole Opry House, and planned structural improvements.

Payment to musicians for appearing on the "Opry" is minimum union scale. Stars get only about $30. One spot on the show will pay only $10 for a sideman with $4 for each additional spot. A bandleader may only earn $15 to $18 for doing a show on the "Opry," but we heard no complaints in Nashville. Although a star will appear on the "Opry" for a token fee, it is the exposure and the affiliation with the "Opry" that may help him get $1,500 to $2,000 for one-night stands outside of Nashville. The "Opry" roster was recently cut down to include only those who appear twenty-six times a year.

If the hubbub in the Opry House audience is great, if the spectacle on the stage is a sort of controlled chaos, the scene backstage is beyond description! Here is a cramped, stuffy meeting place for musicians who work hard and long, traveling thousands of miles each year to do personal appearances around the world. There is a strong feeling of fraternity among the country musicians that is unlike anything else in America's jazz, classical, pop, or folk-music worlds. There is concern when one of their number is ill, and there is tragedy when one of their number dies.

It has almost seemed as if the "Opry" were stalked by tragedy. From the death of Hank Williams in 1953 to the death of Jim Reeves in an airplane crash outside Nashville in the summer of 1964, the toll of continuous air and motor travel and hard living has been high. A tragic crash on March 6, 1963, of a private plane cost the lives of three of the most beloved performers on the "Opry"—Patsy Cline, Cowboy Copas, and Hawkshaw Hawkins. Almost as if to underline such songs of death and tragedy that country singers lean to so much, such as Copas' "Hillbilly Heaven," these losses on the "Opry" were not soon forgotten.

Reeves, who had been very popular on several European tours, was to have the post-

199   The late cowboy Copas and daughter

200 The Jordanaires; l to r, Neal Mathews, Gordon Stoker, Ray Walker, Hoyt Hawkins, Jerry Byrd, steel guitar; Hawkshaw Hawkins at piano and Patsy Cline

humous honor of having his recordings break many sales records in Scandinavia, Britain, West Germany, and South Africa. Robert Cooper, general manager of WSM, put these losses into the tradition of show business by remarking: "Eight members of the 'Opry' lost their lives in four separate accidents in a little over a year; the show went on."

It would be impossible, within the confines of this survey, to discuss every performer who has played a role in "Grand Ole Opry" in the last forty years. It would be impossible to mention the contribution of the large staff of directors, announcers, technicians, and others who pull the show together each week.

In the space available we cannot include the stories that have grown, like stalks of corn, about the "Opry" stars and others associated with the show. For instance, that boy from East Tupelo, Mississippi, named Elvis Presley who once slapped a bass on the "Opry." Or that lovely young Vanderbilt graduate, named Fannie Rose (later Dinah) Shore, who passed through the "Opry" on

201 The late Jim Reeves

202   Marty Robbins

203   Porter Wagoner and his band

204   Stonewall Jackson at the "Opry"

205   Kitty Wells

her way to becoming a national singing star. The Everly Brothers passed through, too, on their way to rock 'n' roll fame.

It would take a whole book to recount the story of each of the artists. We know they and their fans will appreciate that we are not slighting them by only including a photo. We know they'll understand that the contributions of the Craigs, Harry Stone, Ralph Emery, Jack De Witt, Marvin Hughes, the late Jim Denny, Vito Pellittieri, Trudy Stamper, Jack Stapp, Bill Williams, Grant Turner, Len Hensel, and others cannot be given in detail. It would be easier to list the few people in country music who have *not* had some contact with the "Opry."

206 The Ernest Tubb broadcast after the "Opry" at the Tubb Record Shop. Here, with his youngest son

The Solemn Old Judge has gone into retirement since the late 1940's, and Uncle Dave Macon died in 1952. Ott Devine took over the reins of the show as general manager and tries to accommodate the wide range of tastes that now stand for "country music."

When traditionalists hear the modern sounds of country music they are often disturbed, feeling the "Opry" has gone off course. But Devine maintains "we have to keep pace with the times." In general, the change in the show reflects the change in the whole area of country music.

"Grand Ole Opry" is a large and emotional institution. It rings with rebel yells and the reverent cheers of fans who have traveled for days to see their favorite performers. It has been on the air each Saturday night since November 28, 1925, except for an occasional Fireside Chat by President Roosevelt. It has generally reflected the course and development of country music, from the scraping sounds of an eighty-year-old fiddler to the up-to-the-minute novelty tunes of Roger Miller. It has seen its controversies and tragedies. But it has been the loudest, strongest, longest single voice in country music.

It helped the emerging country-music industry to form a nucleus within a few blocks of where it was being broadcast, and it soon had its imitators all around the nation. Films have been made about "Grand Ole Opry," and untold records and personal appearances have carried the banner of the "Opry" around the world. It has become, in its forty clanging, ringing years, the sound of country music today.

207   Irma Frost and Ernest Stoneman, 1925

6   THE BLUEGRASS GROWS ALL AROUND

Few styles of country music are more exciting in rhythm or drive than Bluegrass. This string-band music has been called "folk music with overdrive." It has been compared to the sprightly sounds of Dixieland jazz or the energetic, driving gypsy bands of Eastern Europe.

Bluegrass is a very strong link in the chain of country music, connecting old-time banjo and fiddle duets of the nineteenth century to such modern sounds as the background music of the popular TV show "Beverly Hillbillies."

You hear the bright strains of "Flint Hill Special" or "Molly and Tenbrooks" and a picture of the typical Bluegrass band leaps into your mind. There are five or six colorfully jacketed musicians with string bow ties and broad-brimmed Stetsons. One member of the band, the bassist probably, is in a tramp's costume, with baggy trousers, galluses, and a clown's hat. The Bluegrass band clusters in a semicircle, then almost breaks into a dance as the players bob and weave to get close to the mike.

The faces are placid, unemotional. But the music is not. The banjo crackles with showers of notes, flying about like metal confetti in a windstorm. The fiddler whips his bow across the strings, doing daring slides and audacious double-stops. The bass is slapped gustily. The Dobro, a steel guitar fretted with a metal bar in the Hawaiian fashion, makes a purring sound. The mandolin, suggesting a brittle, nervous cat walking a telephone wire, scampers at dangerous speed. Above it all, riding high and penetrating, is a tenor voice, or several voices in two- and three-part close harmony.

Bluegrass is folk music, handed down by tradition, enriched by new ideas, but still part of a long line of descendants. Even though some of the songs date from the string-band era of the 1920's and before, Bluegrass has nothing if not a fresh sound. It can almost have a jazz quality of freewheeling voices and instruments weaving in and out, some for rhythm, others up front for melody.

While the fascinating story of Bluegrass is planted in the hills and flatlands of the Southeast, it can also be told by the young musicians and fans of Northern cities and college campuses. In the middle and late 1950's Bluegrass began to take the cities by storm. Soon not only were there large audiences for rural Bluegrass bands in the North, but a large coterie of city folk musicians were also learning Bluegrass songs and banjo runs.

This form of country music has built the principal bridge between rural and urban music fans. There was a Bluegrass band at Yale, the Gray Sky Boys; another at Harvard, the Charles River Valley Boys. Roger Sprung brought Scruggs-picking up to the Sunday free-for-alls at Washington Square Park in New York, the Greenwich Village gathering place for folk fans. Mike Seeger, another who helped popularize Bluegrass, played for a time with the band of Ralph and Stanley Carter. Eric Weissberg, a New York youth who studied at the Juilliard School of Music, became such a wizard at playing Scruggs-style banjo that even Earl Scruggs sang his praises. A city Bluegrass band, the New York City Ramblers, and banjoist, Bob Yellin, won awards at the nation's oldest continuous country festival, the forty-year-old Old-Time Fiddlers' Convention at Union Grove, North Carolina.

Although Bluegrass has captivated the city folk audience, its largest following remains in the rural areas. Two names dominate the Bluegrass picture: Bill Monroe and Earl Scruggs. Monroe is credited with being the "father of Bluegrass." His various bands

209   Charlie and Bill Monroe

208   Charlie Monroe and Kentucky Partners

210   Bill Monroe and his Blue Grass Boys on "Grand Old Opry", 1942

211   Bill Monroe and his Blue Grass boys today

212   Bill Monroe, 1947

Bill Monroe today

have been seedbeds for the formation of the musical and vocal style which derives its name from his band, the Bluegrass Boys, and his native Kentucky, the Bluegrass State.

Monroe was born in 1911 in the heavily wooded Jerusalem Ridge section near Rosine, Kentucky. He began his professional career in 1930 as a mandolinist and tenor with his older brothers, Charlie and Birch Monroe. By October, 1939, Bill Monroe and His Bluegrass Boys had built a sufficient reputation to earn him a place on the roster of "Grand Ole Opry." When he marked his twenty-fifth anniversary on the "Opry" he had become a keystone of the traditional music offered on the show. Steadfastly, despite the many changes of those years, he had clung to one of the recognizable traits of Bluegrass—unamplified instruments.

Since about 1944, according to a story by Ralph Rinzler in *Hootenanny* magazine (March, 1964), the Monroe band has achieved a regular format which has become an approximate standard for all Bluegrass bands. That instrumentation is guitar, bass, mandolin, fiddle, and banjo.

Rinzler, a city mandolinist and singer who has been the talent and folklore coordinator for the Newport Folk Foundation since 1964, has been greatly influenced by Monroe's artistry. Rinzler gave up his own thriving career as a performer with the city Bluegrass band, the Greenbriar Boys, to help serve the Monroe band. Here is how Rinzler described the Monroe legend:

"Monroe is a legendary figure in the world of country music; his regal bearing, pride almost to the point of arrogance, terse expression and profound musical dynamism have given rise to countless tales among the few who know him and the many who admire him.

"His vocal range has set a standard that produced the popular boast: 'I'll bet he can sing higher than Bill Monroe,' or the jest: 'That was so high, it would take Bill Monroe to sing bass to it.'

"His virtuoso compositions for mandolin and other Bluegrass lead instruments are standard fare for city and country musicians alike. His songs and ballads, sung in his often-imitated, cavalier style, have provided material for many artists' recordings and repertoire.

214 The Stoneman Family, 1953

215 J. E. Mainer's group today

216 Jim and Jesse McReynolds

217 The New Lost City Ramblers, Tracy Schwarz, Mike Seeger and John Cohen

"Bill Monroe is a musician's musician. His respect for his own music is, according to Mike Seeger, like the attitude that a concert artist has for his work. Known as the Father and King of Bluegrass Music, Bill Monroe continues to carry on his function as a leader and an inspiration to other musicians — not as a commercial faddist, but as the profound artist and creator that he is."

Monroe has virtually run a "Bluegrass school" with his bands, sending "graduates" all over the country. Among them are Mac Wiseman, an exceedingly able singer, who is, incidentally, one of the few country performers to have studied at a classical conservatory; Don Reno, a fabulous banjo virtuoso who went on to form his own band with Red Smiley, the Tennessee Cut-Ups.

Jimmy Martin was with Monroe five years before he formed his own band, now heard frequently on WWVA, Wheeling. Other alumni of the Monroe band are Carter Stanley, Gordon Terry, Sonny Osborne, Clyde Moody, and Chubby Wise. Wise, incidentally, was the fiddler from Florida whose smooth bowing and flashy effects gave much of the outlines to subsequent Bluegrass fiddling.

Another city performer, besides Rinzler, who has played with Monroe is Bill (or Brad) Keith, a young Bostonian whose banjo became a brilliant addition to the band in 1963.

In describing the songs of the modern Bluegrass bands, Mike Seeger wrote in his notes to the excellent album "Mountain Music Bluegrass Style" (Folkways):

"The songs themselves are mostly built on traditional patterns, 4-line verse, 3 or 4 chords, and in simple 2/4 or 4/4 time: instrumentals are usually in a breakneck 4/4 time and, like the songs, are performed with great skill. Often new songs are made from the old with a change of words, harmony, treatment, or pace. The subject matter is most usually unsuccessful love, but also covers home, mother, catastrophes, religion, and almost anything else. . . . Monroe has written a number of

218   The Stoneman Family rehearsing on "Jimmy Dean Show"

219 Flatt and Scruggs at Carnegie Hall, 1964

his own songs, as do many other artists.''

Few are those who can forget Monroe's singing of "Mule-Skinner Blues" and "Kentucky Waltz" or the burning religious fervor of his "Wayfaring Stranger." It is ironic to recall that the first song recorded by Elvis Presley was a composition by Monroe, "Blue Moon of Kentucky."

The most famous alumni of the Monroe band went on to become such national celebrities that they nearly obscured the important role that Monroe had played in the development of Bluegrass. Earl Scruggs and Lester Flatt worked with Monroe during the pivotal period, 1945 to 1948, when the style of Bluegrass crystallized. In 1948, they left to form their own band, the Foggy Mountain Boys, which has enjoyed much renown since the mid-1950's. They can be heard singing "The Ballad of Jed Clampett" on TV's "Beverly Hillbillies."

The rise in popularity of Flatt and Scruggs and the Foggy Mountain Boys has been in three areas: country, city folk, and flour! The group's sponsor, Martha White Mills, even has a singing commercial in Bluegrass style by the band.

Scruggs captured the imagination of city banjo-pickers as have few country instrumentalists. His unique manner of three-finger picking, which makes possible speed in phrasing and fluid, almost ribbon-like, runs, has become known as Scruggs-picking. If any instrumental sound gives the identifying quality to Bluegrass, it may be said to be the five-string banjo picked in Scruggs' fashion.

While still a toddler in his home in Shelby, North Carolina, Scruggs fell under the influence of two country musicians, Snuffy Jenkins and Smith Hammett. "Smith was a distant cousin of mine," Scruggs recalls. "I heard him play three-finger style when I was only five or six years old. I thought it was the prettiest playing I ever heard." He tried to reproduce the sound Hammett got on his banjo. One day, in a sort of daydream, he was fingering the old tune "Reuben." "I found that roll! I ran into the kitchen and yelled: 'Mama! Mama! I've done it!'"

This was the birth of the famous Scruggs-picking, a style now widely imitated. It has caused Scruggs to be considered to have the same relationship to the five-string banjo that Paganini has to the violin. By sharply accentu-

220 The Stanley Brothers, 1964

ating the melody line, Scruggs makes it stand out clearly in a shower of notes. His playing is heavily syncopated, bright, and often filled with cunning subtlety.

In 1951, Scruggs made another innovation, the Scruggs peg, a small cam near the conventional tuning pegs that enables him to change the pitch of a given string, then to return it to its former pitch. This admittedly attention-getting device has helped to heighten the appeal of the banjo as a virtuoso instrument.

As brilliant as Scruggs' banjo work is, the whole band works together with a cohesiveness that is smoothly professional by any musical standards. Flatt's vocals have the easygoing lilt of a rural Bing Crosby. Curly Sechler's mandolin provides a bright, brittle, agitated sound. The fiddling of Paul Warren is showy and witty, but always musical, as it soars and glides over the ensemble. An unusual instrument in the band is the Dobro, a steel guitar fretted in the Hawaiian manner with a steel bar. This gives a wonderfully tangy, almost biting quality, as played by Buck Graves. (Graves and Shot Jackson are two of Nashville's finest performers on the Dobro, making a sound that electric steel and pedal steel guitars have built upon.) Finally, the Foggy Mountain Boys have in Cousin Jake (English P. Tullock) a comedian-bassist-singer who brightens the proceedings

with his outlandish costume. He is often the butt of a lot of good-natured leg-pulling.

Flatt and Scruggs stand today at the height of country and folk music success. They are no strangers to the Hollywood Bowl or Carnegie Hall and have shared bills with top names of Nashville and such folk stars as Joan Baez. They have had their own radio and TV shows out of Nashville besides appearing on the Columbia Broadcasting System "Beverly Hillbillies." Each year the Foggy Mountain Boys travel some 100,000 miles in a specially outfitted bus. Their fame has spread as far afield as Japan.

Flatt and Scruggs are among the stanchest traditionalists in Nashville. Although they have at times been recorded with drums, they have never forgotten for long where their music came from or where it is going. Here is how Scruggs described it, in an interview with Nat Hentoff in the May, 1963, issue of *Hi/Fi Stereo Review:*

"It's like a dream come true to see how our music is taking hold in places I'd never expected it to. But just as we've never been willing to alter our course to accommodate rockabilly, semi-pop, and all those other moves away from what country music ought to be, we're not going to leave the people who made us. After all, they're people who don't change their minds about what they like. We're not about to forget that the core of our

221 The Kentucky Colonels, Newport Folk Festival

fans are people who get up early in the morning and bake a lot of biscuits."

Although the Monroe and the Flatt and Scruggs bands are at the summit of Bluegrass, the mountainside is full of other able ensembles. Scores of professional Bluegrass bands have sprung up in the last decade, and there may be one hundred amateur bands playing elsewhere.

A few will be mentioned in passing: An Ozarks-born group that has achieved a wide following on television and recordings is the Dillards. The group has undeniable charm and appeal, musically, and through the whimsy of its spokesman, Mitch Jayne, a teacher and writer who plays bass with the group when not joking.

Traditionalists have found the Stanley Brothers and the Clinch Mountain Boys one of their favorite Bluegrass bands. Coming from the area of southern Virginia where the Carter Family lived has given them a strong link, geographically, as well as spiritually, to the early country-music group. City listeners at the University of Chicago Folk Festivals and concerts by the Friends of Old-Time Music have been struck by the beautiful part-singing of Carter and Ralph Stanley, and the unpressured mellowness of the band's ensemble sound.

A group that has been very firmly rooted in the Boston area, where many rural and relocated Southerners have gravitated since the beginning of World War II, has been the Lilly Brothers and Don Stover. Of them, Betsy Siggins wrote in the November, 1964. *Hootenanny* magazine:

"They settled in this most Southern of Northern cities and acquired their following largely through their appearances at the Hillbilly Ranch (a night club), numerous radio shows and the large country and Western shows organized by Nelson Bragg in the early fifties. This following has remained loyal and discriminating through the last thirteen years."

A band that got its biggest push in Los Angeles is the Kentucky Colonels, formerly the Country Gentlemen. The band features the brilliant guitar-playing of Clarence White, who is still in his teens. Another alumnus of the Bluegrass band, Don Reno, continues to record on the King label dazzling banjo flights with his band, the Tennessee Cut-Ups.

The nation's capital has had as many as a dozen little bars, from Georgetown to across the Virginia line, where fine country Bluegrass bands can be heard. Out of such a bar, The Famous, sprang another Bluegrass success story. For years, one of the earliest country-music men to record, Ernest (Pop) Stoneman, and his family played twice weekly there. With the help of a feature article in *The Washington Post and Times-Herald,* the Stonemans have become very well known in the last three years. The band includes two attractive girls, Donna and Ronnie; a fine fiddler, Scott, and the genial patriarch of the clan, Pop Stoneman, who only regrets that it took forty years for America to discover his music.

Another Bluegrass band known mostly through King records is Wade Mainer and the Mountaineers, an offshoot of a famous string band of the 1930's. The Mainers' contribution to Bluegrass has been mainly in recording and keeping alive fine old tunes of the 1920's.

Jim and Jesse McReynolds and the Virginia Boys have been equally as well received on "Grand Ole Opry" as at The Newport [R.I.] Folk Festival of 1964. Jesse's excellent mandolin-picking is in a league with such other masters of the instrument as Monroe, Frank Wakefield of the Greenbriar Boys, and Joe Val of the Charles River Valley Boys.

The number of city musicians who have grasped the intricacies of Bluegrass is high. Bill Clifton, a stockbroker turned bandleader, has enjoyed considerable success in bringing Bluegrass to Britain. The Charles River Valley Boys of Cambridge have included a great many scholars, intellectuals, and scientists, such as Jim Rooney, Bob Siggins, and John Cooke, the last-named the son of Alistair Cooke, the British writer and pundit.

Probably the most distinguished city Bluegrass band has been the Greenbriar Boys. Its lead singer, John Herald, has captured all the drive, power, and tension of the best country singers in the vein. The banjoist, Bob Yellin, has developed a singular style, somewhat influenced by the Jimmy Martin band, of a loping, erratically metered set of figures that inevitably set one's feet tapping.

Bluegrass began to make a sizable inpact on city music circles after Alan Lomax enthusiastically introduced Earl Taylor and the Stoney Mountain Boys at the "Folksong '59" concert at Carnegie Hall on April 3, 1959.

Now the bridge between country and city is firmly set. Colleges invite Bluegrass country bands to play, and the Greenbriar Boys make guest appearances on "Grand Ole Opry," and even changed personnel to include country-born musicians.

The bridge of Bluegrass is growing wider and wider. Musicians and fans are walking back and forth on it, from country to city, from folk music to country music.

Don Reno, right, Red Smiley, with guitar, and the Tennessee Cut-Ups

223   Silent movie still showing the influence of music in the early 1920's on Western films

7 WAY OUT WEST: SINGING COWBOYS AND WESTERN SWING

*"Oh, come along, boys, and listen to my tale,
I'll tell you of my troubles on the old Chisholm Trail.*

Coma-ti-yi-youpy, youpy ya, youpy ya,
Coma-ti-yi-youpy, youpy ya, youpy ya . . ."
"The Old Chisholm Trail"

On the face of it, most country musicians of 1965 look as if they lived on a ranch, rehearsed in a corral, relaxed by galloping an old bay thirty miles, and had just left their six-shooters in the bunkhouse because they got in the way of their guitars.

Whether they come from the Carolina hills, the Kentucky Bluegrass, or the Indiana plains, a majority of professional country musicians have adopted Westernized costumes, from boots to Stetsons. "Barn-dance cowboys" might be an appropriate phrase to replace the old spoofing term, "drug-store cowboys."

The identification of much of country music with the images of the West is one of the curious anomalies of this business. The irony is all the greater when one realizes that Nashville in general and "Grand Ole Opry" in particular strongly opposed the inroads of Western swing. Yet, through the back door, much of the dress, manners, and, more importantly, the stylistic devices of Western music have all but eclipsed the original mountaineer nature of commercial country music.

The change has been cumulative during forty years. But, as with so much that was to follow him, the impact of Jimmie Rodgers, "the father of country music," is again strongly felt here. Rodgers was something of an honorary Texan. He moved to that state, always enjoyed great popularity there, and made innumerable personal appearances in Texas and other Western states.

Although the first regional home of country music was in the Southeast, by the 1930's country music had become inextricably costumed in the romantic imagery of the cowboy, the Great Plains, the cattle trails and lonely mesas of the West. Rodgers by no means had "invented" the romantic West. He apparently was as caught up in it as was the Alabama boy who followed him, Hank Williams, who ran off to become a cowboy. Dime novels and serialized magazine and newspaper fiction had, by the time of World War I, already tinted the American mythology with the rosy hues of the Westerner. What greater cultural hero have we had in twentieth-century imagination than the self-reliant, ruggedly individualistic, unfettered cowboy?

Radio, silent and sound films, and television have kept the Old West alive in the consciousness of all Americans, city or Southern rural. At an early point, Western dress partially clothed hillbilly musicians more in the garb of Texas than that of Kentucky. From the standpoint of music alone, the songs of the trail and the cowboy had long intrigued folk-song collectors. Two of the earliest printed collections of American folk music were Nathan Howard Thorp's *Songs of the Cowboy* (1908) and John A. Lomax's *Cowboy Songs and Other Frontier Ballads* (1910).

Among the first musicians to record country music were three Texans: Eck Robertson, the fiddler, Carl T. Sprague, and Vernon Dalhart. Among the first sounds to become nationally popular as "the sound of country music" was the bland, gentle crooning of Jimmie Rodgers, a far cry from the more nasal, taut vocal style of the Southeast.

Three states in the Southeast—Texas, Oklahoma, and Louisiana—were to be the fulcrum for the development of a kindred but different style of country music. These states had been largely settled by migrants from the

224   Jimmie Rodgers in Western dress

226   Denver Darling, 1946

225   Arizona Red (Ed McBride)

227   Tiny Dodson and his Circle B Boys

228   Jimmy Wakely Trio, 1943; on the left, Johnny Bond

229   The Maxwell Orchestra, 1925; Billie Maxwell, center. One of the first Western groups to record for Victor, 1929

232   The Ranch Boys; top to bottom, Joe "Curley" Bradley, Hubert "Shorty" Carson, and Jack Ross

230   Tex Owens

231   Smith Ballew

234   The Down Homers; l to r, Shorty Cook, Unidentified, Guy Campbell, Kenny Roberts, 1946

233   Roy Schaeffer, the Lone Star Cowboy

Southeast, but regional identities became established in time. This, in turn, began to affect the region's musical identity. Having followed its own course of development, folk music of the Southwest departed significantly from the folk music of the Southeast. But then a fusion and an interaction developed that were later to make the two forms overlapping and similar.

This chapter will attempt to survey the development of the two principal elements in country music of the West: the singing cowboys and Western swing. Again, as in so much of the story of country music, reference materials are sparse, research is still fragmentary, and the writing of comprehensive histories or bio-discographical studies is in the germinal stage. But it is a fascinating story of real cowpunchers and Westernized hillbillies, of singers who became national idols on the screen in the 1930's and 1940's, and of the big-band style known as Western swing that to millions of listeners and dancers was as important as was the music of the bands of Benny Goodman and Duke Ellington.

It was with poorly concealed bitterness that the well-known Western swing bandleader, Leon McAuliff, could tell this writer in 1964 that Nashville had never been directly receptive to Western music, and yet the influence of Western music was to be found throughout country music—in themes, in the dress of the performers, in the instrumentation and rhythm.

Most of the Southwest had been settled by migrants from the Southeast. Moving westward in the search for land and better living conditions, the displaced Southeasterners moved to Texas, Oklahoma, and Louisiana. They brought slaves, "cotton culture," religious institutions and customs, and, as ever, their folks songs and ballads. In the Southwest, the emigrant music of the Southeast was affected by contact with Negroes of the flatlands, with Mexican-Spanish folk culture, and also with the musical traditions of the French-American Cajuns of Louisiana.

As in the transformation of Southern mountain folk songs into commercial country music, the transformation of cowboy songs into Western music followed a jagged, not easily documented course. For twenty years after the publication of Lomax's *Cowboy Songs*, this landmark collection caused little stir. But by the 1930's radio singers were using texts that Lomax had first printed. The

235 Carl T. Sprague

236 Jules Allen

237 McClintock's Haywire Orchestra

romantic aura surrounding the cowboy was to get its greatest impetus from radio and film, but even before the 1920's the tales and legends of early pioneers on the trail had become a large part of American folklore.

Three of the most interesting singers of the period before the 1930's were Texans who sang authentic traditional music of the cowboy: Carl T. Sprague, Goebel Reeves (the Texas Drifter), and Jules Verne Allen. Sprague can bear claim to the title of being America's first singing cowboy, having recorded in 1924 for Victor songs such as "When the Work's All Done This Fall." He had been reared on a ranch near Alvin, Texas, and learned most of his songs from a cow-punching uncle. While Sprague was studying at Texas Agricultural and Mechanical College, he became impressed with the success of another Texan, Vernon Dalhart, and went to New York to audition with his cowboy songs for Victor. Sprague was content, however, to sing as a hobby, and did not pursue an active music career beyond his recordings. Subsequently, he was to be a coach at Texas A. & M. and to serve as an Army major.

The fact that Jules Verne Allen actively pursued a professional music career probably will make him the likelier heir to the title of "original singing cowboy" than Sprague. Allen was born in Waxahachie, Texas, and started as a working cowboy at the age of ten. During the years 1893 to 1907, Allen gained experience as a rough-string rider and broncobuster. During the 1920's and 1930's, he sang on many radio stations. On at least one of them, WOAL in San Antonio, he was also known as Longhorn Luke.

Goebel Reeves was one of the most colorful figures in early country music, combining the dual roles of cowboy and hobo. Some excellent material on Reeves was collected by Fred Hoeptner for an article in *Country and Western Spotlight* from New Zealand, which is the basis for the material on him that follows:

"Goebel Leon Reeves had a great flair for the dramatic and created an air of mystery about his life, often intentionally. Behind all of this lies a man who turned down social position and family prestige to live as he himself wanted to live, a life of freedom and travel free from the pretentiousness of ordinary life," Hoeptner wrote.

The Texas Drifter was born in Sherman, Texas, on October 9, 1899. To dramatize such mundane origins he later said that he was a cowboy brought up in the wild Pecos. His mother was a voice and piano teacher, and his father went from being a shoe salesman to being a member of the Texas State Legislature. When Reeves was in his teens, he served as a page in the legislature.

Hoeptner wrote: "It was during this period that he first found out about hoboes. He had received a brand-new overcoat from his parents. One cold, wet night he saw a shivering hobo walking. . . . He felt . . . sorry for him and followed him to the 'jungle' where he gave him his new coat. From then on, Goebel was entranced by hoboes. Of course, he got the spanking of his life the next day."

The young romantic was learning such songs as "Hobo's Lullabye," and he also picked up yodeling from a vaudeville yodeler named Al Wilson who was appearing in Austin.

In 1917, Reeves enlisted in the Army. After serving as a bugler he saw front-line action and was wounded, then discharged. "It was in 1921 that he made up his mind to just keep drifting, to become a hobo," said Hoeptner. Odd jobs took him around the country. Whenever he ran out of money he would turn to his guitar and a few songs. While singing in and around New Orleans with one Lucien (Piggy) Parks, Goebel Reeves met Jimmie Rodgers.

The Drifter shipped to Italy as a merchant seaman, then toured Europe. On his return to Galveston, he heard a Jimmie Rodgers record being played in a music store. Thinking that recording was a good idea, he hopped the next freight train for New York. Reeves went to the Gennett Studios on Long Island managed by George Keats. Besides recording on several labels for Keats, he also recorded on Okeh, Brunswick, and lesser labels, using a variety of pseudonyms. (Among them were Johnny Fay, Bert Knowles, George Riley, the Yodeling Rustler, the Broadway Rustler, the Yodeling Wrangler, the Broadway Wrangler.)

In the early 1930's Reeves made some transcriptions for Frank Black of Brunswick Records. While working for Black, Reeves got to know some of the top figures in country music, such as Dalhart, Carson Robison, and Frank Luther. His final group of transcriptions, in 1937 or 1938, were for the McGregor Company in Hollywood, and included songs and poetry with guitar accompaniment.

During this time, Reeves continued to drift around, rarely staying in one place for more than six months. He shipped out to Japan, was active in the Industrial Workers of the World (Wobblies) for a time, and was married briefly. Reeves probably made his first radio appearance over station WDOD in Chattanooga. Later he had programs on stations from Halifax to Los Angeles. One of his favorite songs, which sold well on a song sheet, was "Alabama Tornado," which he wrote after witnessing a storm near Birmingham. He was so popular in Jackson, Tennessee, that he was named honorary mayor of the town. He returned the favor by writing a song called "Miss Jackson, Tennessee."

Of the many songs Goebel Reeves sang, some were traditional and some original and others were his adaptations from the traditional. One of the favorites was "Station H.O.B.O.," in actuality, "Big Rock Candy Mountain" done to an original melody with a spoken introduction. His own compositions were, Hoeptner contends, almost all autobiographical. Among the most popular songs identified with the Texas Drifter, including his own and others', were:

"Little Joe, the Wrangler," "The Texas Drifter's Warning," "The Boatswain," "Hobo's Lullabye" ("Go To Sleep, You

238   Goebel Reeves, The Texas Drifter

Weary Hobo"), "Hobo and the Angelus," "I've Ranged, I've Roamed, I've Traveled" (a song by Reeves recorded by Jimmie Rodgers), "I'm Just a Lonesome Cowboy," "Bar None Ranch," etc.

Hoeptner recounted that Goebel Reeves' "big break" came in 1931. A hard-drinking man in New York invited the Texas Drifter into a posh restaurant, only if Reeves would sing. There he was heard by Graham McNamee, a famous N.B.C. announcer and producer. McNamee introduced Reeves to Rudy Vallee, who tried Reeves· on his network show. Reeves was a success on the show and signed a contract with N.B.C. for "three and a half." (It turned out to be $350, not the $3.50 Reeves expected.

Singing and reading for a sophisticated radio audience was to present problems. The rural listeners liked Reeves because of strong identification with him, but the sophisticates took him as a novelty and a comic. He found the city audiences laughing at material that his rural audiences might have cried at. He did, however, appear on rural radio and made appearances intermittently on the WLS "Barn Dance" and the WSM "Grand Ole Opry."

By the time of World War II, Reeves had retired to Bell Gardens, a suburb of Los Angeles. He maintained a private "museum" there of items he had collected around the world. By this time, Reeves had lost touch with his family and earlier friends, typical of the drifter's way he espoused. In his later years Reeves was active in the American-Japanese community in Southern California.

Hoeptner, who had paid many visits to Reeves, last went there in late January, 1959. He discovered that Reeves had died of a heart attack in the Long Beach Veterans Hospital on January 26.

Leo LeRiche of Maplewood, Missouri, had corresponded frequently with the Texas Drifter. One letter concluded: ". . . Yes, Jimmie was the greatest yodeler America ever had. I taught him to yodel, another mutual friend taught him to play the guitar, and he turned out and beat his teachers. He could play a banjo far better than he could the guitar."

Another early recording star of the 1920's

who similarly dealt in traditional songs of the cowboy as well as the songs of the hobo was Harry McClintock. He was born in Knoxville and, like Reeves, traveled widely and was affiliated with the Industrial Workers of the World in the early part of the century.

The story of Mac McClintock and his famous songs, "Hallelujah, I'm a Bum" and "Big Rock Candy Mountain," has been told at length in John Greenway's *American Folk Songs of Protest*, George Milburn's *Hobo's Hornbook*, Nels Anderson's *The Hobo*, and *Songs of Work and Freedom* by Edith Fowke and Joe Glazer.

McClintock had ranged the open road in 1897 or 1898, often singing for his supper. For "Hallelujah, I'm a Bum," he put new words to an English hymn called "Revive Us Again," the melody of which appears in the overture to *The Miller and His Men*, an English opera of 1813 by Sir Henry Bishop. McClintock had sung it in Tennessee Army camps for troops training for the Spanish-American War. The song became the unofficial theme song of the I.W.W. after a convention of 1908, and McClintock recorded the song in 1926.

Mac had a radio show as early as 1925 on San Francisco's KFRC. He recorded for Victor from 1927 to 1931. Billy Charles Malone summarizes the importance of this Wobbly song leader in these terms:

"Along with such cowboys songs as 'Sam Bass,' 'Jesse James' and 'Texas Rangers,' McClintock's Western labor songs make him one of the important progenitors of Western music during the 1920's."

While cowboys songs and Western bands have grown to large proportions by 1965, it was back in 1924 that the early commercial applications of the Western-style music were first made. Otto Gray formed a cowboy string band, the Oklahoma Cowboys, that for twelve years was to be both a prototype and a pioneer in the modern form of Western entertainment. Zeke Clements, who had worked with the Otto Gray band, described Gray as "always being twenty years ahead of his time."

In early 1924, one Billy McGinty, who had been a "Rough Rider" with Colonel Theodore Roosevelt in the Spanish-American War, organized the Oklahoma Cowboy Band as "a fiddlin', singin' and dancin' unit for the purpose of bringing back to the present generation the music and songs of the early days in the West."

"GREETINGS *To All Our Friends"*

OWEN GRAY

OTTO GRAY
and his COWBOYS
OKLAHOMA COWBOYS

Radio - Stage - Screen Attraction
The Original Oklahoma Cowboy Band Organized in 1924

Traveling in a Caravan of Special Custom Built Cars and Trailers
PERMANENT ADDRESS STILLWATER, OKLA.
OR CARE OF THE BILLBOARD CINCINNATI, O.
AFFILIATED WITH N.B.C. ARTISTS BUREAU, N.Y.C.

OTTO GRAY

OTTO GRAY *And His* OKLAHOMA COW BOYS *from* Stillwater, Oklahoma

239 Gene Autry and Champion

240 Spade Cooley

241 Jimmy Wakely

242 Roy Rogers and the late Trigger

Wilf Carter

244   Rex Allen

245   Stuart Hamblen on Tomboy

246   Red River Dave McEnery

247 Bill (Cowboy Rambler) Boyd

248 L to r, Kid Cason, John Boyd, Bill Boyd, Gar Austin, Julian Akins

Otto Gray of Stillwater, Oklahoma, was named manager and leader of the group, which numbered seven men and one woman (Gray's wife, "Momie") and had an elaborate publicity and advance group of eight more.

The band, recruited from various ranches, made its radio debut on KFRU in Bristow, Oklahoma. By the time the group had disbanded in 1936 they had broadcast from more than 150 different stages. The Oklahoma Cowboys had appeared on all the major live entertainment circuits of the period, including R.K.O., Fox, Loew's, and Publix.

The group traveled in a caravan of fancy, custom-built autos, including a three-ton sedan made to look like a railroad observation car. The Cowboys' sound truck had enough amplifying equipment to rouse a city before a local stage appearance.

Otto Gray's troupe had a wide repertory of Western and country and sentimental parlor songs, including "She'll Be Comin' Round the Mountain," "Who Broke the Lock on the Henhouse Door?" "The Song of the Dying Cowboy," "The Cowboy's Lament," "Sucking Cider Through a Straw," "The Old Maid and the Burglar," and "I Had But 50 Cents." One press release by the Oklahoma Cowboys gives the flavor of the very successful band:

"Some cowboys are only drugstore cowboys and some cowboy bands are only cowboy bands. But some cowboy bands are both (sic) riding, roping, shooting, bronco-busting cowboys and musicians as well. That's the kind of cowboy band that came to town yesterday when Otto Gray and His Oklahoma Cowboys drove in with their custom-built train of autos that are really a sight to see. . . ."

As indicated, Jimmie Rodgers played a strong role in attaching a Texas cowboy quality to country music. The musicians who have claimed Rodgers as their inspiration are legion. None was perhaps more successful nor did more to establish the concept of the singing cowboy than another performer who was heavily influenced by Rodgers, Gene Autry.

Gene Autry is one of the most colorful figures in the history of American show business. He began as a country singer in the style of Jimmie Rodgers, rarely singing anything Western. He became, through his roles as a singing cowboy in the films of the 1930's, one of the best-paid movie stars of all time. Through his own remarkable business acumen, he became a millionaire real-estate operator and a producer of live shows, films, and TV series.

Not a few amiable jokes have been told at Autry's expense either by the real cowboys or by those who could see more than an element of the ludicrous in his rigorously romantic, ultrawholesome film conception of the cowboy. One gag tells how Autry, in a film, is facing disaster and hypothetically talks to himself:

249 T. Texas Tyler

250 Frankie and Johnny Marvin, 1932

"Them bandits have beaten mah mother, ravished mah girl, burned down mah house, killed mah best friend and stolen all mah prize cattle. Ah'm agonna get 'em if'n it's the last thing ah do—but first, folks, ah'm agonna sing ya a little song."

Gene Autry was born on a tenant farm in Tioga Springs, Texas, in 1907. His grandfather, a Baptist minister, taught him to sing so he could help out the church choir. His professional singing career began when he was in his teens, singing at a night club for whatever the collection plate yielded, generally about fifty cents a night. He worked the medicine-show circuit with the Fields Brothers' Medicine Show.

His first musical ambition was to sing and accompany himself on saxophone, but he soon discovered how difficult that is, and took the decisive step of trading his sax for a guitar. At this time, Autry's father was running a ranch near Achille, Oklahoma, from which Gene would drive cattle to the nearby railroad station. By seventeen he was a telegraph operator for the Frisco Lines, and while working the midnight to 8 A.M. shift he had ample opportunity to practice.

One night, while he was working at a station at Chelsea, Oklahoma, a man entered to send a wire. Seeing his guitar, he requested that Gene sing "They Plowed the Old Trail Under." The stranger then sang a version of "Casey Jones" for the young telegrapher. After he left, Autry saw the wire was signed

"Will Rogers." The famed humorist came in several times thereafter and gave Autry some encouragement: "I think you have something," he said. "Work hard at it and you may get somewhere."

Autry's first crack at the entertainment world was at the inspiration of a friend, Johnny Marvin, a radio and phonograph star. In 1928, Autry went to the Victor offices in New York. Unable to get an audition, he just began to sing and play in the waiting room. Nat Shilkret, a Victor official, heard him, then gave him an audition. He liked Autry's voice, but suggested more experience. With a letter of introduction from Shilkret, Autry got a singing stint at KVOO, Tulsa. Not getting any money from the station, Autry worked meanwhile for a railroad to support himself.

Art Satherley of the American Record Company was the first to record Autry, who had begun to write his own songs. By the fall of 1929, Autry made his first records for Victor, which billed him as "Oklahoma's Singing Cowboy."

The KVOO appearances helped Autry to move to the "Barn Dance" on WLS in 1930, where from 1930 to 1934 he was a headliner. The Sears organization was quick to see Autry's potential, and he was soon being recorded on a number of Sears disk labels. The catalogue also featured a Gene Autry "Roundup" guitar for $9.95. The image of Autry as the ranch singer was becoming imbedded at this time, despite the fact that

Best wishes from Gene Autry and J. L. Frank

251   J. L. Frank and Gene Autry

252   Will Rogers

he was still singing the usual hillbilly repertory.

During a personal appearance with the "Barn Dance" troupe in 1932 at the Tivoli Theater in Danville, Illinois, Autry wrote on his dressing-room door, "Gene Autry, America's Biggest Flop." The door was later framed under glass in the theater's lobby.

It has been estimated that Autry wrote, alone or with collaborators, some three hundred songs. During his time on WLS he wrote such numbers as "My Old Pal of Yesterday" and "A Gangster's Wedding." His greatest hit of this period was the 1931 "Silver-Haired Daddy of Mine," written in collaboration with Jimmy Long, a train dispatcher. It was estimated that the song, an all-time hillbilly hit, sold between 300,000 and 500,000 records. Among the hillbilly fare that the future singing cowboy recorded was a song about a radical labor leader, called "The Death of Mother Jones."

It was still a far distance to Autry's becoming established as America's leading singing cowboy. In 1934, he went to Hollywood. Satherley had persuaded Herbert Yates, president of Republic Studios, to take a chance on his protégé. At this time Hollywood was undergoing many changes. The Legion of Decency was cracking down on sex-filled films, and a new style of wholesome family fare was being sought by an industry in flux.

The introduction of sound films in 1928 had opened the way for the use of Western and cowboy music. The films of John Ford in this early period had used traditional Western folk music. *The Western: From Silents to Cinerama*, by George N. Fenin and William K. Everson, describes the advent of the singing cowboy film:

". . . to [Ken] Maynard—rather than to Gene Autry—belongs the real credit for the introduction of the musical Western. Songs in Maynard's films were never introduced for their own sake, and they were integral parts of his films for some five years prior to the advent of Autry and Rogers. 'Strawberry Roan' had its plot built around the theme of that popular Western song. Maynard had a pleasant voice and frequently accompanied himself on the fiddle. Songs in his Westerns were usually sung around the campfire episodes, introduced logically to provide moments of relaxation between melodramatic action. They remained essentially masculine affairs, quite without dance-hall singers or even a vocally inclined heroine."

3 An early photo of Gene Autry

Although Maynard (he first sang four original songs in *Songs of the Saddle* in 1930) and sound-track scores had started the musical Western, it was a producer at Republic Studios who is generally credited with being the father of the singing Western. Nat Levine in 1934 was considering hundreds of candidates for the role of the "tuneful cowpuncher." He decided upon Autry, whose radio and record following was already established. The choice was described in an article, "Tenor on Horseback," in *The Saturday Evening Post* of September 2, 1939, by Alva Johnston:

"The fact that he [Autry] couldn't act was at first considered a negligible flaw, and later an asset. Like Gary Cooper and Jimmy Stewart, Autry has the kind of awkwardness and embarrassment that audiences like."

Autry initially had a small part in a film that starred Maynard. The fan mail was heavy, and in his next stint, a serial, *The Phantom Empire*, Autry meandered through a mythical underground kingdom with his lasso and his guitar. Another Republic producer, Armand Schaeffer, was given the assignment of building Autry into a singing cowboy star. Johnston wrote:

"Schaeffer . . . discovered later that Gene's liabilities could be converted into assets. The songs, instead of interrupting the story and making audiences lose interest, were written to push the plot forward. Autry ditties sway mobs like Marc Anthony speeches. In one picture, Autry sings a message to a pal in prison, as Blondel did to Richard-the-Lionhearted. In other pictures Gene uses his ballads to unmask crooks. He sings good citizens into fury and villains into desperation."

In the musical Western cycle that began in 1935, Autry often appeared with his friend Smiley Burnette, a comic and hillbilly singer and song writer. After appearing in the serial *Mystery Mountain*, the pair did three numbers in a Maynard feature, *In Old Sante Fe*, which set the pattern for many future Autry films.

Autry was billed in his films as Gene Autry, a prestigious factor that led to similar billing for other Western stars. A third singing cowboy star was Roy Rogers, the former Leonard Slye of Duck Run, Ohio. Under the name Dick Weston, Rogers had been a member of the Sons of the Pioneers, and first starred for Republic.

254 Movie still from "Song of Texas." L to r, Hugh Farr, top, Tim Spencer, Bob Nolan, Lloyd Perryman, Carl Farr, Pat Brady

The success of Autry and Rogers led to many imitators of these singing cowboys. Warner Brothers had Dick Foran, Tex Ritter, Jack Randall, Bob Baker, Fred Scott, John King, Smith Ballew, Jimmy Wakely, Monte Hale, and Eddie Dean. Tex Ritter was to use more traditional folk songs than the tailor-made Western songs written or sung by Autry and Rogers.

Fenin and Everson wrote that at the Columbia Studio "a new deal was ushered in with the signing of Tex Ritter and Russell Hayden, restoring pep and vitality to the studio's horse operas." A poor line of musical Westerns at Columbia was replaced when Autry became affiliated with that studio. As the history of these films states: "His Westerns became more realistic in style and omitted the big musical production numbers previously much a part of his films." The film historians had high praise for the last of the Columbia Westerns made by Autry, including *The Last Round-Up*, *Mule Train*, and *Sons of New Mexico*.

The musical Westerns provided a great outlet for the new style of composed Western song. It also catapulted Autry into tremendous international fame. His visit to Dublin, Ireland, on the eve of World War II in 1939, brought three-quarters of a million fans into the streets. In November, 1941, the town of Berwyn, Oklahoma, changed its name to Gene Autry, Oklahoma.

By this time Autry had been established with a show on C.B.S. radio, later on television. In 1953, Autry purchased the Placeritas Ranch, near Newhall, California, where many Westerns had been filmed. The ranch, renamed "Melody Ranch," had seventy-two buildings and extensive acreage. It was here that his first feature film, *Tumbling Tumbleweed*, was made in 1935.

After serving as a flight officer with the Army Transport Command, Autry was discharged in 1945, and has been said to have clocked more hours in a pilot's seat than in the saddle.

At the end of the war, Autry began to build his financial empire in real estate and show business. He formed Gene Autry Productions, which produced thirty-two Western musicals for release by Columbia. The end of the 1940's saw the rise of television, and Autry soon became involved in the new medium. He organized Flying A Pictures, which produced his own half-hour shows and the "Range Rider" series and three subsequent TV series.

Sons of the Pioneers; top, left, Hugh Farr, Verne Tim
ncer; center, Robert Nolan; bottom, left, Carl Farr, Len
e (Roy Rogers) 1936

Dale Evans, the late Trigger and Roy Rogers

Autry also has a traveling show and rodeo, several music-publishing companies, his own record company, Challenge Records, and extensive holdings in broadcasting stations, hotels, and motels.

It is typical of Autry's warm personality that despite his enormous international standing and the millions he has earned, he kept in touch with some of his earliest associates in country music. John Lair and Pappy McMichen speak affectionately of Autry, recalling how thoughtful the star could be toward his old friends. When his rodeo troupe passed through Louisville a few years ago, Autry found time to visit Pappy McMichen's home.

The late 1930's and early 1940's saw the transformation of Hollywood into a mecca for country musicians, comics, and all identified with country music. Some of the old-timers in Western films decried what had happened. Buck Jones, a cowboy star of the authentic school, lamented that children would get "the wrong idea that all you need to stop an Indian or a rustler is a loud voice accompanied by a hillbilly band."

Still, the revolution on the mass audience that Autry had effected in the more than one hundred features for Monogram, Republic, and his own production companies had virtually made the name "Western" synonymous with the music of the Southern rural areas. It became a gentler substitute for the term "hillbilly."

"There were, however, a number of groups who stayed rather close to the cowboy repertory," Malone wrote in his dissertation. He added: "Some of them had been in existence long before Autry achieved Hollywood fame, and many of them had made their headquarters on the West Coast, presumably because of the lure of Hollywood. These groups stressed the performance of Western songs and differed from their Southwestern counterparts in that they placed less emphasis on instrumentation. Among the early California groups were Len Nash and His Original Country Boys, broadcasting from KFWD, Hollywood, as early as March, 1926; Sheriff Loyal Underwood's Arizona Wranglers; Charlie Marshall and His Mavericks; and perhaps the most important of all, The Beverly Hill Billies. The latter group, originating in 1928, broadcast from the Hollywood-Los

257 The Beverly Hill Billies, Hank Skillet, Miranda, Ezra Paulette, Gus Mack, Elton Britt, Lem Giles and Jad Dees, 1932-33

258 The Beverly Hill Billies, 1930, l to r, Hank Skillet, violin; Zeke Manners, accordion; Glen Price, M.C.; **Ezra Paulett** violin; Stuart Hamblen, guitar; Lem Giles, guitar

Milton Brown and his Brownies; l to r, Wanna Coffman, Marshal Pope, M.C., Milton Brown, Jesse Ashlock, Fred Calhoun, il Brower, Ocie Stockard, and Durwood Brown, 1934

Angeles area. Led by Zeke Manners, the accordionist, the group featured country fiddling and Western songs. Over the years, the Hill Billies attracted certain individuals who later became top-ranking country performers. These included Stuart Hamblen, from Texas in 1930, and yodeler Elton Britt (James Britt Baker), from Arkansas in 1932."

Early in 1965, Variety reported that a $2,-000,000 suit filed by four members of the original Beverly Hill Billies against C.B.S., Filmways, and others connected with the popular TV series of that name, had resulted in a "very substantial amount" for the plaintiffs. The surviving members of the original band, who also won contracts for future appearances on the TV show, were Curt Barrett, Charles Quirk, Ashley Dees, and Aleth Hansen.

A Western group that was to become very popular and to be influential in style was the Sons of the Pioneers. Although its members were not from the West—Bob Nolan was a Canadian, Tim Spencer was from Missouri, and Roy Rogers from Ohio—the group developed a strong Western repertory. The three original members went to California in the early 1930's, working with various groups.

Rogers, the lead singer, had been an Ohio farmboy who moved in 1931 to Tulare, California, with his father to work as a migratory fruit picker. Until the formation of the Sons of the Pioneers in 1934 under the original name of the Pioneer Trio, Rogers had played with such Western groups as Uncle Tom Murray's Hollywood Hillbillies, the Rocky Mountaineers, the International Cowboys, the O-Bar-O Cowboys, and the Texas Outlaws.

The threesome, later joined by Hugh Farr, a fiddler, initially had a typical country-music sound. Rogers left in 1937 to become a singing cowboy for Republic. His first starring role was in *Under Western Stars*, although he had been in some Charles Starrett Westerns at Columbia and in some Autry films, too. In *The Old Corral* Rogers had been involved in a filmic fist fight with Autry, who forced him to sing at gunpoint. After a bit of understandable rivalry, a workable relationship between the two singing cowboy stars was worked out. After Autry left to work for Columbia, Rogers acceded to the billing of "King of the Cowboys" and became Republic's leading Western star.

The Sons of the Pioneers continued to thrive after Rogers left them. Their polished,

260 The Light Crust Doughboys on tour; L to r, Clifford Gross, Sleepy Johnson, Leon Huff, Herman Arnspiger, W. E. Lee O'Daniel, Ramon de Arman and Leon McAuliff.

close-harmony singing and such numbers as "Tumbling Tumbleweed" and "Cool Water" made them widely known.

Several other singing cowboys were to make names for themselves in Hollywood, and, strangely enough, in New York.

Texas Jim Robertson, born in 1909 on a ranch near Batesville, Texas, was to have a long singing career on the N.B.C. Blue Network, and recorded for Victor and Bluebird. Jimmy Wakely was featured in thirty films and appeared in a total of nearly seventy. He was born in a log cabin near Mineola, Arkansas, and grew up on an Oklahoma ranch near a town named, of all things, Battiest. He had recorded a number of hits, including some duets with Margaret Whiting, such songs as "Slipping Around," "Wedding Bells," "Too Late," "I Love You So Much It Hurts," and "Let's Go to Church Next Sunday Morning." Wakely left the films in 1949 and continued to be a cowboy singer at such ranches as Ciro's in Hollywood and the Capitol Theater in Manhattan, and on early TV variety shows.

Still another Oklahoma cowboy, who had worked with Wakely in a trio, was Johnny Bond. His musical career started with a ninety-eight-cent ukulele; ultimately he played in the Hollywood Bowl and appeared in more than one hundred films. Bond has written more than three hundred songs, including "Cimarron," "Gone and Left Me Blues," and "Glad Rags."

Maynard has been noted for his trick riding and roping besides his singing. He had worked with the Kit Carson show in 1914, gone on to appear with Pawnee Bill. His first film role was as Paul Revere in a picture starring Marion Davies, *Janice Meredith*. Later he starred in Western films with a half dozen production companies.

T. Texas Tyler went into singing Westerns just as they were beginning to decline, in 1949. He was a distinctive singer known for the "growl" in his voice. He wrote such hits as "Deck of Cards," the popularity of which in 1948 led to his being part of a Carnegie Hall concert. Tyler has since undergone a strong religious conversion and sings only sacred material now.

261   Leon McAuliff on Jimmy Dean show, 1965, with the late Cecil Brower, fiddler, from Milton Brown and his Brownies

One of the finest country voices of all time belonged to a Canadian who started in the Jimmie Rodgers style, became a cowboy, and recorded widely in Canada and the United States. Wilf Carter, as he was known in Canada, called himself Montana Slim on his American recordings, which began for Victor in 1932. He has been identified with such songs as "There's a Love Knot in My Lariat," "I'm Thinking Tonight of My Blue Eyes" and a variety of Rodgers songs.

Another late entrant into singing cowboy films was Rex Allen, who appeared in such Republic epics as *The Arizona Cowboy* and later starred in a TV series, "Frontier Doctor."

Men have not monopolized the singing cowpuncher field. Dorothy Page, the first cowgirl heroine since Ruth Mix, starred in a film called *The Singing Cowgirl*. The glamorous Jan Moore, who calls herself "Little Miss Sweetheart of Rodeo," has doubled as a singing star and a rodeo performer.

The first of the Western stars to have had a large impact on the New York show-business world was the two-time president of the Country Music Association and the latest man to be elected to the Country Music Hall of Fame, Woodward Maurice (Tex) Ritter.

Tex Ritter has had such a varied career in country and Western music that Variety recently described the easygoing, whimsical singer as "an elder statesman" of the field. At fifty-eight, he may object to being called "elder," but his qualifications as statesman are beyond dispute.

His decision to leave Northwestern Law School lost the legal profession a persuasive and articulate man, but thereby show business gained one of its most colorful characters. Ritter was the youngest of six children, born in Panola County, Texas, and grew up in Nederland on the Gulf Coast. As a student at the University of Texas he studied voice with Oscar J. Fox, a "cowboy composer," and headed the university glee club. At Austin he was befriended by J. Frank Dobie, the noted folklorist of the Southwest, and John A. Lomax, the famous collector of cowboy songs.

Ritter used his own collection of Western and mountain songs when he began as a singer on KPRC in Houston in 1929. He traveled with a music troupe the next year and decided to try his luck in New York, where he stayed for five years. Ritter is credited with starting a vogue in New York for cowboy

262   Tex Ritter and White Flash

263   Billie Maxwell, 1925; The Girls of the Golden West, 1936; Cindy Walker, 1940, and Judy Lynn, 1965

songs in the early 1930's. He starred in such radio shows there as "The Lone Star Rangers," "Tex Ritter's Campfire," "The WMGM Barn Dance," and "Cowboy Tom's Roundup." Ritter joined the Theater Guild of New York and got a featured role in *Green Grow the Lilacs*, which later became the revered musical *Oklahoma!* In the original version, Ritter sang four cowboy ballads and understudied Franchot Tone. The success of the show made him greatly sought after for lecture-recitals in many Eastern colleges.

In 1936, Hollywood beckoned, and Ritter began twelve years in musical Westerns, appearing in a total of seventy-eight films for five studios. More recently, he sang the background music in such films as *The Marshal's Daughter, Down Freedom Road* and *Wichita*. He is perhaps most widely known for his singing of the theme song "High Noon" in that famous Western.

Ritter's recording career started with Columbia in the early 1930's and led him to Decca. When Capitol Records was formed in 1942, Ritter was one of the first artists signed. Among his most widely known recordings are "Have I Stayed Away Too Long?" "Jingle, Jangle, Jingle," "Boll Weevil," and perhaps his biggest hit, "Hillbilly Heaven." Ritter's gentle, rich baritone is one of the most pleasant to be heard in country music, and his speaking voice has been such a persuasive one for country music as head of the C.M.A. that he was re-elected as president in the fall of 1964.

Much as the debate has ranged about traditional country music versus commercial country music, so has "cowboy" music been embattled. Some contend that films and TV have slighted the great body of traditional Western song, contenting itself with the work of Tin Pan Alley or Hollywood song writers in this idiom. (See chapter on song writers for discussion of Billy Hill and Bob Miller.) Some students of cowboy and Western music are bitterly outspoken in their belief that the great traditional music of the cowboys is rarely heard in films or on TV. These devotees of authenticity point to the recorded work of such men as the Cartwright Brothers, early Stuart Hamblen, Harry Jackson, Glenn Ohrlin, or Bob Atcher. Jackson and Atcher, interestingly enough, are Midwesterners who went deeply into traditional cowboy material, Jackson by way of a boyhood on a Wyoming ranch, and Atcher through his long career on the WLS "Barn Dance."

One of the more articulate critics of the use of Western music, Jan Kindler, wrote in the January, 1964, issue of *A.B.C.-TV Hootenanny Show* magazine:

". . . In the 35 years since film acquired a sound track, the opportunity to use this rich mother lode has occurred upward of 2,000 times. And it has been missed upward of 2,000 times . . . . The music that had accompanied the six-gun shenanigans of the 1920's was as primitive as the plots. The moment Tom Mix leaped into the saddle (usually from a distant roof) the professor in the pit raced into the overture from 'William Tell,' or, even better, rattled off the appropriate number of bars from von Suppé's 'Leichte Kavallerie.' . . . Hollywood's indifference to folk material is not so irksome as its creation of fake folk songs to be nasalized, during a film's transitional passages, by an unseen darling of the night clubs. . . . Folk art is made by people for their own use or pleasure. The Western is one of the mass arts—even a pop art—made by a small group of people to sell to a large group of people. It may be,

Note the changes in cowgirl clothing styles over the years

167

264 The Hi-Flyers, probably the first organized Western band to start playing take-off solos. L to r, John Rogers, M.C., Elmer Scarborough, Darrell Kirkpatrick, Buster Ferguson, Sleepy Johnson and Andy Schroeder. Photo taken in Oklahoma City, group originally from Fort Worth, Tex.

therefore, that folk music and the Western are not really compatible and that my initial assumption that they should get together, was an unwarranted optimism. . . ."

The entire process by which cowboy-Western music became an umbrella phrase for all country music is described by Malone:

"The growing use of the word 'Western' as a designation for country music was completely inaccurate if viewed in the light of a cowboy-produced music. With the exception of a few cowboy songs recorded by country entertainers, and the employment of cowboy titles and dude cowboy clothing, the cowboy has had no appreciable influence on American popular or country music. No particular vocal or instrumental style, or musical form of rhythm, was contributed by the cowboy that did not exist before. The 'Western music' that became fashionable during the 1930's was not produced by the cowboy."

The Emergence of Western Swing

A distinctive form of folk-derived Western music did arise in the late 1920's and early 1930's in the Southwest. It went under a variety of names — Okie jazz, Tex-Mex music, Southwestern swing and then Western swing. The development of this popular form can be traced to the early 1920's or before, starting with fiddle-guitar combos performing for house dances. If they were available, piano and banjo were added.

The dancing for most of this music began as traditional square-dancing, but, according to Hoeptner, by 1924 it had become half square dancing, half ballroom fox-trot dancing. "The coming of radio was a definite factor," Hoeptner went on. "One informant said WBAP had a string-band jam-session type of program in 1924. . . . They played some pop songs, mostly learned from records. In the later 1920's, the proportion became more pop songs and fewer squares.

"As nearly as I can determine, and subject to later revision," Hoeptner wrote, "the first organized band to start playing take-off solos was the Hi-Flyers, who started on KFJZ in 1929, but didn't start take-off solos until about three years later. Soon it became a matter of pride to be able to play these solos, and those that couldn't were looked down upon by those that could. . . ."

Among the early groups that helped develop Western swing was Prince Albert Hunt's Texas Ramblers. Hunt, who recorded for Okeh, was an old-timer fiddler who played with a guitarist at Texas house parties and taverns until he was shot to death in March, 1931, in Dallas.

The change from Southeastern mountain string bands to Western swing bands has been well-detailed in the "Story of an Early Fiddle Band: The East Texas Serenaders" by Hoeptner in *The Disc Collector* of May, 1961:

"While this band," Hoeptner wrote, "stuck closely to the older fiddle bands in style and never played in Western swing style, it is probably typical in general of the type of band that prepared the way for the change to the swing or jazz style." The band was led by Daniel Huggins Williams, a left-handed fiddler. Hoeptner and the discographer-collector Bob Pinson interviewed Williams in 1959 in the East Texas farming community of Lindale. Williams, born in Tennessee in 1900, was the son of an old gourd-fiddler. He

formed his first group in the mid-1920's with a guitarist, a three-string-cello player, and a tenor banjoist. The Serenaders played house dances, on some rural radio, and at various church and civic functions. "At a typical house dance they would play mostly popular songs of the day, 'Five Foot Two,' 'I Love My Baby,' and 'Down Yonder,' and later 'Rosetta' and 'Stardust.' The people did round dances to these songs. . . . They also played many square-dance tunes, called 'breakdowns,' but the squares, while popular, were not done as often as the rounds."

The Serenaders recorded two masters for a Columbia regional salesman on December 2, 1927. Later Williams' group recorded for Brunswick and Decca. All the sessions were in Dallas. The recordings were instrumental waltzes and breakdowns, material drawn from old popular minstrel songs and early ragtime pieces. The Serenaders drifted apart in the mid-1930's, while the leader worked as a professional until the late 1940's. "They have preserved on phonograph records some of the best examples of the early Western folk instrumental style," Hoeptner wrote.

In 1928, in Greenville, Texas, a similar

65 Milton Brown and his Brownies. Cecil Brower stated that the food in front of the band was the admission price to the radio broadcast, 1934, height of the depression. It was distributed free to the needy after the show. L to r, Milton Brown, vocal; Fred Calhoun, piano; Ocie Stockard, banjo; Jess Ashlock, violin; Durwood Brown, guitar; Wanna Coffman, bass; Cecil Brower, violin, nd Marshal Pope, M.C.

266 Johnnie Lee Wills and orchestra, a Western band, led by Bob Wills' brother

267 Bob Skyles and his Skyrockets, 1936

269 Doug Bine's Orchestra, 1937

270 Adolph Hofner and his Tex
1940. This group was one of the
known bands in the Southwest,

272 The Village Boys, a Western swing band from the Houston area.
Notice the piano, an oddity in Western bands

273 The Bar X Cowb
from Houston, 1938

268 The Tune Wranglers. L to r, (standing) Tom Dickey, Bill Dickey, Buster Coward, George Timberlake; (seated) Eddie Fielding, accordion; Eddie Duncan

271 Jimmie Revard and the Oklahoma Playboys, 1936. A Western swing group composed of some members of Adolph Hofner's Band

d dance halls in Texas
a. They were also
SA, San Antonio

274 Charlie Herald and his Round-up Rangers, Charlie is on bass.

171

band, called the Cowboy Ramblers, was [or]ganized by Bill and Jim Boyd. The Ramble[rs] who began recording in 1934 for Blueb[ird] drew on country, popular, and jazz for t[heir] instrumentals. Considered their most succ[ess]ful disk was a fiddle-guitar version of a[n] march tune, "Under the Double Eagle."

Malone has found that "Southwester[n] sicians had revealed a tendency to imp[rovise] and experiment with melodic variations [much] earlier than their counterparts in the [other] Southern states . . . perhaps because diversity of cultures in the Gulf Coa[st] It has been suggested that South[western] string-band music, strongly influe[nced by] Louisiana jazz, may have taken on liar regional stylings when oil work[ers] from Louisiana to Texas during th[e]

The trail of Western swing mov[ed] some of the names that were to be In the late 1920's a two-man formed by Bob Wills and Herma[n] for playing at house parties a Worth. The duo, called Wills'

recorded f
earlier sign
sponsor, to
he even ha
fiddling so
his own da
Texas Play
of two thou
Wills'
Negro coun
well as the
more urba
the late 1
Benny Goo
Swing." (A
to the mus
America, a
bands throu
not a line
bands who
west of the
ada.)

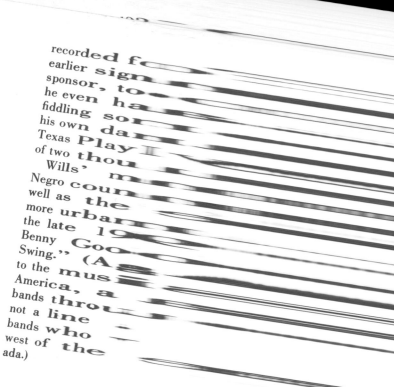

275 Bob Wills and his Texas Playboys, 1945. Rear, Jac[k] Ramsey, Kelso, Laura Lee Owens, Tommy; (front) Noel Cameron Hill

268 The Tune Wranglers. L to r, (standing) Tom Dickey, Bill Dickey, Buster Coward, George Timberlake; (seated) Eddie Fielding, accordion; Eddie Duncan

eaters and dance halls in Texas
Oklahoma. They were also
ed on KTSA, San Antonio

271 Jimmie Revard and the Oklahoma Playboys, 1936. A Western swing group composed of some members of Adolph Hofner's Band

274 Charlie Herald and his Round-up Rangers, Charlie is on bass.

band, called the Cowboy Ramblers, was organized by Bill and Jim Boyd. The Ramblers, who began recording in 1934 for Bluebird, drew on country, popular, and jazz for their instrumentals. Considered their most successful disk was a fiddle-guitar version of an old march tune, "Under the Double Eagle."

Malone has found that "Southwestern musicians had revealed a tendency to improvise and experiment with melodic variations much earlier than their counterparts in the other Southern states . . . perhaps because of the diversity of cultures in the Gulf Coast. . . . It has been suggested that Southwestern string-band music, strongly influenced by Louisiana jazz, may have taken on its peculiar regional stylings when oil workers moved from Louisiana to Texas during the 1920's."

The trail of Western swing moves next to some of the names that were to be influential. In the late 1920's a two-man band was formed by Bob Wills and Herman Arnspiger for playing at house parties around Fort Worth. The duo, called Wills' Fiddle Band,

was joined in 1931 by a vocalist, Milton Brown, and then was called the Aladdin Laddies. They branched out to perform over WBAP, Fort Worth. Later that year the trio got a sponsor in the Burrus Mills. For Burrus, they began advertising Light Crust Flour on Fort Worth radio.

In 1932, Sleepy Johnson, a guitarist and tenor banjoist, replaced Arnspiger. With the addition of Brown's brother, Durwood, the band, first called the Fort Worth Doughboys and later the Light Crust Doughboys, made its first recording for Victor on February 9, 1932. The Doughboys were to be to Western swing what Bill Monroe and His Bluegrass Boys were to Bluegrass music, a seedbed for a style that spread out to affect the whole Western-swing field.

Because of the popularity of the band on Fort Worth radio after 1933 the city became known as "the cradle of Western swing." The Burrus Mills executive who hired the band, and who later was its master of ceremonies, was none other than W. Lee ("Pass

275 Bob Wills and his Texas Playboys, 1945. Rear, Jack McElroy, M.C., Alex Brashear, Billy Jack Wills, Rip Ramsey, Kelso, Laura Lee Owens, Tommy; (front) Noel Boggs, Joe Holley, Louis Tierney, Bob, Jimmy Wyble, Cameron Hill

278 The Spade Cooley Orchestra with some 6,000 listeners at the peak of Western Swing popularity in the 1940's

with this borrowed material came a large number of compositions written by members of the Wills organization and others that differed little from the typical country melodies of the days: ballads, love songs, and novelties. 'Steel Guitar Rag,' written by Leon McAuliff, became a country-music standard and revealed the popularity the instrument would attain. The majority of Wills' national hits did not achieve that recognition until the war years, but one composition, early in 1941, forecast the future popularity that both Wills and country music would attain. This was 'The San Antonio Rose.' It was first recorded in strictly country fashion in 1940 and achieved wide popularity, but in 1941 it was recorded by Bing Crosby and the record sold over 84,000 copies in the month of January alone.''

The emergence of Western swing in the mid-1930's and the later development of a honky-tonk style such as that of Ernest Tubb's Texas band were to have sweeping effects on the sound of country music by the period of World War II. The Western image of the singing cowboys, planted by Jimmie Rodgers and made into an international phenomenon by Autry, was to have a deep effect on country music and the entire country music atmosphere.

Several later Western bands that fused elements from both the Wills band and the honky-tonk style, which put a beat and the sound of electric steel guitars forward, have continued to flourish. No history of Western swing, even in these broad outlines, would be complete without reference to Hank Thompson and His Brazos Valley Boys, Leon McAuliff and His Cimarron Boys, or the bands of Billy Gray and Spade Cooley. McAuliff reports a decline in the playing for dancing since 1955, when the prewar fad had all but died. Only about 30 per cent of the McAuliff band's work now is for dances.

One of the most popular and distinctive performers to emerge in country music in the last few years is Buck Owens, leader of the Buckaroos. Using some elements of Western swing and some of the honky-tonk style fused with rockabilly, Owens has carved out a beautiful and exciting form of vocal and instrumental popular country music.

Western dress costumes are almost standard apparel for country musicians today. Autry's home near Hollywood has some 1,500 square feet of closet space holding 250 Western costumes averaging in cost $275 apiece, and 75 pairs of boots! A latter-day country singer, Judy Lynn, today has a wardrobe of flashy Western clothes designed by Nudie, the North Hollywood "cowboy" tailor, valued at $75,000. It seems to be a question of how are you going to keep them down on the farm after they've gone West?

Not all country musicians have gone

279 The late Cecil Brower, a staff musician on the Jimmy Dean show and former member of Milton Brown's Brownies.

280 The "Bonanza" crew

281 Glenn Ohrlin at the Newport Folk Festival

Gene Autry and Smiley Burnette in "Rootin' Tootin' Rhythm," 1937

Western, however, and some conservatives still wear sports clothes or more Southeastern-flavored costumes. Indeed, had members of such country groups as the Range Riders or the Girls of the Golden West ever ridden the range or been in the golden West?

Westerns on TV have begun to produce a new brand of singing cowboy in Lorne Greene, Harve Presnell, Robert Horton, David Houston, and Pernell Roberts. Although TV in recent years has been wary of singing cowboys on screen, record companies have been pushing these singing actors heavily in the last years. (After the success of Lorne Greene's single, "Ringo," it was suggested that Ringo Starr of the Beatles might try recording a song called "Lorne.")

By the fall of 1964 several changes in attitude toward the Western element of country music were becoming evident. No one has suggested placing a statue of Autry's horse Champion or Rogers' horse Trigger in Nashville, or changing the name of the "Grand Ole Opry" to "Horse Opry," but other straws in the Western wind are obvious. The naming of Tex Ritter to the Country Music Hall of Fame took direct cognizance of the importance of Western music.

Perhaps of even more tangible significance was a gala opening, twenty miles northwest of Nashville, at Ashland City, Tennessee, of the Fort Aldrich Movie Ranch, in the fall of 1964. Charles Aldrich, the road manager of several stars of leading TV Western series, said of his new amusement park and ranch that he had "commitments with several low-budget Western motion-picture companies to film Western series and 'Wild West shoot-em-ups' for TV and movies at Fort Aldrich."

The Western promoter turned Tennessean ranch owner had previously operated the Lone Ranger Movie Ranch in Hollywood, the old Paramount Movie Ranch and the Riverside (Calif.) Rancho Ballroom that had featured country and Western music acts.

How are you going to keep them down on the ranch after they've seen Nashville?

283 Vaughn Horton, Tex Ritter, Ted Daffan, Floyd Tillman and Roy Horton

8 TIN PAN VALLEY: THE SONGS AND THE SONG WRITERS

"Country songs use the words that Lincoln used. . . ." — WESLEY ROSE.

*"You ask what makes our kind of music successful. I'll tell you. It can be explained in just one word: sincerity.
When a hillbilly sings a crazy song, he feels crazy. When he sings 'I Laid My Mother Away,' he sees her a-laying
right there in the coffin.*
*"He sings more sincere than most entertainers because the hillbilly was raised rougher than most entertainers.
You got to have smelt a lot of mule manure before you can sing like a hillbilly. . . ."* — HANK WILLIAMS.

All the strengths and all the weaknesses of country and Western music can be found in the songs produced by its song writers. Although this book has taken a primarily positive view of country music, it would be a distortion to indicate that all country songs have merit. The Nashville tunesmiths have turned out enormous amounts of trivial, shoddy material. There are hundreds of country songs that ceased to be of interest — musically and otherwise — almost as soon as they were put to paper or recorded.

But by and large, the "respectable" world of music has overlooked the positive achievements of country song writing. The melodic richness, the beauty of many lyrics, and especially the attitudes and values reflected in those lyrics, have given the forty-year storehouse of country and Western music a load of treasures.

The emergence of a Nashville music industry has not stopped the writing of folk songs. Now these songs are produced by professionals instead of by gifted hill country amateurs. The purpose of writing has changed, inevitably, from one of self-made entertainment and self-expression to the production of a commercial product. But there remains enough first-rate song composition in the grand tradition to show that the feelings that went into the writing of the folk songs of today are still at work. Some of what is being written by the professional songsmiths of Nashville can be considered as the material for the folk songs of tomorrow.

The use of popular music as a social barometer to document what people are thinking, hoping, and feeling has long fascinated students of popular culture. This "sociology of music" can give us an entire profile of what the millions who live by country music look like. Someday a group of social psychologists

and folklorists may team together to make a serious, detailed study of "the meaning of country music," from its folk origins to the Nashville Sound. Until such a study is made, we must rest content with just a few surface observations about the content and the oddities of human expression in country music.

Perhaps the most fascinating thing about country songs is how they differ from the songs of Tin Pan Alley. Both reflect attitudes toward life, standards of conduct, ideals or broken ideals of behavior, social practices, feelings about family, life, love, work, marriage, religion, history, and nearly every other human activity.

In this brief survey of the content and nature of country songs, a few conclusions can be made. In general, country music deals in more reality than other popular music of the United States, which is usually oriented toward escape from the real world. Country music usually chooses to meet life head on, rather than to deal in the sort of fantasy life suggested by Tin Pan Alley songs. Country music is unabashedly sentimental, often tragic (for reasons to be delineated later), and displays an "obstacle course" approach toward love.

Let's take a look at some of the oddities and curiosities of country songs by scanning a few titles or topics that have been dealt with. Emotionalism of the baldest sort is used in country music: "If Teardrops Were Pennies and Heartaches Were Gold" or "Mother, the Queen of My Heart." Love is also treated in everyday language without the necessity for consciously poetic imagery: "My Shoes Keep Walking Back to You," "I'm Biting My Fingernails and Thinking of You," "Let's Get Married," "My Love for You Has Turned to Hate," or "I Betcha I Getcha."

In its attitude toward reality, country music will speak candidly about wild times and dissolution: "Cigarettes, Whiskey and Wild, Wild Women," "If You've Got the Money, I've Got the Time," "I'm Gong to Tie One On Tonight," and this curious mixture of wild times and religious morality, "It Wasn't God Who Made Honky-Tonk Angels." Other "wild side of life" songs are "Here I Am Drunk Again" and "Playin' Dominoes and Shootin' Dice."

In country music, love is the favorite topic, as with other popular musics, but it may appear in the guise of larger world problems, as in "Cold War With You." Or love may be placed on the earthiest basis, with barnyard imagery, as in "Henhouse Serenade."

To continue with the novel themes of country song lyrics, consider more unusual material: Immortality and reincarnation, a movement that has many adherents in the country-music world, from song writer Floyd Tillman to the late Jim Reeves and Cowboy Copas, are reflected in these titles: "You Must Be Born Again," "Will We Meet on That Isle in the Sky?" and "Hillbilly Heaven."

When was the last time you heard a Tin Pan Alley song about food? Country music has "Sidemeat and Cabbage." Or the famous novelty song, "Did the Chewing-Gum Lose Its Flavor on the Bedpost?" A strange mixture of imagery comes in the sad love song "Bubbles in My Beer." A bit of advice to return to real values is offered in "Get a Little Dirt on Your Hands." Although Nashville writers shy away from songs touching on integration or segregation, Sheb Wooley's Tex-Mex song "When Mexican Joe Met Jole Blon" mentions the ethnic diversity of Mexican and Cajun in Louisiana. "The Pretty Quadroon" by the Happy Chappies laments the death of a mulatto girl friend.

Urbanization and its rewards and problems are discussed in many songs. "Texas Millionaire" and "Good Deal, Lucille" admonish country folks not to let money and sophistication turn their heads. Although one can find more reflection of teen-agers' attitudes in rock 'n' roll than in country music, there are such songs as "Too Young to Tango." Even suicide becomes a subject for a song in "Three A.M."

284 Floyd Tillman and Lew Childre with Mr. Pooch, 1943

285 Merle Travis

286 Marvin Rainwater

287 Tennessee Ernie Ford

Family finances are discussed frankly in "Walking Shoes" by M.K. Rainwater, while Justin Tubb's "Keeping Up With the Joneses" tackles the very real situation of social rivalry. A variety of songs talk about poverty ("Busted") and social inequality ("Po' Folks" and "The Wrong Side of Town").

Migration from country to city is dealt with in many songs, such as "Country Love," "Big City Blues," "I Wanta Go Back to Baltimore," "You Can't Take the Country From the Boy," and "I'm Going to Hollywood." "Detroit City" complains about the life of a Southern migrant, while its answer song, "Detroit City #2," recalls that life back on the farm wasn't all that great.

A theme rarely touched on by Tin Pan Alley songs, marital infidelity, has become as prevalent in country music as actual infidelity has evidently become. "Slipping Around," "Back-Street Affair," "One Has My Name and One Has My Heart" all touch on the triangle theme. A dimension beyond that is "Let's Invite Them On Over," which is almost an implicit reference to wife-swapping.

Work songs or songs about occupations also play a big part. Songs about work or songs to make work go easier have always been part of the world's folk tradition. Commercial country music has not let this tradition die, but makes its own distinct contribution. Merle Travis' songs of coal-mining are among the best. The wide fame enjoyed by his "Sixteen Tons" as recorded by Tennessee Ernie Ford has been one of the shining moments in country music. (Travis' work carries on with Jimmie Key's 1963 song, "Last Day in the Mines.")

A similar vein of occupational songs is the writing of Alex Zanetis, a pop-country song writer. In the *LP*, "Alex Zanetis Writes and Sings the Story of The Oil Fields," on the RIC label (with liner notes by no less an authority on oil than Winthrop Rockefeller), Zanetis sings of the life of the oil-field worker as Travis did of the Kentucky miner. Dave Dudley, a fine balladeer whose style is obviously influenced by Johnny Cash, has recorded for Mercury "Songs of the Working-Man," which touch on truck-drivers, track-layers, steelworkers, miners, and taxi-drivers.

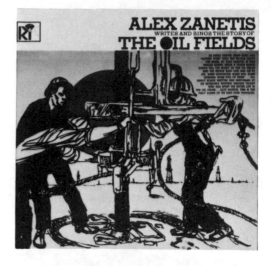

288 Alex Zanetis

An interesting trend has been the recent emergence of the truck-driver song, which reflects one of the deep-rooted values of American life—the lonesome hero pitting himself against danger. The truck-driver has replaced, or rather continues, the heroic symbol of lonely courage and mobility that was earlier held by the Daniel Boone-like trapper-frontiersman, the pony-express rider, the cowboy, the hobo, the railroad man. Now, the lonely American who drives a giant Fruehauf semi-trailer diesel is celebrated in songs.

"Idaho Red" is a tale of a freewheeling truck-driver "with a gal at every coffee stop." "Widow Maker" speaks of the "diesel driver's code," which in this case means a driver's sacrificing his own life rather than plowing his truck into a pickup filled with children.

A fascinating collection of these songs by nine performers is heard on the Starday "Diesel Smoke, Dangerous Curves and Other Truck-Driver Favorites." The songs present an alternately romantic and realistic picture of the life, doubts, and thoughts of the teamsters who ply the American highway.

Insights into other channels of the thinking of rural people are reflected in country songs. Divorce, an increasingly prevalent topic, is the subject of "Dear Judge" and "Married by the Bible, Divorced by the Law." A curious approach to death is reflected in "I'm an Old Old Man" by Lefty Frizzell, in which a man wants to paint the town red with a young girl

before he dies. Conversely, Bob Wills and Cindy Walker had some encouragement for the geriatrics set with "Don't Be Ashamed of Your Age."

There is a hint of voyeurism in Sheb Wooley's "Peeping Thru the Keyhole," in which a man learns to "dance and kiss" by spying on his friend through a keyhole. "I'm Going to Tear Down the Mailbox" voices a common complaint about what the mail brings —letters from sheriffs, tax collectors, and "moneysucking women." Death in childbirth, which no Jerome Kern or Cole Porter ever wrote about, is found in "Little Angel With the Dirty Feet." There are, of course, C.&W. songs to nearly every Southern state and to many Southern towns.

Love is the overridingly popular theme of country music, but even here, there are vast differences from the love reflected in many other musical forms through the ages. How love is treated may vary from the sublimity of "Maid of Constant Sorrow" to the mundane imagery of "Billy Broke My Heart at Walgreen's and I Cried All the Way to Sears."

A stimulating study of country songs by Joe Goldberg in *The American Record Guide* of August, 1960, found some startling parallels between country songs and medieval troubadour songs of eight hundred years ago. In the article entitled: "Why So Pale and Wan, Fair Lover?" Goldberg wrote:

"The basis of country music lies in a direct transference into contemporary terms of the

182

289 Jimmy Davis

290 Simon Crum (Ferlin Husky)

rules of courtly love and the poetry that stemmed from it." He quotes several definitions of the courtly love of which the medieval troubadours sang, such as one by the writer-philosopher C.S. Lewis:

"The sentiment, of course, is love, but love of a highly specialized sort, whose characteristics may be enumerated as humility, courtesy, adultery and the religion of love. The lover is always abject. Obedience to his lady's slightest wish, however whimsical and silent, acquiescence to her rebukes, however unjust, are the only virtues he dares to claim."

Tracing this tradition through the romantic poetry of Keats, Byron, Swinburne, and the Marquis de Sade, the commentator presents strong support for the fact that songs by Hank Williams and Johnny Cash and many country writers are really carrying on this same tragedy-wracked approach toward love. He cites the fact that Cash ". . . has recorded the most romantic of all titles, 'I'd Rather Die Young Than Grow Old Without You.'"

Another country song writer found to document this startling theory is Ray Price, in "Heartaches by the Number," "Same Old Me," and "Crazy Arms." The article concludes with a reference to a couplet from Hank Williams' "Lovesick Blues," which Goldberg maintains, "gets to the root of the entire question posed by country music, the dual heritage it represents, and the lives of the millions who lived by its standards:

"I'm in love, I'm in love with a beautiful girl, That's what's the matter with me."*

A comparison breakdown of the content of a contemporary country-music collection with a collection of older folk-country songs may give some ideas about the scope of this music. While obviously not meant to be scientific, two collections were used in this research task by Steve Oberkirsch. Scanning 350 songs in the catalogues of Southern Music-Peer International and *100 Great Country & Western Songs*, published by Hill and Range Songs, Inc., he found this breakdown:

65% were "weepers," sad love songs.
 5% were happy or optimistic love songs.
 4% had Western themes.
 5% were sacred.
 1% were dance tunes.
20% were on miscellaneous topics.

Turn now to a collection of old-time hillbilly songs, most of which dated from the early period before there was conscious song writing for a commercial country music industry. This book, *The New Lost City Ramblers Song Book* (Oak), was carefully culled by two city musicians who have done so much to popularize early string-band music, Mike Seeger and John Cohen. Their criteria for inclusion were obviously different from those of Southern Music-Peer International and Hill and Range.

* © Acuff-Rose Publications, Inc. Used with permission.

183

291 Carson Robison

292 Frank Luther

At any rate, the breakdown from the New Lost City Ramblers collection revealed:

11% sad love songs.
8% murder ballads.
10% dance tunes.
10% topical and protest songs.
15% rambling-gambling, hobo and train songs.
2% work songs.
7% children's songs.
3% sacred songs.
5% nonsense and humor songs.
29% miscellaneous topics.

As indicated, these random samplings of song collections cannot be used to document statistically the nature of country music. Some conclusions are inescapable, however. There is a greater breadth of topics in country songs, whether from the folk-oriented "Golden Age," or from the post-1941 period, than can be found in the composed songs of Tin Pan Alley. (One Nashville publishing house, Cedarwood, today has as its working slogan: "If you need material, call us. . . . If we don't have it, we'll write it.")

The statistical breakdowns are also helpful as an indication of the diversity of themes treated in country music from its inception. Inevitably, general impressions of the nature of a music are made in the popular mind. As Archie Green says, "1,000 country songs may have 900 songs on love and the remaining 100 on 49 other themes. Still, the over-all impression is set by the 900." The over-all impression of country songs, however wrong this may be, is that country music is sad, sentimental, stressing the tragic side of love. A disk jockey from KAYO in Seattle wrote a letter published in *Billboard* December 7, 1963, asking:

"Why not more happy tunes? Don't they sell? Have they really had a chance? One of the comments most often heard by the C. & W. disk jockey is: 'Why are all the songs we hear so sad?'

"I know that most of our songs are taken from actual situations in life. I know that the events in any person's daily life which are likely to have the most emotional impact are tragic events, but there is happiness in most lives, too. Look at the current C. & W. Top

Fred Rose, 1933

294 Fred Rose much later

40. About 80 per cent of the songs have as their theme the triangle situation in which one, or both, of the central characters is married, and one, or both, sings about the tragedy and unhappiness of illicit love.

"Granted, this situation happens often enough in real life to make Dr. Kinsey blush, but even in these situations, surely, there must be some happiness, at least at first. Every love affair that ends in tragedy must have started as a love affair that gave the participants enough joy to make them want to sing a happy song. . . ."

— Bashful Bobby Wooten

This complaint from the not-so-bashful Mr. Wooten is more often heard from those hostile to country music than "within the family." That sad songs had their appeal was indicated in an article on Johnny Cash in *Variety* on February 11, 1959, by Mike Gross:

"There's been a shift in the mood of the record-buying audience that's turning unhappiness into a thing called dough. Tunes dealing with hanging ('Tom Dooley'), gunplay ('Don't Take Your Guns to Town'), burying ('Springtime in Alaska'), prison ('Life to Go'), and solemn vows ('I Walk the Line') are moving out of their folk and country and Western origination and into pop areas long dominated by rock 'n' roll. . . ."

The prevalence of tragic songs in both folk and country and Western songlore stems from a variety of complex reasons. It must be kept in mind that commercial country music is only about forty years old, but the folk-music tradition in the American South runs at least one hundred years prior to that and for countless years earlier in the British Isles and Ireland. The backgrounds of many attitudes, tragic or joyful, in country music can be traced to folk origins. Again, we'll quote from Billy Charles Malone:

"The Southern taste in ballad and song ran the gamut from the ridiculous to the tragic—from 'Froggie Went A-courting' to 'The Fatal Flower Garden.' Although the songs depicted every aspect of rural life and temper, the rural taste ran heavily toward the mournful and lonesome tunes. In part, this inclination was a legacy from the British tradition, because many of the songs dealt with somber themes and were cast in minor-sounding keys which seemed to evoke a melancholy response in the minds of the singer and listener. The sad songs continued to be loved by later generations of Southerners even after the melodies became constructed in the major chords.

"The preference for the mournful derives its existence from several sources. One source was the religious life which stressed an other-worldly attitude and the depiction of this world as a vale of sorrow. Southern backwoodsmen, imbued with the doctrines of Calvinism, labored under a conviction of sin. It is not surprising that their choice of songs and style of singing would reflect this tragic outlook. The average rural dweller in the pre-1920 period needed few reminders to know that life was indeed a tragic epoch — an epoch that was filled with sadness and disappointment and ultimately ended in death. Rural life, especially that of the pioneer period, was fraught with arduousness, deprivation and suffering. In such an existence, it is not surprising that death would become a major theme of the songs. The isolation of rural living led, too, to a fondness for the 'lonesome' tunes which seemed to mirror so well the existence with which the people were accustomed. Many of the popular sentimental tunes from Tin Pan Alley filtered into the rural areas and, finding a natural habitat, remained there. Such songs as 'I'll Be All Smiles Tonight,' and 'The Fatal Wedding' experienced their births in urban areas and gained considerable popularity in a 19th-century America that, despite its rapid industrialization, was still basically rural in values and outlook. Long after these songs had faded into obscurity in other areas and had ceased to be known by 'popular' music fans, they continued to be known and loved by rural Southerners who held onto the simple and sentimental values of a bygone era. As a result, the sentimental songs of the 19th century, and later songs similar to them, became a vital part of the commercial country recordings of the 1920's."

In the early years of the recording of country musicians, most, but not all, of the material used was traditional. The first known hillbilly disk recording, of A.C. (Eck) Robertson and Henry C. Gilliland, on June 30, 1922, had used the traditional "Sally Gooden" and "Arkansaw Traveler." Henry Whitter's recording in New York in March, 1923, was the traditional "Wreck of the Old 97," one of the first hillbilly hits. The song, dealing with a train wreck in Virginia in 1903, was believed to have been composed by David Graves George, a farmer who saw the wreck. By the mid-twenties the song had become traditional, and his claim for compensation was never

295 Buck Owens

296 Dave Dudley

297 The Carlisle Brothers

298 Dock Boggs

honored. Similarly, Buell Kazee's early Brunswick recordings were of traditional ballads, as were those of Clarence Ashley. Dock Boggs recorded traditional blues songs influenced by Negro singers, and Kelly Harrell, another discovery of Peer, did traditional material in addition to his own compositions. Although A.P. Carter's name is listed as composer of most of the original Carter Family songs, they were traditional material which the family had preserved and made popular by the addition of harmony and the use of instrumental accompaniment.

The search for the early important composers of hillbilly songs would certainly dwell upon the blind Holiness preacher from Jenkinsburg, Georgia, the Rev. Andrew Jenkins. (Prof. D. K. Wilgus of the University of California at Los Angeles has done extensive research on Jenkins, on which the following discussion is partly based.) He married into a musical family which started to broadcast on WSB in 1922. Among the more than eight hundred songs Jenkins wrote before his death in 1956 were such songs as "Little Marian Parker," "Ben Dewberry's Final Run," "Billy the Kid," and, reflecting his career as revivalist and writer of mostly sacred songs, "God Put a Rainbow in the Clouds."

The Rev. Jenkins' best-known composition was "The Death of Floyd Collins," an event song based on the entrapment of a cave-explorer in Kentucky in 1925. Jenkins wrote it on commission from Polk Brockman, the Atlanta talent scout, and it was arranged by his stepdaughter, Mrs. Irene Spain. Brockman paid twenty-five dollars for the song, sold it to Frank Walker, who gave it to Vernon Dalhart, who made it into a national hit.

By all odds, the most important song writers of the early years of country music were Carson Robison and Bob Miller.

Carson Robison, who was also known as the "Kansas Jayhawk" and the "Granddaddy of the Hillbillies," was born in Chetopa, Kansas, on August 4, 1890. He was the son of an old-time fiddler. A large part of his early success came through his association with such leading performers as Wendell Hall, Vernon Dalhart, and Frank Luther.

Robison wrote more than three hundred songs before his death on March 24, 1957. His first radio appearance was on WDAF, Kansas City, in 1922. He went to New York two years later with $3.65 in his pocket. He teamed up with Wendell Hall on a few Victor recordings and later worked as a whistler with dance bands. He also performed with the then-popular Gene Austin and Roy Smeck.

Robison's association with Dalhart until 1927 was to be decisive. His songs "My Blue Ridge Mountain Home" and "Way Out West in Kansas" were among his earliest successes. From these he turned to the event songs about disasters, wrecks, and topical events. Here he was continuing the eighteenth-century British broadside tradition. Many of the songs in this genre were to become leading hillbilly hits of the 1920's. As a modern broadside writer, Robison followed a clear-cut method. He was quoted in an article by Hugh Leamy, "Now Come All You Good People," in *Collier's* of November 2, 1929:

"'First I read all the newspaper stories of, say, a disaster,' he explains. 'Then I get to work on the old typewriter. There's a formula, of course. You start by painting everything in gay colors — "the folks were all happy and gay" stuff. That's sure-fire. Then you ring in the tragedy — make it as morbid and gruesome as you can. Then you wind up with a moral.'"

Robison, who also wrote under the names Maggie Andrews and Carlos B. McAfee, left Dalhart in 1927 and sang later with Frank Luther as Bud and Joe Billings and The Jimson Brothers. Robison also had a band, Carson Robison and His Pioneers, that enjoyed popularity on recordings. His Bluebird disks of the World War II era carried on his topicality to include taunts at Hitler and Mussolini.

Among the best-known Robison compositions were "Carry Me Back to the Lone Prairie," "Life Gets Tee-jus, Don't It?", "Little Green Valley," "Naomi Wise," "Left My Gal in the Mountains," and broadsides about "The Wreck of the Shenandoah," "The Wreck of the 12:56," "The Miami Storm," and "The John T. Scopes Trial."

A song writer from Tennessee who enjoyed popularity from the 1920's on was Bob Miller, who worked in New York but managed to retain his rural roots. He began writing epitaphs for an undertaker in his native Memphis at the age of eleven. He gave up a career as a concert pianist because so many songs coursed through his head. He wrote under twelve pen names (Trebor Rellim, Bob Kackley, Lawrence Wilson, Shelby Darnell, Dinny Dimes). By 1946 Miller had written seven thousand songs of what he called

299   Bob Miller

300   Hank "Sugarfoot" Garland

1 (Standing) Ruby Wright, Wayne Walker, and (seated) Mel Tillis and Red Sovine

"Main Street music." He had written such popular hillbilly hits as "Eleven Cent Cotton and Forty Cent Meat" and "There's a Star-Spangled Banner Waving Somewhere," a World War II hit as recorded by Elton Britt. (The song was later rewritten as "The Ballad of Francis Powers," about the hapless pilot of an American U-2 shot down by the Russians.)

One of the most incredible events in hillbilly song writing was Bob Miller's prophetic penning of a song about the assassination of Huey Long before it happened! He sang it to the Louisiana politician at the Hotel New Yorker two years before Long was shot. Long invited him to Baton Rouge to teach it to the glee club there. "They'll sing it at your funeral, Huey," Miller said. They did.

The song writer also did two versions of the death of John Dillinger to be ready for immediate recording. He carried on the badman song tradition that stems back to Robin Hood ballads with "Outlaw John Dillinger" and "Pretty Boy Floyd," and another about

the gangster "Dutch" Schultz. Miller also was the moralist in "The Morro Castle Disaster," and a courtroom dramatist in "The Trial of Bruno Richard Hauptmann," about the kidnaper of the Lindbergh child.

Commentary in music on social issues was to spread into the rural areas during the Depression, although hard times were no stranger to the country. Some songs of protest and many songs of social comment can be found in the forty-year treasury of country songs. It has been pointed out that it would have been unusual for the makers of commercial records to have used their outlets as a medium for the transmission of protest, but they did.

Songs commented on the life of the displaced Dust Bowl farmer (as in Woody Guthrie's works), the life of the textile worker (in the songs of Dorsey Dixon and Dave McCarn), and of the coal miner of eastern Kentucky (in the songs of Aunt Molly Jackson and Merle Travis).

The work of Dorsey Dixon has been documented in a recording on the Testament label, "Babies in the Mill," edited by Archie Green. The title piece by Dorsey Dixon comments on child labor in the textile plants of the Carolinas. "Weave Room Blues," composed in 1932, was the first song recorded by the Dixon Brothers, for Victor, in February, 1936, in Charlotte, North Carolina. "Hard Times in Here" is similar to "Cotton Mill Girl" and "Cotton Mill Blues," recorded, respectively, by Lester Smallwood on Victor in 1928 and by the Lee Brothers Trio on Brunswick in 1930. One of the most exciting items on "Babies in the Mill" is "Factory Girl," which Green describes as a New England broadside that has lived in oral tradition for 130 years!

Two other songs recorded by Nancy, Dorsey, and Howard Dixon have fascinating histories. One is an industrial song, "Weaver's Life," a textile workers' parody of the sacred "Life's Railway to Heaven." It was first recorded by an influential but obscure country musician named Jimmie Tarleton, for Victor, in 1931, as "Weaver's Blues." (Art Satherley has been quoted as saying that the greatest hillbilly record he ever recorded was Tom Darby and Jimmie Tarleton's "Birmingham Jail" because both, as former convicts, could feel their material so deeply.)

The most famous song by Dorsey Dixon did not protest in the usual sense. His famous moralizing song, "Wreck on the Highway," Green wrote in the album notes, was "initially . . . no more or no less popular than other records by the duo, but after it began to circulate someone brought the song, taught it, or sold it to Roy Acuff in Knoxville. He deleted three stanzas and altered the melody slightly. . . . Acuff recorded 'Wreck on the Highway' for Columbia . . . in May, 1942." The Dixon Brothers had recorded Dorsey's song on January 25, 1938, under the title, "I Didn't Hear Anybody Pray."

A famous singer and song writer who

302 Bill Anderson and Hubert Long with some of their newly received awards.

Martha Lou Carson

304 George Morgan

spoke to and for the coal miners of eastern Kentucky was Aunt Molly Jackson, in early September, 1960, at eighty-three. Her sole commercial recording was "Kentucky Miner's Wife" ("Hungry Ragged Blues") on the Columbia 15,000 series. But much of her work was recorded by the Library of Congress. To the gospel song "Precious Memories" she wrote "Dreadful Memories," a moving tale of children's death from hunger. Other songs from this fabled workers' leader are to be heard on the Folkways recording, "The Songs and Stories of Aunt Molly Jackson." Ironically, she is probably best known as the original "pistol-packin' mama," her song that was later made into a hit by the commercial song writer Al Dexter.

Other songs of social comment and protest of the hillbilly era have been revived by the New Lost City Ramblers, notably "Songs From the Depression" (Folkways). Among the most interesting hillbilly social-comment songs of the 1930's were Bill Cox's 1936 recordings of "Franklin Roosevelt's Back Again" and "The Democratic Donkey Is in His Stall Again." Even Roy Acuff and Uncle Dave Macon reflected the times in such songs as "Old-Age Pension Check," "All I've Got's Gone," and "All In Down and Out Blues." Also commenting upon the life of the textile worker were songs recorded by the Martin Brothers and those of Dave McCarn on Victor, such as "Cotton Mill Colic" and "Serves 'Em Fine."

An early song writer and performer, Bill Carlisle, who worked with his brother Cliff as the Carlisle Brothers, showed a wide range of interests in his song writing, from novelty to risqué songs to prison and hobo songs. Bill Carlisle, who credits Art Satherley, the Columbia recording scout, "with all my success," began his song writing with "Rattlesnake Daddy," a tune that became a national hit. He received all of fifty dollars for it. Bill Carlisle has written about three hundred songs and has a consistent ability to produce hits, largely because of rhythmic vitality in novelty tunes, such as "No Help Wanted," "Too Old to Cut the Mustard," "Knothole," and "Is Zat You Myrtle." (The Carlisles were briefly associated with the colorful Panhandle Pete, a drifting one-man-band showman, around Asheville, N.C.) A comment typical of the prolific veterans in country song writing is Bill Carlisle's recollection that on personal appearances, "old-timers would come up and talk to me and mention songs I'd written and forgotten about."

One of the revered figures in country writing is a Texan named Floyd Tillman, who got into the business at the age of nineteen in the early 1930's. He worked the Texas honkytonks and in various Western string and swing bands. His most famous early composition, "It Makes No Difference Now," was written in 1938. As is often the case with country writers, he sold part of it to another performer, Jimmie Davis, later the Governor of Louisiana. Tillman had earlier turned his writing toward politics, having written for two Texas candidates, Jerry Sadler and Price Daniel.

Tillman was among the first of the rural song writers to break into the pop music of the North. His "I'll Keep on Loving You" was recorded in 1938 by Connie Boswell, Bing Crosby recorded "It Makes No Difference Now," and Ella Fitzgerald recorded his "Gotta Have My Baby Back." In an interview in Nashville in 1964, Tillman saw that today's country trend was toward the "clever song," whereas it used to be toward inspirational.

Tillman also wrote the decidedly noninspirational prototype song about infidelity, "Slipping Around," which has been a perennial since 1948. This song inspired what seems to be a practice unique to country music, the answer song. A year after this song became a hit, in 1949, Tillman wrote its answer in "I'll Never Slip Around Again." (The cycles of answer songs, virtually continuations or negations of the topic of the earlier composition, are fascinating to watch. "Dear John" received its "Answer to Dear John." "Nobody's Darling But Mine" was rebutted by Patsy Montana in "Woman's Answer to Nobody's Darling," and someone else came up with a mournful sequel in "By the Grave of Nobody's Darling."

At least two Louisianans were to gain fame as song writers, Theron Eugene (Ted) Daffan and former Governor Jimmie Davis. Several of Daffan's songs seem, in recollection, to have almost been the theme songs of World War II. One of these was his "Born to Lose." (An interesting argument against this song's pessimism was written by Woody Guthrie, the Oklahoma ballad maker. The poem provides the title for a new book of Guthrie writing, *Born to Win*, published by Macmillan.)

Ted Daffan may have started the currently popular cycle of truck-driver songs with his "Truck Driver's Blues" of 1939. Other songs of his that characterized the melancholy and loneliness of World War II were "Worried Mind" and "No Letter Today."

305 Ted Daffan and his band

Movie still from "Frontier Fury," 1943, with Jimmy Davis (third from left) and Johnny Bond, far right

A song writer who has probably been the leading political figure to be closely aligned with country music is Governor James (Jimmie) Houston Davis. He was born in 1902 in the red clay hills of Northern Louisiana, the eldest son in a sharecropper's family of eleven children.

Davis attended Soule Business College in New Orleans, then worked his way through Louisiana College at Pineville. He received an M.A. degree from Louisiana State University. Although he sang in the Glee Club at L.S.U., he leaned toward the informal cadences of country music. The future Governor began composing country songs while a professor of history and social science at Dodd College. He left teaching to become a full-time professional country and gospel singer.

In 1938, Davis was persuaded to enter politics, beginning as a public service commissioner, then a criminal court clerk in Shreveport. He was Governor of Louisiana twice, from 1944–48 and 1960–64. His first recording had been for Victor in 1928 and he joined the Decca roster in 1936. His longstanding appeal has been based on his relaxing, full-bodied voice and as writer or co-writer of such national hits as "You Are My Sunshine," "Nobody's Darling But Mine," and "Sweethearts or Strangers." Because of his prominent political position, Governor Davis has long been a leading spokesman for country music. (His life story was sketched in the Monogram film, *Louisiana*.)

Writers working in the cornfields and canyons of Tin Pan Alley have made their contribution to country song writing. During the vogue for cowboy and Western songs of the 1930's, several Western hits were written by city writers, for example Nick and Charles Kenny's "Home in Wyoming," and Johnny Mercer's satirical "I'm an Old Cowhand."

A leading Manhattan cowboy was William J. (Billy) Hill, who has to his credit such songs as "The Last Roundup," "Call of the

307   The late Johnny Horton and Band

Canyon," and "Home in Wyoming" (with Peter DeRose). Hill was one of the few conservatory-trained musicians to have made a name in country music. He was born in Boston in 1899, studied at the New England Conservatory of Music, and played violin with the Boston Symphony Orchestra. After a Western tour and contact with the life of the cowboy and ranch hand, he returned to New York in the 1920's. While working as a hotel doorman there he composed songs. After his biggest hit, "The Last Roundup," Hill rose from poverty and obscurity with songs that captured the Western flavor of the horse on the trail. He wrote "Empty Saddles," "Wagon Wheels," and country tunes such as "The Old Spinning Wheel" and "They Cut Down the Old Pine Tree."

A song writer and lyricist team that moved back and forth from Tin Pan Alley to Tin Pan Valley were Nat Vincent and Fred Howard, old-timers who call themselves the Happy Chappies. The pair have worked together since 1926, and have to their credit such songs (some reworked traditional songs) as "Strawberry Roan," "My Pretty Quadroon," "My Dear Old Arizona Home," and "When the Bloom Is on the Sage." After careers in vaudeville and in city entertainment circles, they began to work on radio. They wrote a variety of songs for the original Beverly Hillbillies and recorded as the Happy Chappies on Columbia.

After working on radio in Des Moines, the two split up for a time. Howard was a member of the cast of the "Ma Perkins" radio soap-opera for a dozen years, and Vincent was a divisional manager in California for Ralph Peer's Southern Music, later directing the company's activities in Nashville. Howard, under the stage name Howard Wright, subsequently appeared in films and on TV.

The curious interaction between composed Tin Pan Alley songs and country "folk" songs was described in ironic detail by discographer and music historian Jim Walsh in *Variety* on May 16, 1951:

"Once Southern mountaineer fiddlers and git-tar players swiped much of their faddishly acclaimed 'folk music' from Tin Pan Alley. Now the Alley's executing a neat switch by getting some of its hottest hits — 'Tennessee Waltz,' 'On Top of Old Smoky,' etc. — from the hills. . . . In pre-radio days the average mountain yokel had a cylinder phonograph from which he learned many of the current tunes. . . . The Broadway tunes learned from the records sank back into the redbrush and emerged later, in altered form as folk music. . . .

"In the 1920's, many old-time hits were reissued, having undergone the mountain metamorphosis, with changed titles and sans composer credit. Irving Berlin's 'Ragtime Violin' became 'Fiddle Up' as rendered by Jess Young and his Lookout Mountain Boys.

of the World War II era: "Driving Nails in My Coffin (every time I drink a bottle of booze)," "Stompin' at the Honky-Tonk," "I Ain't Goin' Honky-Tonkin' Anymore," etc.

The war years, as we shall see in the last chapter, did much to spread country people, and with them, country music. With the old bent for reflecting actual events and genuine feelings, country music made significant comment on the World War II experience. Acuff's "Cowards Over Pearl Harbor" was an angry song, and Red Foley's "Smoke on the Water" was a defiant pledge of ultimate victory. Separation from loved ones brought many problems, reflected in a variety of country songs.

The war years also saw a rise in interest in sacred and gospel music, as inevitable a trend as increased attendance at churches during periods of crisis or tension. Although a specific discussion of the large outpouring of religious music that has always been a part of country music is outside the scope of this book, a few pertinent facts should be mentioned. In rural folk music of the United States, it has been estimated that nearly 50 per cent is of a religious nature. A large part of the repertory of such influential traditional singers as the Carter Family was religious music. Such old-time members of the "Grand Ole Opry" as the Bailes Brothers wrote many gospel tunes, such as "Dust on the Bible," that were to be as popular with their audiences as sentimental love and family songs.

One of the greatest, if not the greatest, woman singer in country music, Molly O'Day, recorded many sacred songs, such as "Tramp on the Street." She has, in recent years, become a full-time revivalist in the West Virginia hill country and has virtually left commercial country music. Similar conversions to the dedicated religious life have been reportedly undergone by Stuart Hamblen and T. Texas Tyler.

Sacred songs, hymns, and gospel songs

Jimmi

Gospel at Carnegie Hall, 1964, center stage, Wally Fowler

312 WBMD Country Jubilee with Ray Price, "The Cherokee Cowboy," on right

313 Don Gibson

314 Bernard Cartwright of the Cartwright Brothers from Boerne, Tex., 1928

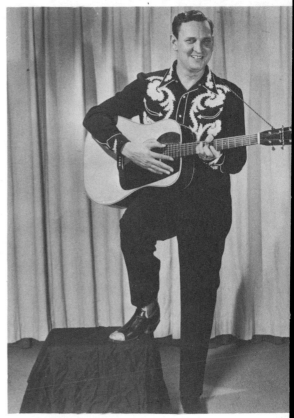

315 Clyde Moody

316   Billy Hill

317   Francis Craig

318   Wilf Carter, "Montana Slim"

are the stock in trade of such country groups as the Chuck-Wagon Gang, the Lewis Family, and many quartets and trios who travel with the Wally Fowler All-Night Sings across the Midwest and Southeast. Nearly every country singer, band, and Bluegrass group has made at least one album of sacred songs. Often they have devoted a large part of their repertory to them. Tennessee Ernie Ford has entrenched himself with many recordings of hymns, spirituals, and gospel songs. Archie Campbell epitomizes an extreme of the sacred-secular dual approach with his racy comedy monologues and songs and his heartfelt gospel songs, often performed one after the other. Tennessee Ernie Ford's comment on religious country songs is representative:

"Of all the singing I do, the hymns, spirituals and gospel songs not only give me great pleasure but seem to be something that truly needs to be done. . . . Many people . . . may get all steamed up about big new love songs that come along, but let's not forget that hymns and spirituals are the finest love songs of them all. . . ."

As World War II served to begin the great dissemination of country songs around the world, the postwar years were to see country music making great inroads into the whole nation's popular-music diet. Some observers have seen 1950 as a peak year for the invasion of popular-music areas by country songs. Among those that had helped build this crescendo of acceptance were "Pistol Packin' Mama," "Sioux City Sue," "Slipping Around," "Lovesick Blues," "I Love You Because," and "Chattanooga Shoe Shine Boy."

The urban folk-music revival, which had its sharpest rise in popularity with the 1958 recording by the Kingston Trio of "Tom Dooley," was also interesting pop-music writers in songs of a folk and country vein. From Tin Pan Alley came such folkish tunes as "Mule Train," "Riders in the Sky," and "Cry of the Wild Goose." The recording in late 1950 by Patti Page of the Pee Wee King – Redd Stewart song "The Tennessee Waltz" served, along with the pop-music recordings of Hank Williams' songs, to establish country music on the popular hit parade. Malone says "it was generally believed that 'The Tennessee Waltz' was the biggest song in modern popular-music history, and was certainly the top song ever licensed by BMI."

The years that followed were not, historically speaking, a distinguished time for country song writing. A taste of the success of the pop-music field led to a watering down of country-music style, a slickening of sound that used vocal groups, violins, and brasses. The pop-country sound was a fusion that tried to serve too many musical tastes at once and ended by probably serving none very well.

By the mid-1950's, however, such country singers as Elvis Presley, Buddy Holly, the Everly Brothers, and Carl Perkins were bringing on a musical revolution. The fusion of country singing with the heavy beat of Negro rhythm and blues gave birth to two related styles, rock 'n' roll and rockabilly. The success of Presley and others in the heavily rhythmic rock 'n' roll made great inroads on country music, especially among younger listeners. The appealing big beat of rockabilly was a direct, and often successful, appeal to win back those listeners who had been seduced by the rock 'n' roll beat and vitality.

The distinction between rockabilly and the style Malone has called honky-tonk would take more space to define than it deserves. Few popular-music styles remain pure for long. Nothing can spread quite so quickly as a musical style that is selling. Whether to place the popular Buck Owens in the rockabilly or the honky-tonk slot seems irrelevant. By either name, his heavily rhythmic approach that steadfastly maintains a country, rather than a pop-music, sound has won him an enormous following, and the highest praise, imitation.

Malone sees the honky-tonk style as growing out of such early Texas performers as Ernest Tubb and Bob Wills. He argues that too many country-music purists fail to recognize its artistic and durable qualities. This writer agrees with him that such exponents of this style as George Jones, Johnny Cash, Dave Dudley, Ray Price, the late Johnny Horton, Little Jimmie Dickens, Buck Owens, and many others are serious country musicians who have found their place in the "grand tradition" of country music. They deserve the respectful attention of even those tradition-directed country fans who want to see only a slow change toward modernization.

After the whole nation appeared to be veering toward the widespread folk-music revival that followed "Tom Dooley," a host of song writers and singers got on a trend of historical or descriptive balladry. Whether

319　An early photo of Elvis Presley, center, with Scotty Moore, left, and Bill Black, right.

320　Harlan Howard at home

stemming from actual or imaginary events, this was a revival of the broadside song in country and popular music, the two frequently overlapping.

From an old square-dance tune, "The Eighth of January," an Arkansas schoolteacher and song writer, Jimmie Driftwood, fashioned a song called "The Battle of New Orleans." The Johnny Horton recording of the song was to be a national hit and helped spur the revival of historical ballads or "saga songs." Many of these songs are to be found on Columbia Records, beginning with Horton's "Springtime in Alaska," a ballad recalling the Robert Stewart Service poems of the Klondike. A large number of Johnny Cash songs were in this vein, notably "Don't Take Your Gun to Town" and several others on his "Songs of Our Soil" and "Ride This Train" albums. Marty Robbins' ballad "Hanging Tree" was in a similar vein.

Another tragically premature death in the sad logbook of country music was that of the Texas-reared Johnny Horton, killed in an auto wreck on November 5, 1960. Between the release of "New Orleans" in April, 1959, and his death, Horton enriched the treasury of country music with such saga songs as "Sink the Bismarck," "Johnny Reb," and "The Battle of Bull Run." (The Civil War Centennial was the occasion for a flood of recordings about the war, from that period or later compositions. Many reflected regional points of view, and the sardonic remark was made that the North won the Civil War but the South won the Centennial.)

Among other notable songs of this period were many that country and folk fans could point to with especial pride as being high standards toward which all country song writers could turn. That these songs enjoyed several years of popularity was a further indication that country songs could stress quality and tradition and still be commercial successes. This list would certainly include many of the songs by Jimmie Driftwood, "Long Black Veil" and "Tennessee Stud," Marty Robbins' "El Paso," and Jimmy Dean's "Big Bad John" and "PT 109."

Malone cites several song writers who contributed quality material to the honky-tonk style singer. Among them are Mel Tillis, Wayne Walker, Jack Rhodes, Merle Kilgore, Justin Tubb, Willie Nelson, Jack Clement, Hank Cochran, Darrell Edwards, and Alex Zanetis. Space does not permit extensive discussion of all the leading figures in country song writing today, but a few should be mentioned.

To single out a few song writers, one must bear in mind the staggering statistics in country music. As of December, 1964, BMI's

1 Redd Stewart and Pee Wee King, co-writers of "Tennessee Waltz," presenting an album of their music to rdon Browning, former governor of Tennessee

Nashville office had six hundred affiliated song writers. There are four thousand more BMI song writers and publishers in the fourteen-state area around Tennessee, a great many of whom can be assumed to be working in country music.

One of the consistent leaders in country song writing is Harlan Howard. In 1961, of the thirty-nine songs named by BMI as the top country songs of the year, ten were written, rewritten, or collaborated on by Harlan Howard. He came to Nashville in the late 1950's, according to a story by Pat Anderson in *The Nashville Tennesseean* of November 5, 1961, "because of a determination to write only country songs rather than shoot for the bigger-paying pop song market."

"'I have no desire to write pop songs,'" Howard said. "'I love country music. If one of my songs goes pop, I'm tickled to death. It's a bonus.'"

He indicated that his songs rarely are built on more than three or four chords. He also likes the forthrightness of lyrics in country songs. "Country people don't mind showing their emotions," he said. In an open letter to country disk jockeys in *Billboard* on April 17, 1965, Howard expressed appreciation for being voted the all-time favorite country song writer.

Howard was born in Lexington, Kentucky, and began writing at the age of twelve. His acceptance did not come until 1956. He attributes his success partially to help from Tex Ritter and Johnny Bond. Among Howard's most successful songs were "Pick Me Up on Your Way Down," "Heartaches by the Number," "Mommy for a Day," and "I Fall to Pieces." One of his most artistic songs was a lament about rural poverty, "Busted," which was recorded by Burl Ives, Johnny Cash, and Ray Charles.

One of the consistently successful song writers is Bill Anderson, also a popular singer and host of his own new TV series. Anderson is a former journalism student at the University of Georgia. One of his finest works, "City Lights," was written, he said in a Nashville interview in 1964, in 1947 while Anderson was working as a disk jockey in Commerce, Georgia. He went to the roof of his hotel at 3 A.M. and wrote the song there while looking out at the city lights. He was unaware that the title was that of a classic Charlie Chaplin film.

Another Anderson work, "99 Years," was a prison song he was inspired to write one night looking at the moving moon while driv-

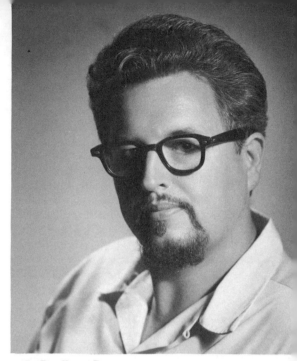

322 Boudleaux Bryant

323 John D. Loudermilk

324 The Great Dixon Brothers

ing. He identified with the man in jail, for whom the moon was always in the same place. A song that clearly falls into the great tradition of country music was his "Po' Folks," another of the folkish, wrong-side-of-the-tracks, social-commentary songs. Anderson wrote the first verse a year and a half before he completed it. He believes that nearly every one of his four hundred songs has been recorded "by someone." Although Anderson has written such banal weepers as "Still," most of his songs have strong imagery, vividness, and sense of realism, or more accurately, naturalism.

One of the more articulate song writers of Nashville and one of its ablest craftsmen is John D. Loudermilk. A former music student at the University of North Carolina, he had a background in folk music and folklore. Coming from a very religious family, he got his first music experience beating a bass drum with the Salvation Army until he was fourteen years old. He came to Nashville in

1959, prepared to give "this town one year. If it didn't work, I was ready to go back to Durham and work in my wife's daddy's hardware store."

Loudermilk said a prayer before his initial meeting with Chet Atkins, and the prayer was rewarded. Atkins offered him a job as an assistant artist and repertory man, listening to material sent in by song writers. He began writing in 1956 and had an early hit with "Abilene." During the revival of historical songs, he scored with "Waterloo." Like Robison and Bob Miller before him, Loudermilk finds many of his songs in the newspaper. He wrote "No Playing in the Snow Today" after reading of a National Health Service warning to children against eating snow because of the danger of radioactivity. In "He's a Scientist" he discusses heroes in American life. Loudermilk, who is especially gifted at keeping a down-home quality in his lyrics, regards his most successful country song as "Tobacco Road," a song that has been recorded more than forty times.

A strong force in country song writing, and a guitar stylist whose name has become attached to a manner of guitar-picking, is Merle Travis. One of the country musicians who has long been revered by the urban folk followers, Travis has kept his music close to its folk roots. He designed and helped build the first "flat guitar," which has since become a standard for guitar manufacturing. He has also contributed many "standard" songs to the country and folk reservoir, such as "Sweet Temptation," "Cincinnati Lou," "So Round, So Firm, So Fully Packed," "Dark as a Dungeon" and "Smoke, Smoke, Smoke." The son of a coal miner from Kentucky, he wrote songs of the coal miners that were as close to life as native folk ballads. His "Sixteen Tons" became one of the popular hits of the century in its recording by Tennessee Ernie Ford. Travis had worked with Pappy McMichen's Georgia Wildcats and later served in the Marines. He has appeared at many folk festivals and has straddled the folk and country-music worlds.

Riding high in 1965 was the charming song writer and singer Roger Miller. In the early part of the year he had two hit LP's and was one of the most sought-after personalities on national television. Because of his songs and his stage manner, he was invited to several folk festivals. Miller has become widely known largely for his song "King of the Road," an effortless little bit of whimsey in the manner of the hobo and tramp songs of the era of Cliff Carlisle and Goebel Reeves. Miller's work proves again that quality and success are not mutually exclusive in country music.

Miller was born on an Oklahoma farm twenty-nine years ago. He described his college education to a reporter for *Time* magazine as: "Korea, Clash of '52." He got his first work in Nashville as a bellhop-elevator operator in the Andrew Jackson Hotel, but soon was attracting attention for his clever lyrics. He has written such bright novelty songs as "Dang Me," "Chug-a-Lug," and "You Can't Roller-Skate in a Buffalo Herd."

Miller is very adept at one of the fascinating devices of the country lyricist, the play on words, as in such lines: "I'm a man of means, By no means"; "Squares make the world go round"; "The moon is high and so am I." There are many examples of this far-from-

325 Buck Owens and His Buckaroos. L to r, Doyle Holly, Don Rich and Owens

326 Roger Miller, 1966

unsophisticated wordplay in country music. For instance, the song "A Fooler, A Faker" by Hank Thompson and Billy Gray:

"You're a fooler, a faker,
A little heart-breaker,
The slyest gal that I've ever known.
Abuser, a chooser, but now you're the loser,
Cause the heart that you've broken was your
    own."[1]

Another good example is Jean Chapel's song "Triangle":

"Triangle, untangle
Don't mingle, don't mangle.
I can't untangle
This crazy triangle."[2]

The roster of leading song writers in country music would include Cy Coben, Cindy Walker, Boudleaux and Felice Bryant, Vaughn Horton, Justin Tubb, Jenny Lou Carson, Don Gibson, Sheb Wooley, Webb Pierce, Wayne Walker, Hank Cochran, the Louvin Brothers, Wayne Raney, and many more.

The folk-music revival spawned many top-flight song writers, some of whose works were to be picked up by Nashville artists. These folk writers include Bob Dylan, Tom Paxton, Paul Clayton, Patrick Sky, Phil Ochs, Dave Cohen, Eric Andersen, Peter La Farge, Billy Edd Wheeler, and others. A young Canadian writer-singer who was beginning to emerge in 1965 in a dual folk and country vein was Gordon Lightfoot.

Although there have been many changes in song writing since the first hillbilly performers used hand-me-down material, there is also an amazingly strong line of tradition and cycles. The broadsides begun in England have reappeared with amazing regularity. These include the songs Bob Atcher wrote to headlines for broadcasts on WBBM in Chicago and these recordings by Zeke Manners and/or the Buchanon Brothers: "Inflation," "No Children Allowed," and "Atomic Power."

The vital importance of songs was underlined in late May, 1965, by the powerful taste-maker Chet Atkins. He was quoted in *Variety:*

"The song's the thing. You can have the biggest and most expensive studio, the best-sounding musicians, and expert engineers and technicians, but if you don't have the song, the artists can't be expected to have a hit."

To which might be added: If you don't have a quality song, you can't expect to achieve quality in country music.

---

[1] © Texoma Music Corporation.
[2] © 1963, Regent Music Corporation.

COUNTRY MUSIC
HALL OF FAME
ELECTED 1961

JIMMIE RODGERS
SEPTEMBER 8, 1897 — MAY 26, 1933

"THE SINGING BRAKEMAN" JIMMIE RODGERS NAME STANDS
FOREMOST IN THE COUNTRY MUSIC FIELD AS THE MAN WHO
STARTED IT ALL. HIS SONGS TOLD THE GREAT STORIES OF
THE SINGING RAILS, THE POWERFUL STEAM LOCOMOTIVES AND
THE WONDERFUL RAILROAD PEOPLE THAT HE LOVED SO WELL.
ALTHOUGH SMALL IN STATURE HE WAS A GIANT AMONG MEN,
STARTING A TREND IN THE MUSICAL TASTE OF MILLIONS.

COUNTRY MUSIC ASSOCIATION

COUNTRY MUSIC
HALL OF FAME
ELECTED 1961

HANK WILLIAMS
SEPTEMBER 17, 1923 — JANUARY 1, 1953

PERFORMING ARTIST-SONGWRITER   HANK WILLIAMS
WILL LIVE ON IN THE MEMORIES OF MILLIONS OF AMERICANS.
THE SIMPLE, BEAUTIFUL MELODIES AND STRAIGHTFORWARD
PLAINTIVE STORIES IN HIS LYRICS OF LIFE AS HE KNEW IT,
WILL NEVER DIE. HIS SONGS APPEALED NOT ONLY TO THE
COUNTRY MUSIC FIELD, BUT BROUGHT HIM GREAT ACCLAIM
IN THE "POP" MUSIC WORLD AS WELL.

COUNTRY MUSIC ASSOCIATION

COUNTRY MUSIC
HALL OF FAME
ELECTED 1961

FRED ROSE
AUGUST 24, 1897 — DECEMBER 1, 1954

SONGWRITER, MUSIC PUBLISHER   FRED ROSE WAS ALWAYS
READY TO LEND A HELPING HAND TO A YOUNG ARTIST OR
A NEW SONGWRITER. HIS GUIDANCE HELPED MANY TO STARDOM.
THE SONGS HE WROTE SHOW THE TOUCH OF SIMPLICITY AND
GENIUS, AND REMAIN WITH US EVEN TODAY, PROVING HIM
TO BE ONE OF AMERICA'S TRULY GREAT COMPOSERS.

COUNTRY MUSIC ASSOCIATION

COUNTRY MUSIC
HALL OF FAME
ELECTED 1962

ROY ACUFF
SEPTEMBER 15, 1903

"THE SMOKY MOUNTAIN BOY"..."FIDDLED" AND SANG HIS
WAY INTO THE HEARTS OF MILLIONS THE WORLD OVER,
OFTENTIMES BRINGING COUNTRY MUSIC TO AREAS WHERE
IT HAD NEVER BEEN BEFORE."THE KING OF COUNTRY
MUSIC"... HAS CARRIED HIS TROUP OF PERFORMERS
OVERSEAS TO ENTERTAIN HIS COUNTRY'S ARMED FORCES
AT CHRISTMASTIME FOR MORE THAN TWENTY YEARS.
MANY SUCCESSFUL ARTISTS CREDIT THEIR SUCCESS TO A
HELPING HAND AND ENCOURAGING WORD FROM ROY ACUFF.

COUNTRY MUSIC ASSOCIATION

COUNTRY MUSIC
HALL OF FAME
ELECTED 1964

TEX RITTER
JANUARY 12, 1907

BORN PANOLA COUNTY, TEXAS....ALUMNUS UNIVERSITY OF
TEXAS. ONE OF AMERICA'S MOST ILLUSTRIOUS AND VERSATILE
STARS OF RADIO, TELEVISION, RECORDS, MOTION PICTURES, AND
BROADWAY STAGE. UNTIRING PIONEER AND CHAMPION OF THE
COUNTRY AND WESTERN MUSIC INDUSTRY. HIS DEVOTION TO HIS
GOD, HIS FAMILY, AND HIS COUNTRY IS A CONTINUING INSPIRATION
TO HIS COUNTLESS FRIENDS THROUGHOUT THE WORLD.

COUNTRY MUSIC ASSOCIATION

COUNTRY MUSIC
HALL OF FAME
ELECTED 1965

ERNEST TUBB
FEBRUARY 9, 1914

"THE TEXAS TROUBADOUR," THAT TALL MAN WITH THE
DISTINCTIVE VOICE AND STYLE, WHO BECAME A
GIANT AMONG THE EARLY PERFORMERS OF COUNTRY
AND WESTERN MUSIC, AND WHOSE CAREER HAS NEVER
DIMINISHED WITH THE SUCCEEDING YEARS. TO HIS
MILLIONS OF FANS, HE HAS BECOME A LEGEND. THEIR
LOVE IS BOUNDLESS. TO THE FLEDGLING ARTIST,
SONGWRITER, OR FRIEND, HIS HAND AND HIS HELP HAVE
ALWAYS BEEN EXTENDED. THEIR GRATITUDE IS UNIVERSAL.

COUNTRY MUSIC ASSOCIATION

9 THE NASHVILLE SOUND: THE RISE OF AN INTERNATIONAL INDUSTRY

"You can change people's tastes. They do it every day on the tube. People buy what is on the market. . . . The only way we'll get people to recognize our music is to destroy the stereotype of the hillbilly. . . ."
JOHN D. LOUDERMILK

"We never use the word [hillbilly] because it was coined in derision. . . . Furthermore, there is no such animal. Country people have a definite dignity of their own and a native shrewdness which enables them to hold their own in any company. Intolerance has no place in our organization and is not allowed. . . ."
GEORGE D. HAY

"Out of the long process of American urbanization-industrialization there has evolved a joint pattern of rejection as well as sentimentalization of rural mores. We flee the eroded land with its rotting cabin; at the same time we cover it in rose vines of memory. . . ."
ARCHIE GREEN

In 1925, the city fathers of Nashville took a bold but inevitable step by authorizing a referendum to vote on a $100,000 bond issue for street lighting and electric traffic signals.

Forty years later parts of the city, especially those that house the Nashville music industry, are as sleekly modern as a Hollywood business center. Record Row along Sixteenth Avenue South makes a startling visual impact with its gleaming talent-agency offices, recording studios, and music-publishing headquarters. Forty years ago Maybelle Carter played and sang with her family in consolidated schoolhouses while kerosene lamps flickered a dim light on the three performers. Today, Mother Maybelle lives in comfort near Nashville. Her dapper, sophisticated manager, Hubert Long, occupies capacious offices of modern design and good taste. (Long is actively trying to encourage more film activity in Nashville.)

These are but a few of the surface changes that have changed the face of country music. The poor man's folk music of the Southern highlands of 1920 has been transformed into an industry of 1965. That industry is led by people who are far from being rubes. They are among the most astute, most imaginative people to be found in American show business. The Nashville music industry has become a powerhouse of influence and promotional skill. It is alive with the sort of energy that many a larger industry would want in its executive and creative personnel.

The change from a home-grown folk music into an international industry that grosses some million dollars a year has been a cumulative series of steps. Talk to anyone in leadership in Nashville today and you will come away with the feeling that this growth is still in its adolescence. The promoters, recording officials, and talent managers speak of the spread overseas of country music. They cite the enormous growth in recording and the use of all electronic means at their disposal to "spread the word" of country music. Even though they know it is a lucrative business, the aims and goals of that business are buttressed by a genuine belief in the basic quality and validity of country music. Convinced, whether honestly or self-deceptively, that their product is good for the United States domestically and abroad, the Nashville music leaders have an almost evangelizing attitude about their work. The jaded, money-grubbing approach of too much of American show business has not yet robbed the country-music industry of its freshness or its sense of purpose beyond profit.

The pivotal year in country music was 1941, the year of our entry into World War II. That year marked the beginning of a period in which the city took over the role of leadership from the rural areas. Malone says: "In a very real sense, America's rural population was liberated by the war. . . . The Southern population, relatively stagnant during the Depression except for some movement into Southern cities, now began to pour into the urban areas." As the people who lived by the cadences and standards of country music moved into Northern cities to enter defense work or mingled in Army barracks with city residents, a new amalgamation of the American population began.

(This writer was only eighteen when he left

Chicago to take infantry basic training at Camp Roberts, California. A city boy, I found in three short weeks that my new friends were buck privates from the country, boys like Curtis Maxey from Norman, Oklahoma, and a tall, rangy Texan from Eagle Pass named Eugene Mabe. In 1944, Maxey and Mabe and the jukebox in the Army Post Exchange began to tell me something about country music. Curtis Maxey loved to sing, and many a long training hike was brightened for our platoon by his drawling Oklahoma voice singing "There was whiskey and blood on the highway, but I didn't hear nobody pray." I had often listened to the "National Barn Dance" on WLS in Chicago, but here was the first contact with country music for a city boy who had wrestled with Bach in piano lessons. Here was my first direct contact with the songs of Acuff, Britt, Tubb, and the other rural music heroes. The city boys laughed at the songs at first, but soon, unconsciously, we were singing along with Curtis Maxey. So it was with millions of others, as the city met the country at service training centers and on defense-plant assembly lines.)

Many students of country music see the year 1941 as the end of a romantic era and the beginning of the decline and commercialization of country music. But this writer agrees with Malone and the others who see a continuum in the great country-music tradition beyond the start of World War II. Popularization led to changes. But just as it seems rigid for the lover of New Orleans jazz to say that "jazz died in New Orleans," so it is incorrect for the lover of tradition-based country music to say that country music declined with the war, with the end of the flourishing nonelectric string bands or the retirement of the Carter Family. A turning point it was, but only the hopeless antiquarian would regard this turning point as a dead end rather than a split in the road.

The war-fostered amalgamation of country and city people and their cultures also led to the general spread of American country music to Europe and Asia. *Billboard* magazine reported in 1943 that the Special Services Division of the European Theater of Operations had at least twenty-five hillbilly bands, and later quoted some Army Special Service officers to the effect that country music was "the most popular of all music with the services." Road shows of country performers associated with "Grand Ole Opry." "The National Barn Dance," "The Boone County Jamboree," and "Renfro Valley" flourished during the war period and set up the routes for the thriving personal-appearance network that today radiates from Nashville and a few lesser centers.

327 Elton Britt

328 Louise Massey and the Westerners

329 Frank and Jim McCravy

330 Uncle Am Stuart

331 Hank Thompson

Several skilled country-music promoters began to arise in the war years during the heightened activity of the barn dance road shows and tent shows, such as the Camel Caravan of "Grand Ole Opry." Among these promoters were such colorful figures as J. L. Frank, Larry Sunbrock, Oscar Davis, Hap Peebles, Lucky Moeller, George Ferguson, Wayne Raney, Tillman Franks, Carlton Haney, Bob Neal, Earl Kurtze, Jim Denny, Dick Bergen, Jim McConnell, Hal Burns, and Foreman Phillips.

Representative of the older school of promoters is Oscar (The Baron) Davis, who worked in vaudeville from 1910 to 1917. Later he worked in motion-picture promotion and started in the country field in 1936 in Alabama. "The Baron" is reputed to have made a million dollars in country music (and to have spent a million and a half). Davis left country music for a time when he saw what was happening with Elvis Presley. Working with the fabled promoter Col. Tom Parker, Davis did most of the advance promotion for Presley prior to the singer's going into the Army. Davis was associated with the 1947 appearances at Carnegie Hall of Tubb and Minnie Pearl and an "Opry" troupe.

Davis described the mechanics of his promotions, involving arriving in a city some weeks before a big country show, lining up radio and TV spots, intensive attempts at newspaper publicity, and so on. One of the last promotions he was associated with may have been the biggest country-music live show of all time. In May, 1963, there were three performances in a day by seventeen country acts, yielding the amazing gross of $43,000. Davis, a silver-haired elder statesman of Nashville, has been partially paralyzed since he suffered a stroke. He is regarded as one of the greatest showmen to ever work with country musicians.

A happy phrase that has entered the language of the music world in the last few years is "the Nashville sound." It is a quality easier to recognize than it is to define. Some say the phrase originated with a New York advertising or promotion man; others attribute the phrase to Charlie Lamb, the tireless journalist formerly with *The Music Reporter* and then the associate publisher of *Music Business*. Some ads for Columbia Record Productions have said that the Nashville sound was born in its Bradley Studios on Sixteenth Avenue South.

Owen Bradley, who built that studio with

his brother in early 1955, defined the Nashville sound with a smile: "It's two German echo chambers turned wide open." Becoming serious, he added: "We have a certain kind of player here, a certain kind of song. We also use a generous echo, which helps to cover mistakes."

Chet Atkins of R.C.A. Victor says: "Technically, there is no such thing as the Nashville sound. It is the musicians. Southern people have a relaxed way of life, a relaxed way of playing."

The Nashville sound emerges, therefore, as a mood, an atmosphere, more than any musical or engineering approach. Recording sessions in New York or Hollywood tend to be pressured, controlled, rehearsed affairs. In Nashville, more than likely, the sidemen are assembled only shortly before a session. The quality of spontaneity and relaxation is there because that is usually the atmosphere of Nashville. Although a few pop singers had tried to record with country musicians in Nashville in the late 1940's and early 1950's, it was not until 1957 that the trend for making pop recordings in the Tennessee capital began. What the pop stars were to find is what the country musicians already knew: gifted sidemen with fast ears had the musicianship to provide a freely relaxed background sound for vocalists.

By 1962, pop singers were recording in Nashville by the droves. Some wag has remarked: "Nashville is a musical Mayo Clinic for ailing acts. The pop singer takes the Nashville treatment and either recovers or dies."

Whatever the mystical qualities of the studios in Nashville, a trend has been at work since 1957 that has made Record Row a mecca for musicians, country or pop. According to a comprehensive survey in *Broadcasting* magazine on January 28, 1963:

"Some of the biggest names in pop music are turning to country-style songs; many are starting to record in Nashville because the studios produce a relaxed type of musical support that performers like and the public buys. . . . The term [Nashville sound] has become a symbol of prestige in an industry that once belittled Nashville as the corn-crib of the music industry."

Oddly enough, the Nashville sound has become so popular in Europe that Elliot Horne of R.C.A. Victor reports that European distributors request that the term be put on record jackets because they sell better. When the young French singer Sylvie Vartan arrived in New York recently, she turned down recording in the excellent Victor studios in New York, but insisted on singing into the microphones in Nashville.

The story of the development of the Nashville recording center goes back, as we have seen, to such venturesome field scouts of the early years of disk recording as Ralph Peer, Frank Walker, Art Satherley, and W. R. Callaway. An early recording official who made four big field trips a year to the South was Eli Oberstein, later to become an influential artist and repertory man in the swing-band boom.

According to his successor, Steve Sholes, now a vice president of R.C.A. Victor, Oberstein used those Southern tours to record music by white country, Negro, Cajun, and Mexican musicians for regional sales. Oberstein coupled his recordings of pop material in the North with these field trips of the 1930's, releasing about five country disks a week on the Bluebird label.

Sholes joined Victor in 1936, working under Oberstein. The latter left in 1939, the year that Frank Walker joined the company. (Another source says Walker joined Victor in 1933.) Walker's reminiscences were published in the *Billboard World of Country Music* of 1963:

"I rode horses into the woods to find people who were individualistic in their singing and who could project the true country flavor—like Chris Boucheron [*sic*, should be Bouchillon], who recorded 'Talking Blues' on Columbia."

Walker had also recorded Clayton McMichen and His Melody Men, Gid Tanner and the Skillet-Lickers, the Leake County Revelers, and Charlie Poole and His North Carolina Ramblers. Sholes gradually took over the work of Oberstein and Frank Walker. After serving in the Army, Sholes handled all country music for Victor from 1945 until 1957. By then the country material had moved from the Bluebird to the Victor label.

Sholes was probably the first record-producer after Paul Cohen of Decca to see the potential of Nashville as a recording center. His first recordings in the future music city were cut in 1946 in a private studio run by the Brown Brothers in a site at Fourth and Union Streets that had been the law office of

332 Wanda Jackson

333 Don Law of Columbia Records

Andrew Jackson. "After the first recording trip to Nashville," Sholes recalls, "I agitated for us to build a studio there." Victor officials were slow, but within a couple of years Victor was the first label to have a studio and permanent artist and repertory man in Nashville.

Sholes recalls that the label shared its studio with a Presbyterian church. An ardent church member found an empty vodka bottle in the studio after a session and said this proved to him the outsiders were Communists! By 1957, Sholes transferred to the Victor pop division in Los Angeles. He remains active in all matters concerning country music.

Ten years earlier Sholes had signed a performer who was to become a major figure in Nashville recording, Chet Atkins. (Sholes had heard a transcription called "Canned Heat," and was impressed with the Atkins guitar-picking, similar to Merle Travis', and tracked him down in Denver through Julian and Jean Aberbach of Hill and Range Songs, a powerful country-music publishing organization.)

Chet Atkins began his own recording in 1947 in New York. It was on the eve of a strike of the American Federation of Musicians and there was a rush to build a disk reservoir. Atkins recorded with such country artists as Texas Jim Robertson, Elton Britt, and Rosalie Allen. The guitarist was born in the Clinch Mountains of eastern Tennessee in Luttrell in June, 1924. "My daddy was a classical musician and singer. I use parts of everything I've ever heard in my music," Atkins says. One of the most versatile musicians in America, Atkins plays classical music, traditional and modern jazz, pop, and of course, straight country music. "The basic guitar style I play was started by a colored guy in Kentucky," he said. (Atkins was probably referring to Jim Mason, a Negro who played a "choke" style of guitar. This style has been traced by John Cohen in *Sing Out!* magazine of January, 1964, to Mason, who taught it to a white coal miner, Mose Reger, and to Ike Everly, father of the Everly Brothers. Travis learned his guitar style from Reger, and Travis, in turn, was "a great influence" on Atkins.) He likes the heavy use of vibrato on the Spanish guitar, but also has been influenced by the guitar work of Les Paul, Django Reinhardt, and others.

After finishing school in Columbus, Georgia, Atkins went to Knoxville to work as a fiddler for Archie Campbell and Bill Carlisle. He told Ren Grevatt of *Music Business:* "I was more interested in my guitar than the fiddle and I'd fool around practicing it whenever I could. One time, the radio station boss heard me playing my guitar in the back seat of his car. He told me to throw away the fiddle for good and he'd give me a job playing guitar. That was how I got started."

Atkins settled in Nashville in the early 1950's, after working there with Red Foley and the Carter Family. Today he is recording director of some thirty stars in country and pop-country music. Atkins has been responsible for much in the modernization of country music. Although not always starting innovations, he was quick to develop them. The first recorded use of a modern vocal group backing with a country artist, Atkins recalls, was behind Ferlin Husky on "Gone." "Elvis Presley changed everything," says the man who touted him to Steve Sholes, if touting was necessary. In a fierce competition for the star of the Sun label, Victor won out over Columbia for $40,000. The rest of the Elvis Presley story is history.

Atkins dates the influx of pop recording stars to Nashville to Rosemary Clooney in 1955 or 1956, with the biggest surge of pop stars coming since 1959. Atkins told Ren Grevatt: "Skeeter Davis is a good example of how we've been able to bring country to pop. I always thought she had a chance for pop, so we took out the steel guitars and fiddles and made her a little more 'uptown' with her over-dubbing of the harmony, and she's done very well."

Because of his gentle personality and his own expert musicianship, Atkins is one of the most popular men in the recording industry. A young sideman told me at the first Country Music Festival I attended in Nashville, in 1961: "Chet Atkins saved country music. He made it respectable."

The story of Columbia gets a bit raveled because so many smaller companies ultimately ended up in the Columbia family. Essentially, though, it is the story of Frank Walker and two Englishmen who became Americans. Art Satherley was born in Bristol in 1891. He came to the United States at twenty-two and worked in record production at Grafton, Wisconsin. In the mid-1920's he joined the ranks of the field scouts, looking for talent among country people. He worked for a variety of companies out of New York: New York Recording Labs, Plaza Music Company, Brunswick, and finally the recording group called the American Record Company. The latter was bought by Columbia Records in the late 1930's.

334   Paul Cohen

335   Gordon Lightfoot

336   Texas Jim Robertson

212

337   Dave Kapp

338   Harry "Hap" Peebles

The roster of country artists recorded by Satherley is long and distinguished, including Autry, Acuff, Willing and McGee, Frank and James McCravey, Little Jimmy Dickens, Al (Poindexter) Dexter, Curt and Louise Massey, Molly O'Day, W. Lee (Pappy) O'Daniel, and many others, until his retirement in 1953.

Don Law was also born in England and is the successor to Satherley. The chief Columbia country A & R man recalls that when he went to Texas he couldn't understand country and Western music at first. He started in the business in 1926 with the Brunswick-Balke-Collender Company as a record audit clerk in Dallas. He was promoted to branch manager of the Dallas-New Orleans-Atlanta district, a district where all forms of country music were to flourish. The early Western swing bands were to be important in the period that Law served in Dallas, until 1942, as were such family gospel groups as the Chuck Wagon Gang of Lubbock, Texas. (Says Law: "I remember when the Chuck Wagon girls were yeah high twenty-seven years ago. Now they are grandmothers.")

Law recalls how the Depression years were almost fatal to the recording business. "The Depression slowed down our releases for five years. The pop field was dead and only the country market kept going. The country market really pulled us through." For three years during the war, Law worked on children's and pop records in the East, but moved into the country field fulltime in 1945. Until Satherley's retirement, the two veteran record producers divided the United States into two regions—Law east of El Paso and Satherley west of the Texas city.

One of Don Law's greatest pleasures in the business is that more than a dozen top-flight Columbia country artists have been with the label for more than ten years. "There is a market for both traditional and modern country music. We cater to both," he says. Law is a well-known figure around Nashville, a tall, dignified, gray-haired, clipped-accented man of great warmth and wit. At the Country Music Convention of 1964, one of the memorable sights was to see this epitome of refinement on the stage of the Grand Ole Opry House in white tennis sneakers playing the tambourine behind a group of Columbia stars. Since the early 1960's Law has been assisted in record production chiefly by Frank Jones, an American-born A & R man who did his early work in Canada.

Decca Records has had a long and significant history in country and Western music since its formation in 1934. It was the first label to explore the riches of the music of the Southwest and is the first label to have cut a commercial recording in Nashville. Dave Kapp and his brother, the late Jack Kapp, got into the country field while running a store in Chicago and working with station WJJD in Chicago. After ten years their store was closed, in 1932, and Jack joined the American Record Company, while Dave started to manage talent. Among the earliest country musicians Dave worked with were a blind duo, McFarland and Gardner, and the International Buckle Busters, an outfit that featured Gene Autry.

Upon the formation of the Decca label, an offshoot of the Decca Company of England, Jack asked his brother to head the country-

213

music operation, which Dave did for eleven years. Dave Kapp made two swings through the South each year, recording all sorts of country musicians, from San Antonio to Charlotte. Portable studios were set up in hotel rooms along the way. (Dave Kapp said recently, "If we would have known we were making history then we would have taken more photos and kept better documentation of our trips.")

Kapp signed the future Governor of Louisiana, Jimmie Davis, in 1934, got some forty-eight sides from Milton Brown and the Brownies, recorded Bradley Kincaid, the Carter Family in the late 1930's, and many others. By the early 1940's, Dave Kapp was into other disk duties, and the country field was delegated to Paul Cohen, who had been a Decca manager in Cincinnati.

Cohen joined Decca in August, 1934, as a salesman, then branch manager in Chicago. To Cohen falls the honor of supervising the first commercial recording session in Nashville. This date is one that the Nashville industry, which is always marking milestones and anniversaries, seems to have lost. Cohen's ledger sheet on the first recording has been lost, but Red Foley, whom Cohen calls the "Bing Crosby of the Hillbillies," believes that he made the first Nashville disks in March or April of 1945: (Foley had recorded earlier for Milt Gabler of Decca in Chicago.)

Foley and Cohen did the session at Studio B of WSM. Foley believes the session was of four sides, only three of which he recalls: "Tennessee Saturday Night," "Blues in the Heart," and "Tennessee Border." (The Hill and Range copyright dates for these songs and the Decca release list for these titles are later than spring, 1945. If Foley's recollection of the historic session is right, Joe Messina of Hill and Range says, it is understandable that the release of the disks and copyrighting the songs were not until much later. Whenever the first date of the first commercial session in Nashville is established, some sort of public celebration will be in order. For now, we will say it was March or April of 1945 by Red Foley.)

Among the many artists that Cohen signed for Decca before moving to its subsidiary, Coral, in the late 1950's were some of the leading ladies of country music: Kitty Wells, the late Patsy Cline, and Brenda Lee, who joined the label at the age of nine. After working with Todd Publishing and Briar Records, Cohen has rejoined his old boss, Dave Kapp, on Kapp Records.

Cohen's successor as the Decca chief in Nashville is Owen Bradley, a pianist, guitarist, harmonica-player, and arranger. This native of Westmoreland, Tennessee, got into the business at the age of ten and became a full-time music man in 1958. Bradley, who

339   The late Jim Denny

340   W. E. (Lucky) Moeller

ran the famous studio purchased by Columbia in February, 1962, had for many years conducted a farm show on WSM. He was eager to credit the strong role Paul Cohen had played in getting Decca established in Nashville. "He was my benefactor, but also, he was the first person, way back in 1947, to say that Nashville was a musical utopia," Bradley said.

Owen Bradley has continued to work with the strong Decca roster, which includes Ernest Tubb, Webb Pierce, and the women stars. Along with Atkins and other leading A & R men, Bradley places great stress on finding good songs, the building blocks of any music. One of Bradley's achievements has been helping Burl Ives to develop a whole new career with Nashville recording since 1960.

Capitol Records has been involved with country music since the label began in 1942. Lee Gillette started the label's country department and Ken Nelson took over in 1950. Hollywood is probably second to Nashville in recording country and Western material, partly because of the leading role that Capitol plays on the West Coast. (Liberty and Dot are also West Coast operations.) Among the performers who have been recorded on Capitol, for Gillette, Nelson, Cliffie Stone, or the label's Nashville producer, Marvin Hughes, are Faron Young, Ferlin Husky, Tex Williams, Tennessee Ernie Ford, Merle Travis,

Sonny James, Jean Shepard, Wanda Jackson, and the current high-riding singer, song writer, and band leader, Buck Owens.

Mercury Records has become entrenched in country music, although a late arrival. Mercury is now part of a family of labels that includes Smash, Philips, Wing, and Cumberland. Mercury entered country music in 1948, recording the Carlisles and then Jimmy Skinner, the singer and former store operator in Cincinnati. By 1952 the first Mercury office on Record Row was opened, with leadership passing from D. Kilpatrick to Don Pierce and finally Shelby Singleton. Singleton was a vice president at the opening of a new Mercury studio in 1962.

The combined labels cut as many pop as country stars. Smash signed the versatile Roger Miller after he had been with Victor for two years. Miller brought a fistful of plaudits to the Smash label by winning, in the spring of 1965, five "Grammy" Awards from the National Academy of Recording Arts and Sciences, something of a record in or out of the record business.

MGM Records rests strong in the country field with the entire recorded library of Hank Williams, dating from the time that Frank Walker was working with that star. His son, Hank Williams Jr., becoming a national favorite although still a teen-ager, records on MGM, as does Sheb Wooley.

Wayne Raney   342   Pappy Dailey   343   Oscar Davis

345 Merle Kilgore

344 L to r, Carson Robison, Pearl Mitchell, and The Mitchell Brothers

A label with a formidable catalogue of country material is King, for twenty years run by Sid Nathan in Cincinnati. Among the country performers who have recorded on King were the late Cowboy Copas, the Delmore Brothers, Jimmy Osborne, Moon Mullican, the Carlisle Brothers, Grandpa Jones, the late Hawkshaw Hawkins, and the legendary promoter and disk jockey, Wayne Raney.

There are dozens of labels dealing with country music, as the discography at the end of this book will show. Two of the most interesting, however, are one very successful and aggressive Nashville operation, Starday, and a small dedicated-to-authenticity label, Rem, in Lexington, Kentucky.

Starday is unique in producing only country records. It has a catalogue that includes scores of the old-timers who were never recorded by the majors or were dropped by the major disk companies. Starday did much to establish the LP in the country market, as a product mostly for adult buyers, and through mail order.

The origins of Starday, although a postwar operation, are almost as complicated as the various shifts of labels in the 1930's. Four Star Records had been run since 1946 by Bill McCall, who enlisted the aid of a leading figure in Texas music, H. W. (Pappy) Dailey. In 1953, Dailey and Jack Starms formed Starday. One of its earliest stars, George Jones, has followed Dailey in his subsequent affiliations to Mercury, United Artists, and now Musicor. From 1956 to 1958, Starday was affiliated with Mercury.

The head of Starday since 1958, and the man who has built the label into an unusually strong country-music voice, is Don Pierce. A volatile, gregarious man with great energy, Pierce is one of the most promotion-minded officials in Nashville, and one of the most imaginative. Some of the groupings on Starday albums are made possible by leasing masters from other companies, and providing many excellent "samplers" or anthologies of railroad and truck-driver songs. In late 1963 Pierce organized a mail-order Country Music Record Club of America, which has in less than two years recruited more than forty thousand members.

If Starday is the most promotion-minded of the labels specializing in country music, then Rem is probably the smallest. The label is run out of a shack behind the Lexington, Kentucky, home of Robert Mooney, a former employee of King Records. He started the label in 1960 and for some time sold his small list of LP's out of the back of his car. Mooney was the last to record the famous Molly O'Day, who had left the business for service with the First Church of God in Huntington, West Virginia. The last Mooney had heard of the singer, she and her husband were running a record shop in Williamson, West Virginia, in the coal fields near the Kentucky border. To record her, Mooney went twenty-five miles up a "holler," to a "little old church house the size of my living room." He described the congregation as having a lot of devoted people who would shout the Lord's praises until red in the face. Says Mooney of his tiny record operation: "I'm going to cut real country-music records whether they sell or not." The dedication of Mooney, a hospital X-ray technician, is typical of that encountered in out-of-the-way places.

There is a wealth of old-time country music lying in disuse in the archives of the large recording companies. R.C.A. Victor, under the direction of a country discographer and fan, Brad McCuen, has taken the lead in reissues of quality country music, from such stars as Jimmie Rodgers to many obscure performers of "the Golden Age." Columbia's Frank Driggs has been working with discographers Loy Beaver and Dave Freeman (producer of reissues on the County label) on a three-disk reissue of early material from the Columbia 15,000 series. Many good reissues are available on the low-priced Columbia subsidiary, Harmony.

As this manuscript was being completed, Decca was planning a reissue of Uncle Dave Macon material and had under advisement a project with Archie Green to reissue old masters of Al Hopkins and the Hillbillies in an album under the projected title of "The Band That Named the Music." Decca owns old masters on the Vocalion and Brunswick labels, in addition to its own fine list going back to 1934.

These unreissued old country disks have been described as "rotting gold" that should be returned to the market. Presumably the growing interest in the history of this field will stimulate more reissues. Interestingly enough, an old six-disk collection on Folkways, "Anthology of American Folk Music," has been the greatest single source of commercial hillbilly material of the 1920's and 1930's. The set become almost a bible for the student of early country music. More such quality reissues, with carefully researched notes, will help fill in the many gaps of country-music history. They will assuredly not become the best-sellers of this field. But their public service value to the growing number of folk and country fans who would enjoy them makes a policy of reissues a responsibility to be met by the recording companies.

The music publisher is an important figure in country and Western music. Where once hillbilly musicians sang songs they had known for years, it became increasingly important for the song writer to have his song published and protected against infringements. (The copyright situation is a complex

346   Al Dexter

347   The late Jim McConnell

legal matter that is outside this book's province.) Of the hundreds of publishers in country music, we'll speak of a few who either have been influential or, by virtue of longevity, have something to tell of their function.

When Troy Martin moved to Nashville, the only other music publisher in town was Fred Rose of Acuff-Rose. For some years Martin was affiliated with Don Law of Columbia. At first the publisher had trouble becoming established because either Acuff-Rose or Hill and Range in New York controlled almost all country songs. Martin has been in the music business for thirty-five years, has recorded for the American Record Company, and was a former vice president of some of Gene Autry's companies on the West Coast. He began as a music publisher with Ralph Peer's Southern Music. He recalls an early comment by Fred Rose about the plight of the music publisher: "Fred said the songs sent in were so bad you had to rewrite them before you threw them away."

Martin's career goes back to the medicine-show era when he was called Doc Martin. "We went to the tobacco market and then to Alabama and Georgia, wherever the farmers had money. There were about six or seven of us in the show. We traveled in the early 1930's in old Big 6 Buicks or Model T's. It got cold, and we had to have lap robes to keep going," he recalled.

Martin had served his medicine-show apprenticeship with a Doc Marshall and a Doc Butler "until I learned their spiels. Then I went on my own, selling laxatives, herbs or iron tonics like Geritol. There was always guitar or piano music with our medicine show. We used to have the Rouse Brothers, Irvin and Jimmie, with Irvin billed as 'The World's Greatest Fiddler.'"

Martin, who is fifty-four years old, started at sixteen as a blackface minstrel, went on to help start radio stations in Danville and Greensboro. When asked why he went into show business, Troy Martin replied: "I was too nervous to steal."

He recalls days as a musician and comic playing shows for ten and fifteen cents. "When we got broke, we went to New York to make recordings, often riding with my partner, Elvin Bigger, in the back of empty trucks." From this start, Martin went on to work with all the major publishing companies and finally to form his own.

Probably the most powerful single man in country-music publishing is Fred Rose's son, Wesley Rose, president of Acuff-Rose Pub-

348   Steve Sholes

349   Chet Atkins

350   Brad McCuen

351   Wesley Rose in his office

lishing. This is the house that published Hank Williams' songs. Rose reports that rather than declining, the royalties from Hank Williams' songs are growing bigger each year. The gray-haired, pipe-smoking publisher wears a dapper mustache and works from an outsize office, one of the few that has not moved to Record Row. "This business used to be here," he said, tapping his desk. "Now it is international."

His formula is one that goes much further than getting a song recorded. He believes in developing name song writers, not just writers who get an isolated mood or inspiration, but professionals who can turn it out. He pointed to the work of Don Gibson, a writer he finds with many of the qualities of Hank Williams.

Rose explained how his operation grew from simply publishing to running a related record label. Hickory; a related management agency; and nine or ten foreign subsidiaries. Despite the scores of new publishing houses that have sprung up in recent years in Nashville, Rose believes only four or five really set trends and have influence on the whole field. "The young song writer can see me any time," Rose says.

Another powerful country-music publishing company is Hill and Range Songs, Inc., which was organized by Julian and Jean Aberbach in 1945. Julian is a German-born naturalized American who learned about country music in the Army. Hill and Range is today part of what is called the Aberbach Group, which has included such member firms as Elvis Presley Music, Gladys Music, Ernest Tubb Music, and Johnny Cash Music.

Of the hundreds of publishers of country music, it would be impossible to list all the houses. To sample the publishing story, we can look at one of the largest, Cedarwood; one of the fastest rising, Tree; and the oldest, Southern Music-Peer International.

Cedarwood Publishing Company is one of the firms connected with the Denny-Moeller Artists Bureau, now Moeller Talent, Inc. It is led by thirty-year-old J. William Denny, who got an early start working at the "Opry," with a summer carnival, and being a disk jockey at WSM at fifteen. He handled publicity for the "Philip Morris Country Music Show," worked with an ad agency and a bank, and then became Nashville studio manager for Columbia Records. When his father, Jim Denny, became ill, he took over as Cedar-

352   Proposed location of C.M.A. Museum at The Tony Rose Park, Nashville, at the head of Record Run

wood's general manager. The publishing company reportedly once spent hundreds of dollars each week returning songs and tapes, but now refuses unsolicited material.

An important place in country publishing is being assumed by the Tree Publishing Company, led by Jack Stapp, who resigned recently as president of Nashville station WKDA to head Tree and its affiliated label, Dial Records. Stapp was the nation's youngest announcer and radio program director, in Atlanta, at seventeen. In New York he became production manager of C.B.S. Radio. After heading programing for WSM, he produced seven network shows a week. Tree has probably won most attention recently as the publisher of Roger Miller's and Justin Tubb's songs.

The oldest publishing company in country music is one started by that pioneer in recording, the late Ralph S. Peer, Southern Music (now Southern Music-Peer International). This goliath of international publishing was born in July, 1927, on West 45th Street in New York, as United Publishing Company. A year later it became Southern, and the years that followed saw the spread of Peer's organization to offices in Mexico, Cuba, Argentina, and London.

Southern-Peer was based in country music on the repertory of Jimmie Rodgers songs. But it spread into Latin-American music and has since moved into all areas of international popular music. The company is now headed by Peer's widow, Mrs. Monique Peer-Morris. Her second husband, David H. Morris, is a vice president of the company, and has outlined plans to expand into Asian music and to develop the country music catalogue for its "tremendous international potential."

One of the key officials at Southern-Peer is "country music's man in New York," the genial Roy Horton. Horton started in country music at the grass roots. He was born in the Alleghenies of Pennsylvania, worked in the coal mines at night, and played guitar at Sunday picnics. With his brother, Vaughn, he worked on "The Crazy Water Crystal Show" and on the Rudy Vallee radio network program. Vaughn became a top song writer, while Roy pursued his deep conviction that country and Western music was "the soul of America."

Becoming a walking library of information about the country field, Roy Horton was hired by Peer to help "revive, reconstruct and promote the massive Peer catalogue." As one of the most tireless advocates of country music, Roy Horton has been one of the key figures in the field.

The talent managers of Nashville spend a good part of their working day on the telephones setting up personal appearances around the world. A refreshing difference can be noted here from other aspects of show business. The talent agent is usually stereotyped as a greedy, implacable money-grubber. My limited contact with the Nashville talent men revealed something quite different. Although they are businessmen, there is a graciousness about them that makes them quite unlike their brothers in Hollywood or Manhattan. Because they realize that their success depends on the success of the entire field, there is a surprising amount of cooperation among agencies to set up large shows.

I asked the help of Mrs. Jo Walker, executive director of the Country Music Association, in finding out the annual number of

Architect's rendering of C.M.A. Museum

354 Mrs. Jo Walker

personal appearances made by country performers each year. She supplied these figures:

Johnny Cash Enterprises	140
Hubert Long Talent	2,500
Buck Owens Enterprises	293
Flatt and Scruggs	180
Moeller Talent	3,000
Don Thompson Agency	250
Bob Neal Agency	841
B-W Music	184
Key Talent Agency	1,000
Hal Smith Artists	675
	9,063

If to this table are added smaller talent-agency performers, those on the West Coast and elsewhere, and the great international roster, especially Canada, the estimate of some fifteen thousand personal appearances a year does not seem too great.

One of the old-timers in country music promotion is Larry Sunbrock, now based in Orlando, Florida. He wrote me:

"In 1930, I was running, at eighteen, the Metropolitan Theater in Cincinnati and starving during the Great Depression, taking in about $20 a night at the movies. Then I heard of The Skillet-Lickers playing over WCKY. I booked them into the theater and grossed $400 a night for three nights. I took them on the road as manager and we played theaters, armories, etc., for several years. In 1933, Natchee, the Indian (whom I named), played a fiddlers' contest against Pappy McMichen and Natchee won. I lined them up again in Louisville, Nashville, Cincinnati, Atlanta, and elsewhere and made a barrel of money and friends. In St. Louis I had 24,000 people turn out for two shows in one day of a band, fiddlers' and yodelers' contest. From

such successes I started barn dances all over the Midwest, but never had enough sense to capitalize on it. In 1935, Cowboy Copas joined me and Natchee and we then used Curly Fox as a fiddling champion against all comers.

"I was the first to take hillbilly music out of the barns and put it in auditoriums. Oscar Davis, Joe Franks all followed me. I left C. & W. for rodeos for some time, but any old-timer can verify that I was the man, the originator, the man that should be in the C. & W. hall of fame as the first promoter of hillbilly or country and Western music."

Another early figure in talent management was James W. (Jim) McConnell, managing vice president of Acuff-Rose Artists Corporation, who died March 6, 1965, after a heart attack. McConnell had been manager of such country stars as Acuff, Ritter, Wilma Lee and Stoney Cooper, Roy Orbison and Bill Carlisle, Red Foley, and even jazz pianist Fats Waller. In the war years McConnell handled booking for N.B.C., then moved to Cincinnati's WLW, where he had earlier managed Bradley Kincaid and the vaudeville act of Salt and Peanuts. He started a successful show in Kansas City, Missouri, called "Brush Creek Follies," named for the town sewer. After serving as talent manager for the "Ozark Jubilee" in Springfield, Missouri, he came to Nashville in 1961 to head Acuff-Rose talent.

An interview with McConnell a year before he died was a retrospective view of many early names of country music. He remembered how Kincaid would sell his "Hound Dog guitars"; how the Nashville merchants hated hillbillies in the early 1930's but changed totally; Arthur Smith and the Dixieliners, Hum and Strum, Gertrude Miller, Denver Darling and Willard Spooner, Silver Yodeling Billy Jones, the comedienne Eloise Boffo, Whispering Smith; songbooks for three cents; the old hymns of Homer Rodeheaver. . . .

Another veteran of country and Western promotion is Harry (Hap) Peebles, who entered the field in Kansas in 1933. At the second annual KFOX Country Music Spectacular in the Hollywood Bowl in June, 1963, Peebles received the Johnny Cash Award for "elevating the image of country and Western music." Besides running country stage shows in a dozen Midwestern states, Peebles has worked with touring Hollywood stars.

One of the top figures in Nashville publishing and management, Jim Denny, died on August 27, 1963. Denny had been manager of "Grand Ole Opry," then went on to establish his own company in 1956. With W. E. (Lucky) Moeller, he developed Denny-Moeller Talent, Inc. Moeller was executive vice president and general manager, and Denny devoted more time to building up the related Cedarwood Publishing Company. Denny and Moeller were instrumental in developing the complex of more than fifty offices along Sixteenth Avenue South called Music Row. (Later called Record Row. There is a move afoot to have it renamed Music City Boulevard.)

On March 1, 1965, the largest talent agency in country music underwent another change of ownership and name to become Moeller Talent, Inc. Moeller, his son, Larry, and his son-in-law, Jack Andrews, now have full ownership of the organization that the elder Moeller and Denny established in 1957. In the 1940's, while vice president of a bank in Oklahoma City, Lucky invested in a night club and then a ballroom. In 1952, Bob Wills sought Moeller as his personal manager. Two years later he moved to Nashville to serve as Webb Pierce's manager. By 1956, Moeller was working with Red Foley and other "Ozark Jubilee" performers. Larry Moeller, now vice president and treasurer of the agency, joined his father in 1958. Andrews, who had also been a banker, joined the agency in 1962 and is vice president and secretary of the new firm.

The roster of Moeller Talent, Inc., includes more than thirty of the biggest stars in the country galaxy, stars who grossed some $1,500,000 in 1962, and more since then. In an interview with Lucky Moeller in 1964, he had some startling facts about the mammoth wheel of personals by country artists that revolve from the Nashville hub:

"We're more popular in the cities than in the rural areas today. Our music is much more popular in the North than in the Southeast. Such areas as Michigan, Illinois, Indiana, Minnesota and the Dakotas are very popular for country musicians. Vaudeville was big in 12 or 15 cities, but we play in towns of 2,000 and up. We can play in virtually every town in a state. Our business is up 20% this year [1964] over last year, and has had a 100% gain over five years ago."

Moeller explained that his agency's performers make a total of between 3,000 and 3,500 personal appearances each year. At their request, these personals are kept to a limited number, for tax purposes and because travel is exhausting. He said that personal appearances are sought by such diverse sponsors as civic groups and state and county fairs. "We've even done shows where the sponsorship was by a local symphony orchestra who used country music to raise funds for their symphony programs!" He recalled a Fire Department benefit in Houston that attracted 27,500 people in two nights with a country show.

Even such professional talent bookers as Larry Moeller express amazement at the way country shows can pull people out of "nowhere." Larry recalled a show at Fulton, Indiana, in September, 1963. "You couldn't see the town from the road. There was just a service station, a grocery store and a consolidated school. We staged two performances in that school's gym. There was nothing but a banner across the highway, and 3,000 people showed up!" He cited the enduring and broadening popularity of such performers as Kitty Wells, who did a total of 265 one-nighters in 1963, and the impact of Webb Pierce, who had twenty-six hit records, one after the other.

The talent managers of Nashville are a colorful lot, with many incredible but true stories. They include Col. Tom Parker, who helped put Eddy Arnold and Elvis Presley on the map; Bob Neal, who helped Presley, Cash, Carl Perkins, and others to get a start. (Neal, who has been in Nashville since 1962, is now working with Billy Edd Wheeler, a singer who has both a country and a folk audience strongly behind him.) The fabled talent managers are the men who handle much of the dirty work of the music business — contracts, reservations, bookings, concert arrangements, travel — and have been

355　Roy Horton, David Morris and Mrs. Monique Peer-Morris

greatly responsible for the field's growth.

Bill Sachs of *Billboard* has described personals as "the bread-and-butter department for countless country artists, bookers and promoters." He estimated the combined dollar income of personals for 1964 at around $5,350,000. He described the bookings at county and state fairs as a "major outlet" for country talent, dating back to pioneer efforts in this area by Denny and Bill McCluskey of the WLW "Boone County Jamboree." He concluded his article in *The World of Country Music* of 1964 with a warning against the phony promoters who occasionally creep into the field, but struck this positive note: "The booking of country music talent is a healthy business—one that is destined to flourish for many years to come."

One of the most resounding, and sometimes most amusing, differences of opinion in American musical life is the recurring civil war between the American Society of Composers, Authors and Publishers and Broadcast Music, Incorporated. Here hangs the tale of the professional barriers against country music and their gradual crumbling. The

complex story of the formation of BMI and the liberating effect it had on country music has been told in objective detail in Hazel Meyer's *The Gold in Tin Pan Alley* (Lippincott) and from an ASCAP point of view in David Dachs' *Anything Goes* (Bobbs-Merrill). The war between ASCAP and BMI rages sporadically, but there are occasional truces. ASCAP is beginning to take serious cognizance of country music and other musics not produced by its writers in New York or Hollywood. ASCAP officials (and even tunes) have appeared at BMI dinners in Nashville.

Such conviviality runs counter to the often acrimonious battles between the two performing-rights groups. The special country-music report in *Broadcasting* magazine of January 28, 1963, described BMI's dominant role in country music:

"This onetime gateway to the West [Nashville] is now 'open sesame' to a new world of music because broadcasters were forced a score of years ago to start a new music source. This happened when they organized Broadcast Music, Inc., in an effort to cope with an ASCAP rate increase they considered intolerable.

"BMI was formed, and at last the frustrated composers who had tried vainly to crash ASCAP's gates now had a market. They still have this market because BMI easily leads the current list of top tunes."

Before BMI was formed by broadcasters, on October 14, 1939, ASCAP had enjoyed a clear field, since 1914, in music licensing and protection in public performance. (SESAC, the Society of European Stage Authors and Composers, later changed to Selected Editions of Standard American Catalogues, had been founded in 1931 as a privately owned corporation by Paul Heinecke, and was until 1939 the only performing-rights clearinghouse for publishers of the musics spurned by ASCAP—spirituals, country, race, jazz, Latin-American and others.)

A contract between ASCAP and radio networks was to expire after five years on December 31, 1940. ASCAP announced its new rates for radio performance rights to music in its catalogues: $7\frac{1}{2}$ per cent of the networks' gross time sales. The National Association of Broadcasters figured this would amount to some $9,000,000 for the year 1941, an increase of 100 per cent over 1939. According to Miss Meyer, "Radio refused to pay, and beginning at midnight, December 31, 1940, it would become an infringement for any radio station to broadcast any ASCAP music over American airwaves."

BMI was initially at a disadvantage because ASCAP controlled most American music written since 1884, having only a few hundred public-domain songs and some material held by SESAC. The July prior to the ASCAP radio ban saw one break in the wall, when the publishing firm of Edward B. Marks, with a large pop and Latin catalogue, joined BMI, as did two publishing companies with large country catalogues, Peer's Southern Music and M.M. Cole of Chicago.

During the ten months of 1941 that the broadcasters and ASCAP were at odds, BMI grew prodigiously, until it held 36,000 copyrights from three dozen publishing houses. The ASCAP monopoly was broken. In place of a music business centered in Tin Pan Alley and Hollywood, a vast decentralization to every state was ushered in by the emergence of BMI. ASCAP settled with the networks, not for the $7\frac{1}{2}$ per cent it had asked, but for $2\frac{3}{4}$ per cent. Many song writers besides the then hitherto unprotected country-music writers found the BMI protection deal appealing. There had been six hundred ASCAP and SESAC firms in 1940, but by 1957 the number was three thousand, with BMI accounting for most of the new houses.

The battle is by no means over. Wrote Miss Meyer: "Adherents to the two performance-rights societies continuously bait each other. BMI followers accuse ASCAP of being snooty; ASCAP champions look down their noses at BMI and condemn it for being corny, phony and cheap. Rock 'n' roll and other crazy music would never have emerged to sully American ears, say some ASCAP writers (who specialize in ballads), if BMI hadn't pried open the manhole."

An often discordant debate about popular-music taste was held in public between BMI and ASCAP factions, in 1956, before the House Anti-Trust Subcommittee, and from March to July, 1958, before the Subcommittee on Communications of the Senate Committee on Interstate and Foreign Commerce.

The 1958 hearings were on a bill to prohibit broadcasting licensees from holding interest in music publishing and recording companies. The bill, which was defeated, also would have forced licensees to divest themselves of interest in BMI. The wind on Capitol Hill blew strong in 1958, with attacks on country music and rock 'n' roll voiced by Dr. Howard Hanson of the Eastman School of Music, Vance Packard and many others. Leaping to the eloquent defense of country music (and thereby to its chief protector— BMI) were a string of broadcasters; Eddy Arnold, Pee Wee King, and other singers; and Senator Albert Gore and Governor Frank Clement of Tennessee. Governor Clement, a noted orator, extolled country music as "our love of life and land, of nation and people, yes, even our love of God. . . ." He said that BMI, by giving writers and publishers of country music the opportunity denied by ASCAP, had made it possible for Nashville to become "one of the major capitals of the world."

Largely because of the competition provided to ASCAP by BMI, there has been an enormous growth in the number of song writers and publishers who can share in performing-rights revenue. In 1939, according to a BMI report, there were 1,000 such writers and 137 publishers. By 1965 that figure had grown to nearly 19,000 writers and about 8,000 publishers!

BMI has had a Nashville office since 1958 and in 1964 moved into its beautiful new $200,000 building on Music Row. The office,

356   Board of Directors of C.M.A. L to r, 1st row seated, Jack Loetz, Columbia Records; W. E. Moeller, Moeller Talent, Inc.; Joe Allison, Nashville Music Publications; Tex Ritter, Mrs. Frances Preston, B.M.I.; Mrs. Jo Walker, C.M.A.; Hap Peebles, The Harry Peebles Agency; Owen Bradley, Decca Records.

2nd row seated, Harold Hitt, Columbia Records; Chet Atkins, R.C.A. Victor Records; Jerry Glaser, WENO Radio; Johnny Bond, Paul Ackerman, Billboard; Wesley Rose, Acuff-Rose Publications; Roy Horton, Southern Music Publishing Co.; Dick Schofield, KFOX Radio, Hal Cook, Billboard.

Standing, Bill Williams, WSM Radio; Bill Denny, Cedarwood Publishing Co.; George Crump, WCMS Radio; J. Hal Smith, Pamper Music; Bob Austin, Record World; Jack Burgess, R.C.A. Victor Records; Wm. Harold Moon, B.M.I. Canada, Hubert Long, Moss Rose Publications; Connie B. Gay, Connie B. Gay Boadcasting Co.; John Brown, Acuff-Rose Publications; Dick Frank, C.M.A. Counsel; Bob Jennings, WLAC Radio; Jack Stapp, Tree Publishing Co.

the largest BMI facility outside of New York, has been headed since 1958 by Mrs. Frances Williams Preston, a BMI vice president. The attractive, able Mrs. Preston is a Nashville leader on just about every level, as board chairman of the Country Music Association, a member of the National Academy of Recording Arts and Sciences, the Nashville Symphony Guild, The American Symphony Orchestra League, and a national board member of American Women in Radio and Television.

A popular figure in Nashville, Judge Robert J. Burton, president of BMI, died in a Vancouver hotel-room fire on March 29, 1965. He had been a leader in the interminable legal fights between BMI and ASCAP and/or the Justice Department. In 1964, the United States had accused BMI of restraint of trade "that tended to exclude other sources of music from the air-waves," monopolizing radio and TV music. The Justice Department wanted broadcasters to divest themselves of stock ownership in BMI. The Justice Department said that in 1948 ASCAP licensed 90 per cent of the nation's popular songs. But ten years later, BMI was licensing 57 per cent and by October, 1964, BMI controlled 80 per cent

of America's popular music. Judge Burton replied, in part: "Far from operating BMI for the benefit of broadcasters, BMI has steadily increased its collections from broadcasters and its payments to writers and publishers."

The battle royal continues between the two giants of music licensing. The year of ASCAP's fiftieth birthday, 1964, saw the first birthday of its office in Nashville with Juanita Jones as manager. *Music Business* quoted a New York ASCAP spokesman: "The establishment of the Nashville office was a slight change in ASCAP policy. It put us in the country and Western music field." The turnout for the ASCAP cocktail party in November, 1964, seemed to one visitor to indicate that many country-music people were gloating over the long-belated recognition by the "good-music" group, enjoying every snack and drink from the hand that had once stung the hillbilly. (ASCAP released a country and Western music catalogue of 121 pages. Hillbilly music had finally made the grade!)

SESAC opened its Nashville branch in January, 1964, headed by singer Roy Drusky. SESAC and ASCAP each have about a dozen publishers in Nashville, while at the end of 1964 BMI listed 600 writers and 289 publishers. The Nashville BMI office has 4,000 more writers and publishers affiliated in the surrounding fourteen-state area.

Another World War II development that had, like the formation and success of BMI, helped spur the development of country music was the recording strike by the American Federation of Musicians, which began August 1, 1942. The union's chief, James C. Petrillo, wanted record-makers to establish an unemployed musicians' fund. He contended that the growing popularity of jukeboxes and all-disk radio programs were the major factors for that unemployment. Many small companies signed with the A.F.M., including many that recorded country music. With such large companies as Decca inoperative until September, 1943, and Columbia and Victor out of the pop-music scene until November, 1944, the country recordings established a beachhead on the national ear-waves. When the majors signed with Petrillo they found an established receptivity for many of the country songs that had been recorded during the strike.

One of the most aggressive groups of boosters in show business is the Country Music Association, a trade group formed in November, 1958, in Nashville, to spread the gospel of country music. The C.M.A. is an incorporated, nonprofit industry association made up of individuals and organizations "interested in promoting and expanding the use of country music, while solidifying the position it has already achieved in today's entertainment world."

The C.M.A. grew out of the Country Music Disk Jockeys' Association, which was formed in 1954. But Harry Stone, the first executive director of the C.M.A., made it clear that although the disk jockeys played an important part in the business, the C.M.A. would represent all elements of country music. Membership is thus divided into nine categories: artist-musician; manager, booker, promoter, agent and ballroom operator; composer; disk jockey; music publisher; radio-TV personnel; record company personnel; trade press and non-affiliated.

The C.M.A. evidently was an idea of several persons, because no single individual is honored as its founder, but Connie B. Gay was the founding president. (Gay operates several radio stations and is a vastly successful promoter who divides his time between the Virgin Islands and Nashville. An "elder statesman" of country music, he was

357 Don Pierce, president of Starday Records, and Biji Kuroda

358 The Columbia Recording Studios, Nashville

359 Skeeter Davis

360   Owen Bradley

361   Ott Devine of WSM

named to a committee of eight American businessmen by President Kennedy to survey the European results of the Marshall Plan.)

Wesley Rose was the first board chairman of C.M.A. The next two leading officers of the group were Ken Nelson, president, and Steve Sholes, chairman. In November, 1962, Gene Autry was named president and Rose was again chairman. In 1963, Tex Ritter was named president and Frances Preston chairman, both of whom were re-elected in 1964. Other officers serving in 1965 are vice presidents Connie Gay, Jack Stapp, Harold Moon, Hal Cook, and Jack Burgess; secretary, Hubert Long; assistant secretary, Bud Brown; treasurer, Dick Schofield; and assistant treasurer, Bill Williams.

Members of the 1965 board of directors are Chet Atkins, Johnny Bond, Hap Peebles, Hal Smith, Joe Allison, Roy Drusky, Bob Jennings, Bill Mack, Roy Horton, Wesley Rose, George Crump, Jerry Glaser, Owen Bradley, Jack Loetz, Paul Ackerman, and Bob Austin. The directors-at-large are Mrs. Preston, J. William Denny, Harold Hitt, Juanita Jones, Lucky Moeller, and Ken Nelson. The chief workhorse on a large team of hard workers is Mrs. Jo Walker, the C.M.A. executive director, a gracious Southern lady who makes every visitor to Music Row at home with the Nashville industry.

The projects of C.M.A. are varied. Encouragement of country radio stations has probably been its greatest achievement. It has conducted radio and TV surveys and established an International Country Music Week. One of the group's leading activities has been to attract the attention and support of the advertising industry. Toward that end, various country-music shows have been produced before hundreds of executives at the New York Sales Executive Club, the Canadian Radio and TV Executives Society, the Detroit Adcraft Club, and the Nashville Area Chamber of Commerce.

The C.M.A. began in 1961 the Country Music Hall of Fame, electing Jimmie Rodgers, Fred Rose, Hank Williams, Roy Acuff, and Tex Ritter. Its most ambitious project is the building of a $300,000 headquarters that will house a permanent Country Music Hall of Fame and Museum. The headquarters, scheduled to open in 1965, will be built on a gift of land from the city of Nashville and Davidson County—the Tony Rose Park, at Sixteenth Avenue South and Division Street, at the head of Music (or Record) Row.

With its membership rising from 225 in its first year to nearly two thousand in 1965, the C.M.A. is a powerful trade group that has given country music a nearly unified voice. Such services as a handbook for song writers and the encouragement of more research into country-music history are among its least-known activities. Jo Walker serves as a principal go-between for the group and the public and the press, and has won many friends for the industry with her gracious help. But almost all the C.M.A. members are walking boosters of country music.

The need for thorough study of the history of country music is the challenge facing the John Edwards Memorial Foundation. John Edwards was a young Australian who studied the music and the careers of American hillbilly and country musicians. Although he never visited this country, he amassed probably the greatest collection of country disks and memorabilia known. He died in an auto crash on Christmas Eve, 1960, at

362   Mrs. Frances Preston, B.M.I.

twenty-eight, his greatest work undone. Professor John Greenway wrote of his work in *Western Folklore* in April, 1961: "John Edwards' untimely death was tragic in any consideration, but most tragic in that he has not lived to see his dearest wish fulfilled — the acceptance, recognition and elevation to academic respectability of the material ignored by those who knew of its existence."

Edwards was considered the world's leading authority on American-folk-hillbilly-country music of the period 1923 to 1941 (a period he called the "Golden Age of Country Music") as documented on commercial recordings. The discographer-researcher left a will stating that he wanted his vast holdings of "disks, tapes, dubs, files, photos and all printed matter relative to my collecting interests to be used for the furtherance of serious study, recognition, appreciation and preservation of genuine country or hillbilly music."

To achieve these ends, friends and associates of John Edwards established in 1960 a nonprofit educational corporation, the John Edwards Memorial Foundation, Inc., which has its headquarters in the Folklore and Mythology Center at the University of California at Los Angeles. Incorporated on July 19, 1962, the J.E.M.F. has begun its great tasks in the Social Science Building of U.C.L.A. with limited funds. The work of the foundation deserves the attention and active support of everyone in country music.

A brochure lists the purposes of the foundation:

"1. To further the serious study, public recognition, and preservation of that form of American folk music commonly referred to as 'country,' 'Western,' 'country and Western,' 'hillbilly,' 'Bluegrass,' 'mountain,' 'cowboy,' 'old time,' and 'sacred'; to study and preserve parallel material referred to as 'race,' 'blues,' and 'gospel.'

"2. To gather, store and maintain phonograph records, photographs, biographical and discographical information, scholarly works and articles, and other material pertaining to such music.

"3. To archive, catalogue and index this material so that it can be most useful to interested persons.

"4. To compile, publish and distribute bibliographical, biographical, historical, and discographical material.

"5. To publish and distribute scholarly articles in this area; to reprint and republish, with permission, works originally appearing in this area, in books, magazines, and journals.

"6. To sponsor and promote field collection of such music.

"7. To stimulate academic research in this area, and to instruct and educate the public to the value of such music as part of its cultural heritage."

The work of the foundation began in the summer of 1961. But it was only after the J.E.M.F. received a $5,000 pilot grant from the Newport Folk Foundation that its real work got under way. In 1964, the foundation began an index of its thirty thousand songs in folios, an index of the artists in the folios, an index of fan club and other journals (of the

363   The late Judge Robert J. Burton of B.M.I.

fifty such periodicals it holds), and an index of recordings.

The directors and advisers of the John Edwards Memorial Foundation make up some of the most knowledgeable people in the world on country music. They are: Eugene W. Earle, president; Archie Green, first vice president; Fred G. Hoeptner, second vice president; D. K. Wilgus, secretary; and Ed Kahn, treasurer and executive secretary. The panel of advisers includes John Cohen, Jim Evans, E. Linnell Gentry, Garth Gibson, John Greenway, Wayland D. Hand, Bess Lomax Hawes, Will Roy Hearne, Willard Johnson, Brad McCuen, Guthric T. Meade Jr., Joseph Nicholas, Bob Pinson, Ralph C. Rinzler, Earl Scruggs, Charles Seeger, Michael Seeger, Stephen H. Sholes, Merle Travis, and G. W. Tye.

A question arises: How many officials of C.M.A. or J.E.M.F. know the officials of the other group? In a field where everyone can benefit from a mutual exchange of information and concerted efforts, the two groups should work hand in hand. The Edwards Foundation is sorely in need of money and other support to continue its work with archives, documentation, and so on. It would also seem that the C.M.A. needs all the expert help it can get in building displays and files for its new Country Music Hall of Fame and Museum. Certainly the affluent country-music industry could make a few tax-free donations to help the Edwards Foundation in its painstaking historical work, work that can only lend dignity and acceptance to country music. The

fact that the Edwards Foundation has been running on grants from the Newport Folk Foundation does not add stature to the Nashville industry, but it is a shortcoming easily rectified. (By 1965, a new cooperation between C.M.A. and the J.E.M.F. scholars was becoming a reality.)

If the Edwards Foundation people and the country-music industry are at a distance as to communication, cooperation, and purposes, there is an even greater gulf between Nashville and the urban folk revival. The fault here is on both sides. As one who feels as much at home in Nashville as in Newport, I strongly believe that both the city folk revival leaders and the country-music world have much to gain from each other. Many folk fans are so interested in traditional music that they tend to ignore or exclude almost anything in country music past that magic year of 1941. To them, it was the early string bands, ballad and shape-note singers, pre-Bluegrass or Bluegrass bands that were most important. (The Bluegrass rage on the campuses reflected this attitude. Although a post-1945 development, Bluegrass's city and collegiate fans found the unamplified instruments and the old songs and singing styles an acceptable extension of old-time music.)

It seems that there are some narrow attitudes on both sides, some failures to see the country-music picture in its entirety. Nashville has far from ignored the Carter Family. But slipping a drum or an electric instrument behind Mother Maybelle Carter is sacrilege to folk fans. They might well consider that the Carter Family originally broke with tradition very sharply. It is partially because they broke with the past that they were to be as influential as they were. It was "modernization" for the Carter Family to have changed their singing from the old modal patterns to the more communicative major-minor scales. It was "modernization" for the Carter Family to have added guitar accompaniment to what had earlier been purely unaccompanied singing. Now the old Carter Family is held up as a paragon of pure country style, yet how many folk purists would have believed that they had done the equivalent of "gone Nashville" in the late 1920's?

Such a point of view does not mean that all modernization in country music can be defended as an improvement. Many within Nashville have felt that the late 1950's saw a tremendous decline in quality in country music as it tried to become "pop country." One

364 The new R.C.A. Victor Studio in Nashville

can well appreciate the many reasons—money, prestige, and a growing sophistication—for country musicians to get out of "a rut." But was "pop country" an improvement?

The most telling criticism the city folk revivalists make against country music is commercialism. Country music is a business, a big business, and no one begrudges it that role. But it is also a mass art form, and some standards have to be held on to, even while change is taking place.

One of the things most glaringly absent from country music is criticism. It would be difficult to expect criticism to come from trade papers, whose function is primarily to document sales and popularity and evaluate new recordings not from a standpoint of artistic quality but from the standpoint of commercial stability. There have been in *Billboard*, from time to time, some guidelines suggested by such astute observers of the country scene as Paul Ackerman. Steve Sholes suggested in *Billboard* to Nashville artists that they "remain unhip," and Mitch Miller wrote about the great tradition of country song writing. This criticism, and mine, seems less ironic when one considers that someone "outside" can often see what the insiders are too close to see. Their perspective from a distance is very helpful. One of the greatest contributions that the C.M.A. could make would be to start encouraging the artistic evaluations of recordings. This might step on a lot of toes at first, but if the ultimate goal is a better, as well as a more popular, music, what better place for criticism should there be than "within the family"?

(*Music City News*, a monthly in Nashville, has probably done the best job in recent times of debating some of the questions about style and quality. The discussions in its letters column about "keeping country music country" and about Western dress versus conventional dress for performers has been one of the few critical outlets. This sort of self-evaluation is necessary for any art, and any business, to keep itself on the right track.)

Unfortunately, commercialism rides entirely too high in country music. Everybody is in business. Everybody wants to make money and be successful. But the "hit compulsion" that affects almost all elements of the popular-music world seems particularly out of place in an area of music where sincerity and honesty are old passwords. One day, it is to be hoped, the disk jockeys and trade papers and, ultimately, the record-makers and the musicians themselves, will kick all the clichés of Tin Pan Alley out of Tin Pan Valley—charts, ratings, "hot 100," hit, hit, hit. (The writer of this book has frequently succumbed to this epidemic, talking about money, sales, and hits. This language has so permeated the industry or "the art form" of country music that it is next to impossible to avoid it.) The industry leaders would do well to begin soft-pedaling the commercial aspects and amplifying the quality aspects. There should be no choice between being good *or* commercial. The country performer is in a unique position to be good *and* commercial.

The folk fans had their introduction to country music on their home ground from the singing in the 1940's of Burl Ives. Pete Seeger has probably done more to popularize the five-string banjo than any other American. Woody Guthrie, the Almanac Singers, Lee Hays of the Weavers, and the late Cisco Houston retained a strong country sound. Jack Elliott and others acquired it. In the folk revival that began in 1958, there started a new interest in country music, especially of old-time music. People like Roger Sprung, Mike Seeger, Ralph Rinzler, and John Cohen took a leading role in recording or "importing" country artists to the North. Groups like

The R.C.A. Victor Studio will comfortably hold 100 performers

66 Carl Smith, 1965

7 The Carl Smith Ranch, 350 acres, at Franklin, Tenn.

the Friends of Old Time Music put on many city concerts of old country musicians. Tom Ashley and Doc Watson became virtual "ethnic stars" in the Northeast, as did Mother Maybelle Carter. Recordings of Buell Kazee, Bascom Lamar Lunsford, Jean Ritchie, and Dock Boggs enjoyed popularity with the deep-dish city folk fans. The Blue Sky Boys appeared at the University of Illinois and other college campuses.

Nothing so dramatizes, however, the different points of view of Newport and Nashville than the fact that the Newport Folk Foundation sponsored special concerts in New York, Boston, and Philadelphia by Sam and Kirk McGee and Arthur Smith, old-timers around Nashville. I heard more playing by the McGees in one New York concert than I had heard in half a dozen "Grand Ole Opry" shows.

The reverse of this situation is the fact that the folk movement has ignored much that is artistically excellent in modern Nashville music. Perhaps the three most highly rated singers and song writers of recent years have been Johnny Cash, Buck Owens, and Roger Miller. Although Cash and Miller have appealed to city folk fans, Buck Owens, with his dedicated country approach (he made a pledge to keep his music country-oriented) and with his beautiful voice, has not become known to the folk movement yet. *Sing Out!* magazine, a folk-music bimonthly, has virtually ignored modern Nashville developments for almost thirteen years, but at last is beginning to stir. Gradually the folk narrowness is breaking down. (In Britain, country music is big, and it is common knowledge that the Beatles were strongly influenced by three country singers turned rock 'n' rollers, the Everly Brothers and Elvis Presley.

The folk fans have been rather harsh on Ott Devine's running of "Grand Ole Opry," always suffering by comparison of his hit-orientation to the traditional vigilance of Judge Hay. Being young and idealistic, the folk fans are appalled at such industry slogans as "Nashville is Cashville." They have taken an extreme view of the commercialism of Nashville to the point where they do not know about Loretta Lynn or Kitty Wells or Dave Dudley's high-quality, sincere singing.

The debate is endless, because there is always much to find in the vast C. & W. activities to defend as good music. Nashville can say that the fine old-time fiddler Curly Fox is still on the scene and working, that the fiddle hasn't died out as a symbolic instrument of fine country sounds. (There is even a new group in Lincoln, Nebraska, led by Dolores DeRyke called the American Old Time Fiddlers Association, and there is Glenn White's Western Bands of Yesterday Association in Oklahoma City.) Modern Nashville defenders can point to the fact that Ernest (Pop) Stoneman has been on "The Jimmy Dean Show." (Stoneman recorded "Sinking of the Titanic" and "The Face That Never Returned" for Ralph Peer on September 1, 1924, and three years later recorded some sacred songs of the Powers Family for Victor. He claims he suggested the name Hillbillies to Al Hopkins for what Archie Green has called "the band that named the music" and worked on the Keith circuit from 1925 to 1929.) The country-music people say that there is a growing interest in the history of the field and that the folk purists are too harsh on them.

The area that folk fans find the most difficult to accept is segregation and the general overlooking of the contribution to country music by Negroes. Admittedly, they have struck the South's Achilles heel here. The re-examination of the status of the Negro is slowly beginning to affect the country-music world as well as all institutions of the South. Bob Cobbins of station WDYL in Richmond told me some years ago that a listener survey found that 40 per cent of his country-music listeners were Negro. A similar survey of the whole field might well change a lot of attitudes in country music.

Certainly, the influence of Negro style has been great throughout country-music history. John Cohen of the New Lost City Ramblers did an exploratory article on "The Folk Music Interchange: Negro and White" in Sing Out! of January, 1964, that ought to be widely reprinted. He cited the contribution of blackface minstrel music, which directly affected such performers as Uncle Dave Macon. Slave songs have appeared on early hillbilly recordings. The impact of the blues and Negro spirituals is so enormous that this need hardly be cited. White country folk musicians such as Roscoe Holcomb, the late Hobart Smith, and Dock Boggs all clearly cited influences by Negro singers.

The first player to appear on "Grand Ole Opry" after the judge named the show in 1927 was DeFord Bailey, playing the harmonica. (Some critics of the "Opry" have said that Bailey was treated patronizingly as a "mascot," and one white Nashville musician told me that he was often cheated out of his money.) Another of the disparities between the folk and country-music attitudes is that Bailey was invited to the 1965 Newport Folk Festival to play banjo, guitar, and harmonica.

Nearly every one of the country-music influentials has had significant contact with Negro musicians. Jimmie Rodgers freely discussed the importance of Negro singers to him. A long friendship existed between the Carter Family and Leslie Riddles, a Negro from Kingsport, Tennessee. Riddles, according to Cohen's article, accompanied A. P. Carter on collecting trips, serving as a "song-learner," and influenced Maybelle Carter's guitar style during a period when he lived with the Carters. Bill Monroe cites the influence of Arnold Schultz, a Negro fiddler with whom he played at square dances. Similarly, "Tee-tot" was Hank Williams' first music teacher.

All this is known to students in the field, but industry leaders could do much to let the average country-music fan know how important have been these communal sharings, musical and personal, between Negro and white. Of course, the fabulously successful "Modern Sounds in Country and Western Music," two LP's recorded by Ray Charles, stand in recording history as the greatest boon to spreading country music since "Tennessee Waltz," Hank Williams' songs, or wartime country recordings by Bing Crosby. Many country stars have all but adopted certain Japanese country musicians, thereby showing they are free of racial prejudice, but this is only a beginning, and a long way from home. Negro musicians have helped shape white country music, and the Negro audience has helped support it on radio and by buying disks. The contribution here should be brought out as often as possible in these trying days of social change. To quote a new Johnny Cash song, "All of God's Children Ain't Free."

As they say on those 1,000-watt stations, "It's getting a little late, folks," so we'll start to bring this survey of country music to a close. The story is far from complete, because each new days sees growth. The growth on radio and television has been little short of phenomenal. More than 2,200 stations now program country music, and with the active prodding of C.M.A. and others, the number increases monthly. In Chicago, a

On Tuesday, October 2, 1928, DeFord Bailey recorded for r in Nashville. Of the eight masters cut, three sides were l. Was this the first record session in Nashville?

Ray Charles

major radio outlet, WJJD, has just become an all-country station. On the West Coast, such powerful stations as KFOX (Biff Collie, Hugh Cherry, and others) are reaching the great country-music audience that has brought an influx of Southern people into Southern California estimated at 86 per cent of the population. In New England, all-country stations have increased, and the regional stereotype is being broken all around the nation. A total of two hundred and ten radio stations today program only country music and news. The New York area will get its first full-time country station in the fall of 1965 when WJRZ in Newark converts to a new policy.

Television is also succumbing to country music, performers, and themes. Besides the many Westerns or country situation comedies already mentioned, there stands foremost the hour-long A.B.C. "Jimmy Dean Show," now going into its third season. The show has made the lanky, amiable singer "the dean of country music." His program has been the greatest single TV outlet for country music. Nashville folks like to recall that the show's fate was uncertain until country radio disk jockeys rallied enormous support for the program with their listeners. Nearly every country star of any proportion has been on the relaxed-paced Dean show. It has heavily stimulated interest in country music, and *Billboard* has called the program "one of the most potent vehicles for country music to hit the national scene since the 'Grand Ole Opry.'"

Carl Smith, another tall, rough-hewn Nashville performer, who lives on a $250,000 ranch outside the Tennessee capital, has been appearing on a Canadian network TV show out of Toronto. (Nothing so clearly dramatizes the appeal of country music on radio as the experience of station CFGN in Ontario. Gordon Symons, the program director, reports the station has signed up sixty thousand listeners as members of the station's Country Club. Mr. Symons told me of the tremendous growth of country music in Ontario recently and expects his club will soon number one hundred thousand members. Even a smaller station such as KHAT in Phoenix, Arizona, has more than ten thousand members in its Country Music Club.)

Other television country shows are growing at a rapid pace. Song writer and singer Bill Anderson has been syndicating a TV show since February, 1965, a half-hour country show that has seventy-five outlets signed.

The show was being filmed in Charlotte, North Carolina, because, reported Red O'Donnell in his *Variety* "Tin Pan Valley" column: "All local [Nashville] facilities are booked solidly through 1965 by other syndicate operators."

In the summer of 1965, WSM-TV began production of thirty-nine half-hour television "Grand Ole Opry" shows for sponsorship by the National Life and Accident Insurance Company. The show was already slated for ten major stations, with more expected, with "Opry" talent rotating. Another straw in the turbulent country TV wind has WSM-TV syndicating a country variety show starring Hickory Record's Bobby Lord, who has had a daily TV show on WSM for two years.

The mushrooming trend of country music in broadcasting can be shown simply. In 1961, there were 81 full-time C. & W. stations. By 1963, that number had reached 115. It is now at the 210 mark.

If the rapid gains being made by country music in the United States are causing wonderment, what has been happening in Canada and around the world is as dramatic. High on the popularity charts of England and Sweden nearly a year after his death were recordings by Jim Reeves. In Western Europe, the vogue for the Wild West is so great that the May, 1965, issue of *Town*, a British men's magazine, carried an extensive report on cowboy clubs in Britain, France, and Munich. Tours of South Africa, Western Europe, Australia and New Zealand, and Japan are now part of the regular itinerary for Nashville-based artists.

An official of Starday Records ranks the highest interest in non-United States countries in country music in this order: Canada, England, Germany, Scandinavia, Austria, South Africa and Japan. Part of this interest can be traced back to World War II again, to various hillbilly musicians and fans with the armed services. More recently, however, the experiences of a Tennesseean named Bill Carrigan, from 1948 to 1952, helped build the European audience. While serving in Germany, Carrigan headed hillbilly music for the American Armed Forces Network out of Frankfurt. As "Uncle Willy," Carrigan ran a disk show called "The Hillbilly Gast Haus" on the AFN radio network. Heavy mail not only from GI's but also from civilians in twenty-two countries indicated the show's popularity. Carrigan even organized a European "Grand Ole Opry" show that played

live in Frankfurt to overflow audiences of more than three thousand each Saturday night, topping attendance for Bob Hope.

With regional differences and in the cyclical ups and downs that affect all music popularity, country music is continuing a trend of greater overseas popularity. In the spring of 1965, Radio Luxembourg was conducting a five-night-a-week show, "Nashville, U.S.A.," run by a disk jockey from Gallatin, Tennessee. He plays all country music except Bluegrass to an estimated total of eight million English-speaking listeners. As to Bluegrass overseas, this seems to be one of the most popular forms of country music in Japan. A report in *Autoharp*, the publication of the Folksong Club at the University of Illinois, reports that "of the people interested in U.S. folk music, Bluegrass is the most popular." There are four hundred members of an American folk-song club in Osaka, and each Bluegrass record to appear in Japan sells about six thousand copies. Although no American Bluegrass group has yet played Japan, some three hundred different Bluegrass records have been distributed there.

Hank Snow toured Japan in early 1964 and returned ecstatic: "In the history of my career I have never played before a greater audience," he said. His first show in Tokyo filled all six thousand seats in the auditorium. A Victor representative in Japan says that the American Armed Forces Network helped build an audience for C. & W. in Japan, an audience quickly catching up to the jazz audience.

Similar glowing-reports came out of Amsterdam when Connie B. Gay's "Town and Country" show ran eighteen days as part of the United States Food and Agriculture Exhibition. The show played a command performance for Queen Juliana and Prince Bernhard at the Hague. Lucky Moeller predicted that many country artists would turn to recording in the local languages of Europe. "I see a tremendous upsurge in personal appearances by our artists in those countries," he was quoted in *Billboard*.

From Britain, Bill Clifton, a folk and country performer, reported to *Close-Up*, the C.M.A. paper: "The interest and enthusiasm for this form of music are steadily growing and have risen to new heights in each successive year since the mid-1940's." He cited the tremendous growth in publications in Britain dealing with country music. Since *Country & Western Express* started in 1954, there have been five other magazines entering the field.

0 The Music City area, Nashville

So go the world conquest and vistas of country music. In the whaling town of Hobart, Tasmania, Johnny Cash gets a standing ovation. In Norway, listeners find similarities to their own folk music in Nashville sounds.

Perhaps the most eloquent discussion of the international appeal of country music was an article Jim Reeves wrote for *Billboard's World of Country Music* just before he died. He wrote, in part:

"Our State department has sent and continues to send jazz groups to all parts of the world, including Communist countries. Let us not forget the Polish or the Russian farmer, the rancher in Argentina, the cowboy in Australia. The simple folk around the world need country and Western music. Country and Western music has never failed to fulfill its mission—to make people happy. . . . A country boy strumming a guitar and singing a story in which an American and a Russian share a common interest will do more to ease tension between the U.S.A. and the U.S.S.R. than all the threats and counterthreats of the past decade. . . . Remember, as the world grows smaller, country and Western music gets bigger."

It is a far cry from the "kerosene circuit" played by Uncle Am Stuart in the 1920's to the new $750,000 studio R.C.A. Victor opened in Nashville in March, 1965, or the half-million-dollar expansion of Columbia facilities planned to open there by September, 1965. These buildings and the new BMI and C.M.A. headquarters indicate that this is no popular-music trend, but a lasting part of the American cultural scene and of American show business.

On many other levels, it is perhaps premature to have already called one period the "Golden Age of Country Music," because another "Golden Age" may be with us again. The interest in the simple words and direct statements of country songs to even non-English-speaking peoples speaks volumes of the appeal of the music. And to the city person who has a sense of loss about the rushed, tense life that urbanization has brought and the attrition of values, country music is a reminder of another life for the American. *A Vanishing America: The Life and Times of the Small Town* was a nostalgic book published in 1965; so, too, was *Sick Cities*. Reminding us of where we have been and where we can go, the best traditions in country music speak to the small town or rural person as well as to the city dweller.

This survey has not, of necessity, been able to touch on every aspect of country music or to discuss every important contributor toward its history. Nor have we been able to tell the full story of the loyal country-music devotee. The stories left untold will be told another time, for this book is only a beginning. Country and Western music will be here as long as those bricks stand in the new buildings and studios of Nashville. And probably long after those bricks have crumbled.

A SELECTIVE LIST OF COUNTRY AND WESTERN LP RECORDINGS

CHAPTER 1: POOR MAN'S MUSIC BECOMES AN INDUSTRY

All Star 25 Years of Songs (King 807)
All-Time Country & Western (Decca 4010)
The Best of the Best (Capitol 1654)
Country Boys and Country Girls (Wing 12275)
Country Classics (RCA Victor 2313)
Country Cousins (Musicor 2053)
The Country Music Hall of Fame (Starday 164)
Country Music Hits (Camden 689)
Country Music U.S.A. (Starday 263)
Country Music Who's Who (Starday 309)
Country Oldies but Goodies (Smash 27016)
Diamonds by the Dozen (RCA Victor 2668)
Galaxy of Country and Western Golden Hits (Mercury MGD – 12)
The Great All-Time Country Hits (Harmony 7292)
Great Country Favorites (MGM 4211)
The Great One (Capitol 1718)
Greatest Country and Western Hits (Columbia 1257)
The Honest to Goodness Country Music Hits (RCA Victor 2564)
Kentucky Derby Day (Columbia 2231)
1964 Country & Western Award Winners
Original Greatest Hits of the Great Country
& Western Stars (Mercury 20825)

CHAPTER 2: THE GOLDEN AGE OF COUNTRY MUSIC

Anthology of American Folk Music
(Folkways 2951 – 53; 6 disks)
Bascom Lamar Lunsford (Riverside 645)
Blue Sky Boys (Camden 797)
The Blue Sky Boys (Starday 205)
Buell Kazee (Folkways 3810)
Cliff Carlisle (Rem 1002)
Doc Watson (Vanguard 9152)
Dock Boggs (Folkways 2351)
Hobart Smith (Folk-Legacy 17)
Instrumental Music of the Southern Appalachians (Tradition 1007)
The Legend of Pete Cassell (Hilltop 6023)
Maple on the Hill and Other Old Time
Country Favorites (Camden 898)
Mountain Ballads (Country 502)
Mountain Fiddle Music (Country 501)
Mountain Music of Kentucky
(Folkways 2317)
Mountain Music Played on the Autoharp (Folkways 2365)
New Lost City Ramblers Vol. 1 – 5
(Folkways FA 2395 – 9)
Old Time Get Together with Lew Childre (Starday 153)
Old Time Music at Clarence Ashley's (Folkways 2355, 2359)

Old Time Music at Newport (Vanguard 9147)
Old Time Southern Dance Music: String Bands (Old Timey 100)
Smoky Mountain Ballads (RCA Victor 507)
Southern Folk Heritage Series
(Atlantic 1346–52)
Southern Journey Series (Prestige 25001–12)
Southern Mountain Folk Songs & Ballads
(Washington 734)

CHAPTER 3: THE JIMMY RODGERS STORY (ALL ON RCA VICTOR)

Best of Legendary Jimmie Rodgers (3315)
Hall of Fame (2531)
Jimmie the Kid (2213)
My Rough and Rowdy Ways (2112)
My Time Ain't Long (2865)
Never No Mo' (1232)
Short but Brilliant Life (2634)
Train Whistle Blues (1640)

CHAPTER 4: THE INFLUENTIALS

Roy Acuff
Best (Capitol 2103)
King of Country Music (Hickory 109)
The World of Country Music (Capitol 2276)
The Carter Family
A Collection of Favorites by the Carter Family (Decca 4404)
Famous Carter Family (Harmony 7280)
Great Original Recordings (Harmony 7300)
Original and Great (Camden 586)
Johnny Cash
Bitter Tears (Columbia 2248)
I Walk the Line (Columbia 2190)
Orange Blossom Special (Columbia 2309)
Woody Guthrie
Dust Bowl Ballads (RCA Victor
LPV 502)
Woody Guthrie Library of Congress Recordings (Elektra 271–72)
Woody Guthrie Songs (Folkways 2483)
Hank Williams
Hank Williams' Greatest Hits
Vol. 1–3 (MGM 3918, 4040, 4140)
Lost Highway (MGM 4254)
On Stage (MGM 3999)

CHAPTER 5: "GRAND OLE OPRY" AND OTHER RADIO BARN DANCES

All-Time Favorites — Eddy Arnold (RCA Victor 1223)
Bradley Kincaid (Blue Bonnet)
Country Music Festival (Starday 274)
The Ernest Tubb Story (Decca 8871 – 72)
Grand Ole Country Hits (Camden 737)
Grand Ole Opry Spectacular (Starday 242)
More Hank Snow (RCA Victor 2812)
Opry Old Timers — Sam & Kirk McGee (Starday 182)
Opry Time in Tennessee (Starday 177)
The Red Foley Story (Decca 7177)
Renfro Valley Gathering (Renfro Valley Barn Dance)
Saturday Night at the Grand Ole Opry, Vol. 1 – 2 (Decca 4303, 4539)
Stringbean (Starday 142)
Uncle Dave Macon (Folkways 51)

CHAPTER 6: THE BLUEGRASS GROWS ALL AROUND

Bluegrass Goes to College — Hylo Brown (Starday 204)
The Bluegrass Sound of Bill Clifton (Starday 159)
Bluegrass Special — Bill Monroe (Decca 4382)
Bluegrass Special — Jim & Jesse (Epic 24031)
Charles River Valley Boys (Prestige 14024)
Country Music & Bluegrass at Newport
(Vanguard 9145)
Cutting Grass — Osborne Brothers (MGM 4149)
The Dillards (Elektra 232)
Early Bluegrass Music — Monroe Brothers (Camden 774)
Flatt & Scruggs at Carnegie Hall (Columbia 2045)
Flatt & Scruggs Recorded Live at Vanderbilt University (Columbia 2134)
Greenbriar Boys — Ragged but Right (Vanguard 9159)
Knee Deep in Bluegrass — Bill Monroe (Decca 8731)
New Dimensions in Banjo & Bluegrass (Elektra 238)
Rose Maddox Sings Bluegrass (Capitol 1799)
Stanley Brothers (King 615)
The Stanleys in Person (King 719)
World's Best 5 – String Banjo — Reno & Smiley (King 861)

CHAPTER 7: WAY OUT WEST

Authentic Cowboys and Their Western Folksongs (RCA Victor Vintage 522)
The Best of Bob Wills & His Texas Playboys (Harmony 7304)
Bob Wills Special (Harmony 7036)
Border Affair — Tex Ritter (Capitol 1910)
Country Fare — Sons of the Pioneers (RCA Victor 2855)
The Dancin'est Band Around — Leon McAuliff (Capitol 2016)

The Dean of Cowboy Singers—Bob Atcher (Columbia 2232)

Favorite Cowboy Songs—Sons of the Pioneers (RCA Victor 1130)

Gene Autry's Greatest Hits (Columbia 1575)

Golden Country Hits—Hank Thompson (Capitol 2089)

The Hell-Bound Train—Glenn Ohrlin (University of Illinois 301)

Johnny Bond (Starday 227)

Mr. Words & Mr. Music (Liberty 3194)

The No. 1 Country & Western Band—Hank
Thompson (Capitol 1741)

Rex Allen Sings and Tells Tales (Mercury 20752)

Roy Rogers & Dale Evans (RCA Victor 1439)

A Swing Legend—Bob Wills & Tommy Duncan (Liberty 3182)

Wilf Carter (Camden 527)

CHAPTER 8: SONGS AND SONG WRITERS

Al Dexter (Capitol 1701)

Alex Zanetis Writes & Sings the Story of the Oil Fields (RIC 1001)

All Aboard: For the Railroad Special (Starday 170)

Babes in the Mill—Dorsey Dixon (Testament 3301)

Back Home—Merle Travis (Capitol 891)

Behind These Walls—Hank Ferguson
(Folk Legacy 45A–13)

Bill Anderson Sings (Decca 4499)

Dang Me—Roger Miller (Smash 27049)

Diesel Smoke, Dangerous Curves & Other Truck-Driver Favorites (Starday 250)

First of the Famous—Various Artists (Capitol 2275)

Floyd Tillman's Best (Harmony 7310)

George Jones Greatest Hits (Mercury 20621)

Hits from the Heart—Hank Cochran (RCA Victor 3303)

I Wrote a Song—Don Gibson (RCA Victor 2702)

Jimmy Driftwood Sings Newly Discovered Early American Folk Songs (RCA Victor 1635)

Johnny Horton Makes History (Columbia 1478)

Mr. Country & Western Music—George Jones (Musicor 2045)

The Prisoner's Dream—Charles Lee Guy III (Capitol 1920)

The Return of Roger Miller (Smash 27061)

Saginaw, Michigan—Lefty Frizzell (Columbia 2169)

Slipping Around (Starday 261)

Songs of the Coal Mines—Merle Travis (Capitol 1956)

The Songs & Stories of Aunt Molly Jackson (Folkways 5457)

Songs about the Working Man—Dave Dudley (Mercury 20899)

Trouble Is a Lonesome Town—Lee Hazlewood (Mercury 20860)

The Voice of Johnny Horton (Hilltop 6012)

The Ways of Life—Hank Locklin (RCA Victor 2680)

You Are My Sunshine—Jimmy Davis (Decca 8896)

CHAPTER 9: THE NASHVILLE SOUND

America's Favorite Ballads (Vol. 1–6)—Pete Seeger (Folkways 2319–23, 2445)
Coronation Concert—Burl Ives (Decca 8080)
Country Hit Parade—Goldie Hill (Decca 4492)
Guitar Country—Chet Atkins (RCA Victor 2616)
I Don't Care—Buck Owens (Capitol 2186)
I've Got a Tiger by the Tail—Buck Owens (Capitol 2283)
Last Date—Floyd Cramer (RCA Victor 2350)
Modern Sounds of Country & Western Music—Ray Charles Vol. 1 & 2 (ABC Paramount 410, 435)
Molly O'Day (Rem 1001)
Night Life—Ray Price (Columbia 1971)
Our Man in Nashville—Chet Atkins (RCA Victor 2616)
Queen of Country Music—Kitty Wells (Decca 4197)
Songs Our Daddy Taught Us—Everly Brothers (Cadence 3016)
A Touch of Velvet—Jim Reeves (RCA Victor 2487)
The Unforgettable Molly O'Day (Harmony 7299)

ACKNOWLEDGEMENTS

The author and photographer-designer of this book gratefully thank a host of people whose unselfish assistance made this work possible. Nearly every page of text and every photograph represents the generous help of someone in this field. Only a few can be mentioned here.

Especial thanks should go to Archie Green and other members of the John Edwards Memorial Foundation of the University of California at Los Angeles and to Jo Walker and Roy Horton of the Country Music Association, whose recurring help and encouragement kept us going.

While research materials in country music are sparse, many scholars gave freely of their knowledge. Archie Green's monograph, *Hillybilly Music: Source and Symbol*, was a cornerstone of early history. A basic book in country-music scholarship is the unpublished dissertation by Billy Charles Malone of Southwest Texas State College in San Marcos. Malone's oft-quoted *A History of Commercial Country Music in the United States, 1920 – 1964* is a bible of pioneer scholarship. Extended research material was provided for the chapter on Jimmie Rodgers by Nolan Porterfield, one of the country's leading scholars on Rodgers and his music. Thanks also for additional material and insights on Rodgers to Johnny Cash, Brad McCuen of R.C.A. Victor, and Jim Evans, the devoted head of the Jimmie Rodgers Society in Lubbock, Texas.

Thurston Moore of Heather Publications in Denver obligingly provided back issues of his *Country Music Who's Who* and *Country Music Scrapbooks*. Linnell Gentry's *A History and Encyclopedia of Country, Western, and Gospel Music* (Nashville, 1961) was a useful compendium of early magazine articles and biographical data. *The Western from Silents to Cinerama* by George N. Fenin and William K. Everson (Bonanza Books, New York, 1962) was a fine source for material on singing cowboys. Fred Hoeptner also helped us greatly on Western swing.

Tracking down old periodicals and fan magazines was an adventure. Joe Nicholas of *Disc Collector and Country Directory* made his back files available. Joe Lacke of the Melody Lane Record Ranch in Elmont, Long Island, made available back issues of *Country Music Jamboree, Country Song Round-up, Trail, Hillbilly, Cowboy Hit Parade* and *Cowboy Songs*.

Members of the trade press, who were among the first to be aware of the importance of country music, have been helpful, especially Paul Ackerman, music editor of *Billboard* and editor of the annual *World of Country Music*. Thanks also to Ren Grevatt and Charlie Lamb of the former trade weekly *Music Business*, and to Roger Scutt, Don Schroeder and the staff of *Music City News*. Smokey Aleshevich supplied copies of several British country-music periodicals, and Bill Legere of Toronto supplied information on cylinder recordings. Other valuable information on "the Golden Age of Country Music" was supplied by Leo LeRiche of Maplewood, Missouri, and Dick Spottswood of Arlington, Virginia. Jo Walker of the C.M.A. and Trudy Stamper, Bill Williams and Len Hensil of the WSM "Grand Ole Opry" were stalwarts of help and hospitality in Nashville. Thanks also to Russell Sanjek of Broadcast Music, Incorporated; Pat Anderson, formerly of *The Nashville Tennessean*, and to the two Nashville columnists Phil Sullivan and Red O'Connell. Thanks to George D. Hay for permission to quote from his pamphlet history of "Grand Ole Opry." For repeated help in New York on vexing questions, thanks to Roy Horton of Southern Music-Peer International for his patience.

Many collectors and country fans generously supplied photographs for use in our collection. Bob Hyland of Springfield, Ohio, and Dr. Bob Healy of Alamosa, Colorado, were especially helpful in supplying old-time and Western swing photographs. Thanks also to Johnny Cash, Phoebe Allen, Hubert Long, Owen Bradley and Clayton McMichen for photographs and memorabilia. Other wonderful photos were supplied by Grandpa Jones, Ted Grant, Cliff Carlisle, Wesley Rose and Gladys Carter Millard. Thanks to Mildred Wyatt, librarian of the Stephen F. Austin State College Library in Nacogdoches, Texas, and to Gertrude Parsley and Fred Estes of the Tennessee State Archives for help in tracking down visual and other material.

Sears Roebuck supplied back catalogue material, and many fine old pictures came from George C. Biggar of WLBK in De Kalb, Illinois. Thanks also to the late Cecil Brower for assistance on Western swing pictures and to the staff of the Jimmy Dean Show and Buddy Atkinson. Gerry Miller of R.C.A. Victor, Mark Brody of Decca, and Sol Handwerger of M-G-M Records were of considerable assistance with photos.

The photographer-designer wishes to thank Jeanne Goldblatt for her "researching, filing and help in keeping some semblance of order in a mountain of material." The author wishes to thank Steve Oberkirsch for nine months' work as an editorial and research assistant and also Midge Paxton for similar help. The patience of Mrs. Norma Mitchell in typing the manuscript was rivaled only by that of the author's local bartender.

Dozens of persons gave freely of their time for interviews that made the work go easier. Those who are quoted at length in the text are hereby thanked for the lengths to which they went.

Finally, a word of gratitude to the late Bill Raney, the editor at Bobbs-Merrill who envisioned the promise of this work although he did not live to see that promise fulfilled.

PHOTO CREDITS

INDEX

NAME INDEX